VIRGINIA COLONIAL ABSTRACTS

Vol. XVI

Richmond County Records

1692 - 1704

Deed Book No. 1 1692 - 1693

Deed Book No. 2 1693-4 - 1696

Deed Book No. 3 - Lost

Miscellaneous Records 1699 - 1704

Abstracted by

Beverley Fleet

Book Publishers

Greenville
South Carolina

These volumes were reproduced
from 1940 editions located in the
Publisher's private library
Greenville, South Carolina

Please direct ALL correspondence and book orders to:
Southern Historical Press, Inc.
PO Box 1267
375 West Broad Street
Greenville, S.C. 29602-1267

Originally printed & ©: Richmond, VA. 1942 & 1943
Reprinted by: Southern Historical Press, Inc.
Greenville, S.C. 2022
ISBN #0-89308-823-4
Printed in the United States of America

PREFACE

Explanations of the self evident start many a preface. Here is more of that unappetizing diet.

So first of all, for those who may not know, Richmond County had nothing whatever to do with the City of Richmond during the Colonial Period. There was no City of Richmond then. It is now in Henrico County, many miles from Richmond County.

The records of Richmond County are at Warsaw, Virginia. For years they have been in the intelligent and actually affectionate care of Mr. E. Carter Delano in the Clerk's Office there. Needless to say, they are in especially fine condition. They contain so vast an amount of data concerning the foundations of Virginia history, that it seems but folly to send forth this small fragment. Much work and little to show for it.

The County was formed from old Rappahannock County in 1692. The records from this date hark back to the middle of the 17th century. While tempted to take abstracts from a later period as being much more interesting, it seemed best to start at the dull beginnings. So here are the first land records and the beginnings of those most interesting Miscellaneous Records. We will have to be satisfied with the fact that the Rappahannock was once the Richmond River, that Col. Nathaniel Pope was alias Bridges casting a sidelight on the Washington background and such detail. If one must know more, ask Mr. Delano. He knows. Indeed thank him for this volume. I could not have made it but for his kindly and generous assistance.

Beverley Fleet

October 10th 1942.

Richmond County
Virginia

Deed Book. No. 1
10 May 1692 - 20 Dec. 1693

p. 1. Deed. 14 April 1692 ("in the year of our Lord according to
Computation of the Church of England"). Angell Jacobus of the parish
of North Farnham in the County of Rappahannock, Cooper, and Elizabeth
his wife, to William Yates of the same par. and Co., for 3720 lb tobo.
100 acres in same par., adj land of Daniel Jackson " which said land
descended to her the said Eliz'a by the death of one John Clarke,
brother to her the said Elizabeth".

Wit: signed   Angell Jacobus (seal)
Elias Yates   Eliz'a Jacobus (seal)
Wm. Eale
James Ellis   Rec. 10 May 1692

p. 3. Power of Atty. 4 May 1692. Eliz'a Jacobus to "my neighbour and
friend David Barrick" to ack. above.

Wit: signed   Eliza Jacobus (seal)
Georg Eale
Thomas Woode
the mark of A
John Anderson

p. 3. Deed of Release. 30 April 1692. Whereas Francis Triplett and
Saml. Bowen of Rappa. Co. sold to Josiah Ship of same Co., for 4000
lb of tobo and cask "a certain parcel of Land being part of a patent
containing one thousand and fifty acres as by a conveyance past from
them the said Triplett and Bowen to him the said Ship bearing date
the first of August 1685"

Wit: His
William Scott   signed   Josiah x Ship (seal)
Wm x Thomas   mark
                    Rec 10 May 1692

p. 4. Virginia
        Whereas there is a Tract of land lying and being in the
freshes of Rappa near adjoining unto a place commonly known by the
name of Powmans in Run formerly belonging to Mr Warwick Cammock
whereof a moiety of Six hundred acres of the said Tract of Land

having formerly been confirmed conveyed and made over unto Mr
Ammaree Butler and from the said Butler Confirmed conveyed and made
over unto Mr William Underwood Sen'r as marrying the sister of the
said Mr Ammaree Butler and from the said Mr William Underwood confirmed conveyed and made over in leiw and by Exchange of the thirds
of Lands belonging unto Mrs Eliza Coumbs with Consent of the said
Mrs Elizabeth Coumbs unto William Underwood Jr, John Coumbs, William
Coumbs to them their heirs Ex'ors, admors or assigns forever, Now
be it known that I William Underwood Junior do for a valuable Consideration x x sell x x unto William Tomas of the parish of Washington
in the County of Westmorland x x all my right x x of the said moiety
of the said six hundred acres of Land belonging unto me, which is to
be understood two hundred acres x x I have hereunto set my hand and
seale this 11 day of December 1691.
Wit:

Thomas Tyrwhitt   signed William Underwood (seal)
William Underwood
John x Pitman   Rec 10 May 1692
                           Test
                               Jo Almond Dep Cur

p.5. Deed. 4 April 1692. William Griffin of Rappa. Co., planter, to
Alexr Doniphan of same Co. "a certain parcel of land lying in the
freshes of Rappa river on the river side the North side the river",
acreage not shown.
Wit: signed Wm Griffin (seal)
Nabu: Jones
James Orchard   Rec. 10 May 1692

p. 5-6. 30 April 1692. Josiah Ship to Triplett and Bowen. see p. 3

p.6. Deed. 30 March 1692. Joseph Beckley of Rappa Co. and parish of
Sittenburn to Josias Ship of same Co. and parish, for 3000 lb tobo
and cask, 100 acres on N. side of Rappa river in same Co. and parish,
adj land of William Jett, along the old line of Joseph Beckley
Wit:

Peter Rawlls   signed   Joseph Beckley (seal)
Francis x Triplett   Mary Beckley   (seal)
William x Thomas   Rec. 16 May 1692
                           Test
                               Wm Colston Cl Ct

Deed Book No. 1

p. 8. Power of Atty. No date. "Joseph Beckley and Mary my wife" to "our loving friend Saml Bowen of Rappa County" to ack foregoing sale.

p. 8. Deed. 2 Nov. 1691. Alexan'd Domphan of St. Mary's Par. Rappa Co., Gen't. "and Margaret my wife" to Nebuchadnozzor Jones of same Co., for 4300 lb tobo and cask, 105 A. in Rappa Co. on N. side of river "it formerly belonging to Mr George Motts and by the said Motts given to Mary Creed and she dying the said Land Returned to the aforesaid Motts children againe which Domphan marryed one the aforesaid Land being his wifes messuage Tenm't and Tract of Land". Adjs land of David Brennahs.

Wit: signed Alex'r: Domphan (seal)
James Harison   Margarett x Domphan (seal)
Jno Deane

                          Rec. 25 May 1692
                              Test
                                  Wm Colston Cl Ct

p.10. Deed. 1 June 1692. John Eyles and Elizabeth his wife and Lewis Farde, both of Richmond Co., planters; to Xpher Ascough of said Co., planter, for a valuable consideration, "one devident or neck of Land situate lying and being neer Rappa Creek bounded as followeth beginning at a sandy valley being the bounds of James Bendall and Tho Stiff downe the County Road S.S.W. to the head of a Branch x x"

Wit:
Tho. Newman   signed   John x Eyles   (seal)
John Craske   Eliz'a x Eyles   "
John Almond   Lewis x Fards   "
                          Rec. 1 June 1692

p.10. Deed. 1 May 1692. John Forsaker, Gent., of St. Mary's Par., Rappa. Co., to Wm. Brennah of the same Par. and Co., planter, for "Two Cows and Two Calves and a Steer and Two hundred Pounds of Arenoco Tobo to him in hand Payed", 135 A. being part of 1640 A., "Knowne by the name of Creeds Land", adj land of David Brennah, and Heaberds land. Refers to "sd John Fosaker and Elizabeth his wife".

Wit:
Alexr Damphan   signed   John Fosaker   (seal)
Alexr Domphan Junr   Eliz x Fosaker

                          Rec. 8 June 1692

Deed Book No. 1

p.12. Power of Atty. 1 June 1692. John Fosaker to James Harison to ack foregoing. Also Power of Atty. 30 May 1692. Elizabeth Fosaker to Mr James Harrison for the same.

p.13. Deed. 27 February 1691 (1691/2). "John Waugh in the Colony of Virginia Clerk" to Wm Fitzhugh, for 9000 lb tobo in cask, 2 parcels of land in Rappahannock County in the Freshes thereof, being part of a patent of 2000 acres granted to Col. John Catlett the 2nd of June 1666 "and by severall means purchased now in my possession being the lowermost part thereof being designed for Dan'll Meriott Contayning Three hundred acres and the lowermost thereof". "The other hundred acres designed for John Corbin", along the Rappa River, adj the said Dan'll Meriotts 300 acres.

Wit: signed   Jo: Waugh
Charles Calvert
Richd x Henward   Rec. 8 June 1692.

Power of Atty. 27 Feb. 1691/2. John Waugh to Mr Wm Colston Clerk of Rappahannock Court to ack above.

p. 14. Deed. 11 April 1692. Edward Lewis, Tho: Lewis and John Landman of Rappa Co. to Tho: Walker of same Co., for 429 lb tobo and cask, 92 1/2 acres "Lying and being near Totuskey Creek in the said County of Rappahannock", adj land of Geo Eale, William Smyth and the land of the said Tho: Walker whereon he now dwelleth according to a survey under the hand of Capt Wm Mosely. Refers to Tho: Lewis and Mary his wife. "The sd John Landmans Part Conteyning Sixteen acres of Land which was taken into Edward Lewis and Tho Lewis part of the over plus within the old Line of Tho: Robertson and Edward Lewis being the Remainder of the Eleven hundred and forty acres entire"

Wit:
Jos: Dike   signed   Edward x Lewis
Lewis x Richards   Tho: Lewis
                                                 John Landman

Rec. 22 August 1692

p.15. Power of Atty. 2 May 1692. Mary Lewis wife of Edward Lewis of Rappahannock County, planter, to " my very good friend John Morgan" to ack. above.

Wit: signed   Mary x Lewis
Tho Lewis
Wm Smith

Deed Book No. 1

p. 16. Power of Atty. 2 May 1692. Mary Lewis wife of Edward Lewis to "my very good friend Luke Williams" to reling dower rights in fore-going deed.

p. 16. Deed. 2 Sept 1691. William Griffin of Sittenburne Par. in Rappa Co. and "Rebecca my wife", to Edward Price of same Co. for 2950 lb tobo. 112 acres in Rappa Co "it being part of a Devident or parcell of Land formerly bought of Mr John and Mr Geo. Motts by William Griffin Esqr". This land on N. side of river.

Wit: Signed   William Griffin
Tho Parke   Rebecca x Griffin
Charles -illegible-possibly Shee
Geo x Proctor   Rec. 22 Aug. 1692

p.17. Power of Atty. 2 Aug. 1692. Rebecca Griffin wife of Wm Griffin, planter, to Tho: Parke of Essex Co. to ack sale of land to Edward Price of Richmond Co. 'Tayler'.

p.18. Deed. 13 July 1692. John Fosaker and Elizabeth his wife to David Darnell, for 10000 lb tobo, 600 acres "being part of a greater Tract granted by Patent To John and Geo Mott Brothers, which Patent bears date Septem'br 1670 the said George being father to the above-said Elizabeth wife of John Fosaker which said Geo Mott having foure Daughters Elizabeth, Margarett, Ann and Ellen did by his last will and Testament give and bequeath his moyety and Part of the abovesaid Land to be Equally divided amongst his Daughters vizt Elizabeth Margarett Ann and Ellen, and to Confirme and Ratefie the abovesaid will of Geo Mott John Mott Eldest Brother and survivour did by his last Will and testament give and bequeath unto the abovesaid foure Daughters of Geo: Mott Eliz: Margarett Ann and Ellen all his Land being the other Moyety of the abovesaid Tract granted by Patent Septemb'r 1670. All which will more at large appear Recourse being had to both the said Wills as proved and Recorded in the Records of Rappahannock County Court Therefore wee the said John Fosaker and Elizabeth his wife do for ourselves our heirs Executors and assigns do Covenant give grant makeover and confirme unto David Darnell the abovesaid Six hundred acres of Land lying and being in now Richmond County part thereof on the Branches of Muddy Creek and part on the Branches of Potomek Creek in Stafford County The said Six hundred acres of Land being part of 1246 1/2 acres which did accrue and come to the Part of the said Elizabeth wife of John Fosaker after a full survey and Voluntary and free devision by consent of all therein

Concerned and bounded as followeth, beginning upon five hundred acres
part of the 1246 1/2 acres surveyed and layed out for Mr Sampson
Darrell of Stafford County South with 146 1/2 acres the Remainding
part of the abovesaid 1246 1/2 acres East with the Land of Richard
Shipway who marryed the Daughter Ellen, West with the Land of Capt
John Clendening who intermarryed with the Daughter Ann".
Wit:

Alexan'r Doniphan   signed   John Fosaker
Alexr: Doniphan Junr   Eliz x Fosaker

Recorded 29 Sept. 1692

p.19. Power of Atty. 2 Aug. 1692. Elizabeth Fosaker of Richmond Co.
to "my Loving friend M'r James Harison" to ack. above.

page 20. Deed. 6 Sept. 1692. Tho: Pace of Rappa. Co., planter and
Jane his wife and Rowland Thornton of the same Co., planter, and
Eliz: his wife one of the Daughters of Alexand'r Flemming dec'd to
Fran: Thornton of the same Co., Gentleman, for 5 shillings Sterling,
320 acres, now in occupation of the said Thomas "being on the River
side on the North Side Rappa River in the County aforesaid and is
that part of the Tract or divident of Land Nine hundred and sixty
acres of Land given by the said Alex'r Flemming betwixt his wife and
Two Children which three hundred and Twenty acres was the divident
alotted to the said Tho Pace and Alexia his late wife the other of
the Daughters of the said Alexander as by the Platt and devident made
by Edwin Conway Surveyor Warwick Canook Fran: Stone Wm Clapham
Fran: Sterne and David Sterne will more fully appeare"
Wit:

Hen: Berry   signed   Fran Thornton
Ja Roy   Tho: Pace
                                               Joane x Pace
                                               Row: Thornton
                                               Eliz: x Thornton

Recorded 29 Sept. 1692

p.22. Power of Atty. 6 Sept 1692. Eliz: Thornton wife of Rowland
Thornton of Richmond Co., to Arthur Spicer to ack above and roling
dower rights. Wit: Fran: Thornton, Tho: Pace.

p.22. Bond for foregoing deed.
p.23. Bond for foregoing deed.

p.23. Deed. 28 March 1692. "John Fosaker and Elizabeth his wife of Rappahannock County in Virginia which said Elizabeth is the Eldest Daughter of Mr. Geo. Mott late of the County aforesaid dec'd" to Capt George Mason of Stafford County in Virginia, for 6630 lb tobo and cask, 337 1/2 acres, being parcell of the Grand Patent of 15654 acres and part of the devision lott or "proporcoon" of the said Elizabeth being in Rappa Co upon the N. side of the river. Adjs land of Richd Shipways, "the Path leading to Parson Woughs", "the Land where the said John and Eliz: now dwell", and land now in possession of Geo. Mason. Deed refers to land making up the grand patent as : 1200 acres patented 23 Sept. 1663, and 10 Sept 1668; 2500 acres 17 Oct 1670; 11954 acres 17 Oct. 1670, issued to John and Geo: Mott. See page 18 for detail of inheritance.

Wit: signed   John Fosaker
Hugh Macaullock   Eliz x Fosaker
Geo Anderson
Jno Glendening
Robt x -illegible-.   Rec. 8 Oct. 1692

p.26. 26 May 1692. Certificate, Alex'r Doniphan, Justice of Peace for Richmond Co., re. foregoing.

p.27. Power of Atty. 5 Sept. 1692. Elizabeth Fosaker to Mr. James Harrison to ack foregoing deed. Wit: Alexr Doniphan, Eliz x Callaway, John Fosaker.

p.27. Certificate. 3 Nov. 1691. William Moseley, Surveyor of Richmond County regarding above.

p.27. Deed. 12 Oct. 1692. John Jacob of Farnham in the County of Richmond, planter, to Isaac Webbe of the same, Gent. "that the said John Jacob as well for as in consideration of one shilling to him in hand Payed by the said Isaac Webbe as for the natural love and affection he the said John Jacob hath and beareth unto John Jacob his son", sells Webb 100 acres adj land formerly belonging to Richard Powell, Maidstones swamp, "which Land was granted by David Mauswell unto the said John Jacob the elder by deed dated the 29th day of June 1665 and by the said John Jacob sold unto Domeniok Rice by Indorsement on the same Deed but Repurchased of him againe the consideration being given back". Refers to a part of the original tract having been sold by John Jacob the elder to Tho: Chitley. Land in this deed, 100 acres, "unto the said Isaac Webbe and his heirs to and for the only proper use and behoof of the said John Jacob the son", "and the said John Jacob doth

Deed Book No. 1

hereby constitute and appoint his Loving friend John Tavener his
attorney to acknowledge these presents "in due forme of Law".
Wit:
Mark Inne   signed   John Jacob
Wm: Miskell
Tho: Chitty

Power of Atty. 4 Oct. 1692. Isaac Webbe to Mr. Den: McCarty to ack.
foregoing. Wit: Alex'r Swan, Raw Travers.

Rec. 15 Oct. 1692

p.28. Deed. 3 March 1690/1. Dan'll Swillivant of Par of Farnham in
Co. of Rappa to John Trapley (Tarpley) of same parish and county,
for "one younge Negro man" and 17808 lb tobo, 398 acres "it being
part of a Tract of Land granted to my father Dennis Swillevant dec'd",
being at head of Tatoskey Creek, and adj "Land of Mr John Newton Sold
him by me", near the plantation of Fran: Elmore.
Wit:
John Oakley Jun'r   signed   Dan'll Swillivant
Geo Glascook
Chas Barber   Rec. 18 Oct   (year omitted from record)
                                                     (however of course 1692   )

p. 30. Assignment. 21 March 1691/2. John x Derry and Barbary his wife
of Rappa Co. to Tho Gladman, land, acerage not shown.
Wit:
Tho Lewis   signed   John x Derry
Mary x Lewis   Barbary x Derry

Rec. 18 Oct. 1692

p.31. Power of Atty. No date. Barbery x Derry of Richmond Co. to Mr.
Wm. Smyth to ack above and relinq dower on above assignment.

p.31. Assignment. 9 Dec.1692. Thomas Gladman "and Katherine my now
wife" to Evan Thomas, right and title to foregoing assignment"of a
Parcell of Land"
Wit: signed   Thomas x Gladman
John Chapman
Jno x Ellis   Rec. 18 Oct. 1692

Deed Book No. 1

p.31. Deed. 2 May 1692. Wm Barber of Farnham Par in Rappa Co., to John Newton of Copley (sic) Parish in Westmorland Co., one acre of land in No. Farnham Par. "on the South End of Toluskey Mill dam and adjoining to the said mill, and now in the terms Possession and occupation of the said John Newton by virtue of his purchase of the said mill, and formerly layed out by Lt Colo John Hull and Majr Sam'll Griffin by order of Rappa County Court to and for the use and benefitt and behoofe of the said mill by virtue of an act of assembly enjoyning the same"

Wit: signed   Wm Barber
Raw Travers
Ed: Jones   Rec. 18 Oct 1692

p.32. Agreement. 2 May 1692. John Newton of Copley Par. Westmorland Co., to William Barber of Farnham Par. in Rappa Co., for a valuable consideration "oblige myself my heirs x x that he the said Wm Barber x x shall and may from time to time every Monday morning, is and shall be hopper free and have his Corne ground That is all for the use of his now dwelling plantation and dovident of Land".

Wit:
Raw Travers   signed   John Newton
Ed: Jones
                             Rec 18 Oct, 1692

p.32. Power of Atty. 2 May 1692. John Newton to Mr Edward Jones to ack above.

p.32. Deed. 28 Sept 1692. John Glendening of Richmond Co "and Ann his wife one of the Daughters and co heirs of Geo Mott late of Rappa County dec'd and one of the neices and Co-heirs of John Mott late of the aforesaid County of Rappa dec'd" to William Fitzhugh of Stafford Co., for 16000 lb tobo, 1248 acres, etc (see page 18). Land adjs main branch of Muddy Creek, Mr Wm Thornton's line and Mr Whitehead's line.

Wit:
Alexr Doniphan   signed   John Glendenning
John x Amee   Ann x Glendenning

                             Rec. 5 Oct, 1692

p.34. Power of Atty. 3 Oct,1692. John and Ann Glendenning to Mr Wm Colston to ack above.

Deed Book No. 1

p.34. Deed. 26 Sept. 1692. "John Waugh of Stafford County in Virginia Clerke" to William Fitzhugh of same Co., for 20000 lb tobo, 1090 acres "being in the forest between the North side of Rappahannock River and the South side of Potomack Creek comonly called or known by the name of Whiteheads Plantation and being part of a Devident of Two Thousand acres sold by one Tho: Comer (?) of New Kent County to me the said John Waugh by lease bearing Date the third of February 1689/90 and by Release 4th of April 1690 and both recorded in the County Court Records of Rappahannock the 4th of June 1690". The 2000 acres being part of a greater tract, by patent 1670, granted to John and George Mott and conveyed in fee to Tho Comer. "Part thereof being part of a Plantacon lived upon and seated by one Geo Shepherd". Surveyed by George Morris surveyor of Rappa. Co.
Wit:
John Withers   signed   John Waugh
Robt Brent

                    Rec. 18 Oct. 1692

p.36. Power of Atty. 26 Sept.1692. Jo. Waugh to Mr William Colston to ack above.

p.36. "Mr Colston
          Sr   These are to desire you to Record one heifer about three years old marked with two swallow forks branded on the neare shoulder with the Letter (M) for Mary Sewell and all the female increase of the said heifer to go to the said Mary and her assigns and the male increase to me
                              John Williams
                    Record'd
                              Test
                                Wm Colston Cl "

No date of record shown but actually recorded 18 Oct. 1692.

p.36. Deed. 16 April 1692. John Fosaker and Elizabeth his wife, eldest daughter of Mr. Geo Mott late of this county dec'd, etc., to Capt Sampson Dorrell of Stafford Co., for 6500 lb tobo and cask, 500 acres, part of Mott patent of 15654 acres, adj land now in possession of Mr Sampson Dorrell "by Reason the said five hundred acres of Land conteyned in the premises is forest or back Land not having the convenience of water wharfe or Landing thereunto belonging the want of which would Render the said Land inservicible Therefore it shall

Deed Book No.1

and may be Lawfull for him the said Sampson Dorrell his heirs and
assigns to Land themselves their Servants Slaves Goods Wares and
Merchandize on some convenient Landing on the Part of the Land of the
said John Fosaker and Elizabeth his wife where now they do live next
and adjoyning to the premises And to make a Convenient Cart way from
thence (that is to say) from the said Landing through the Lands of
the said John Fosaker and Elizabeth his wife to the Land in this
Indenture".

Wit: signed   John Fosaker
Alex Doniphan   Eliza Fosaker
Alex Doniphan Jun'r
John Fosaker   Rec 19 Oct. 1692

p.39. Certificate regarding above. 30 July 1692. Signed Alex
Doniphan, Justice of Peace for Richmond Co.

p.39. Certificate regarding above. 16th April 1692. Signed "Wm
Mosley, sur R:C:", surveyor.

p.40. Power of Atty. 30 July 1692. Eliz'a Fosaker to Mr. Alex'r
Doniphant or Mr Robert Brent to ack above.

p.40. Patent. 28 Sept 1681. Hen: Chicheley Knt their Majties
Deputie Govern'r of Virginia with the consent of the Counsell of
State to Edwin Conway, 900 acres in Rappa "beginning at Tacapacon
Spring, the beginning of a Patent for 5275 acres of Land granted to
Thos Chetwood and John Prosser and running along said Chetwoods and
Prossers Line N and by W 720 perch to an Indian tree mencon'd in
their Patent x x to the River of Rappahannock, thence up along the
said River and Pocason West ninety-three perches to the Place it
began x x".

p.40. Assignment of above patent. 5 May 1692. Edwin Conway of
Lancaster County to Wm Reynolds, for 1500 lb tobo, "all my Right
Title and Interest of in and to the said Patent x x except what of
the said Land lyes and falls into a Certain Tract of Land formerly
by the said Conway surveyed for Mr Symon Miller"

Wit:
Alex'r Swan   signed   Edwin Conway
Jos Lewis

Rec. 5 Oct. 1692.

Deed Book No. 1

p.41
October the 21th day 1692
In obediance to an Order of Court bearing date the 6th day of this
Instant This day John Burkett William Clapham and Wm Payne have mett
and view'd the three severall Tracts or Parcells of Land that did
belonge to David Sterne Dec'd and it is our Judgments that such Tract
of Land is one as good as the other Considering Quantitie and Qualitie
and Nich'o Smyth in Right of his wife is Possessed with one of the
said Tracts it being Judg'd to be a Just third part of it Joyning
upon Mr William Clapham as Witness our hands the day and date above

                                   John x Burkett
                                   Wm Clapham
                                   Wm Payne

                    Rec. 8 Nov. 1692

p.41. "To all to whom these Presents shall come Greeting Wee John
Deane and Wm Clapham both of the County of Richmond having marryed
the Two only Daughters of Mr Silvester Thatcher of the County of
Rapp'a now Richmond dec'd and by virtue of the said Thatchers last
will and Testament was vested and seized of a Certaine tract of Land
Conteyning One Thousand and fifty acres situate and lying on the
South side of Rapp'a River and now within the County of Essex and
upon Portobaco Swamps which land was lapsed and by us the above said
Deane and Clapham taken up againe according to Law and now lies in
Co partner-ship between us the said Deane and Clapham Now know yee
That Wee the said Deane and Clapham do by these presents bind our-
selves our heirs x x firmly by these Presents x x to stand to and
abide the devision of the aforesaid tract of Land as it was formerly
Ordered x x by the Last will and Testament of the abovesaid Mr
Silvester Thatcher" x x x.
Wit: signed   John Deane
Nicho Smyth   Wm Clapham
Philip x Comens
                    Rec. 19 Dec 1692.

p.42. Deed. 7 Dec 1692. Moses Barrow of Sittenburn par. Richmond
Co., planter to Nich'o Smyth of same par and Co., planter, for 4000
lb tobo, 200 acres in same par and Co. Adjs land of Peter Fexon, land
of Roger Richardson, land of Mr James Scott. "all and every its
Rights x x thereunto belonging x unto the aforesaid Nich'o Smyth x
during his Naturall Life the Remainder thereof to Agatha his wife and

Deed Book No. 1

to her assigns for and during her naturall Life The Remainder thereof
after their said severall deaths of Nich'o and Agatha unto Ann the
Daughter of the said Agatha and David Sterne dec'd for and during her
naturall Life" x x x "and the said Moses Barrow doth x x agree to and
with the said Nicholas Smyth Agatha his wife and Ann Sterne x x".
Wit:
John Doane   signed   Moses x Barrow
Rees Evans
Arthur Spicer   Rec. 19 Dec. 1692

p. 44.   Deed. 19th Nov. 1692.   Rich'd Winter and Abigall his wife of
Farnham par. Richmond Co., planter, to Rich'd Adams of the County
of Northumberland, planter, for 5500 lb tobo, 100 acres "being in the
forest between the Two Rivers of Potomack and Rappahannock upon some
branches of Toteskey Creek beginning at a marked white Oake standing
nigh on in a great branch of the said Creek Called hogg Town branch"
x x "to another greated white Oake standing in the said Hog Town
branch neigh opposite to the now Cleared plantacon of Hugh Harris".
Wit:
Wm Lambert   signed   Rich'd Winter
Hugh x Harris   Abigall x Winter
Alexr Swan   Rec 20 Dec. 1692

p. 45.   Powers of Atty. 19 Nov. 1692. Rich'd Winter and Abigall Winter,
both to Alex'r Swan to ack. above.

p. 46.   Deed. 14 Dec. 1692. John Craske of Richmond Co., planter, and
Elizabeth his wife one of the Daughters of Wm Moss late of Rappa Co.
dec'd to James Orchard of Richmond Co., planter, for 4700 lb tobo
in cask, 150 acres in Richmond Co. "and was part and taken out of
Herman Keldermans Pat or Tract of Land and by the said Herman sold
unto Patrick Norton late of Rappa County aforesaid Planter Dec'd and
was surveyed for the said Patrick the 24th of November 1677 by Edwin
Conway Surveyor" x x "and was since sold by the said Patrick to the
aforesaid Wm Moss and by the said Wm Moss in and by his Last will and
Testament given and bequeathed unto the said Elizabeth".
Wit:
Fran: Jordan   signed   John Craske
Rees Evans   Eliz: Craske
Jo Almond
(See next page)

p.48. Surveyors plat. 24 Nov. 1677. "a Tract of land lying and being on the north side of Rappa River in Rappa County the said Tract taken out of Herman Keldermans seat Conteyning 150 acres for aid (?) of Patrick Norton".

The plat shows "a Bay of the Maine Branch of Rappahannock Creek". To the north a small house and barn marked "Wm Moss Plant", to the south a small house and larger barn marked "Herman Keldermans Plantation".

Plat signed Edwin Conway Surveyor.
Date recorded not shown.

p.48. Deed. 12 Dec. 1692. Nich'o Smith and Agatha of Richmond Co. to Wm Clapham, for 7000 lb tobo, 150 acres "lying in the County abovesaid and adjoyning upon the Land which the said Clapham now dwells" Wit:

John Deane	signed Nich'o Smyth
Charles Spee	Agatha x Smyth

Rec. 28 Dec. 1692

p.49. "Whereas his Majties King Charles the second etc And whereas all the Right Title of in and to the said Land and premises etc is by Deed made over unto Thos Lord Culpeper etc and whereas King James the second hath been gratiously Pleased by his - Patents etc to Confirme the said grant etc to the said Thos Lord Culpeper his heirs and assigns forever etc and the said Thos Lord Culpeper being since dec'd all the Right Title and Interest etc descending on the Hon'bl Mrs Catherine Culpeper sole Daughter and heir etc and Alexander Culpeper Esq etc and whereas the said Proprietor have thought fitt etc Now know yee that I the said Phillip Ludwell Esqr by the Power and Authorite to me given and granted as aforesaid Do hereby under the Condicons and provisons etc make over and assigne unto Roderick Jones of Richmond County Two hundred acres of Land scituate lying and being in North Farnham Parish in the said County formerly called Rappa County and on the branches of Totuskey beginning at an Hickory neer the Plantacon of Tho Colley being the place where formerly stood a Red Oake Corner tree to Rich'd Powell and Robt Bedwell x x x which said Two hundred acres of Land is supposed to Escheat unto the Hon'ble Proprietors and according to the Rules prescribed in the Hon'ble Proprietors office hath preferred his Peticon for the first preference

Deed Book No.1

and the said Phill Ludwell Esqr do by these presents give and grant
the aforesaid Land as Escheatable unto the said Roderick Jones and
his heirs forever". x x x. Dated 10th October 1692.

Signed   Phill: Ludwell

p.50. Assignment of above. 2 January 1692/3. Roderick Jones "of the
County of Richmond als Rappa Tanner with the Consent and assent of
Mary my wife" to Wm Glew, for 9000 lb tobo, all right, title and
interest in above 200 acres.

Wit: signed   Roderick x Jones
James Samford   Mary x Jones
Edward Jones
Sam'll Samford   Rec. 10 Jan. 1692/3

p.50. Power of Atty. 2 Jan. 1692/3. Mary Jones the wife of Roderick
Jones of Farnham Par. Richmond Co., to Edward Jones to ack above and
relinq dower rights.

p.51. 99 Year Lease. Dated 26 December 1692/3, doubtless meaning
26th December 1692.

"Know all men by these Presents That I Moses Barrow of the County of
Richmond do for and in Consideracon of one eare of corne to be Payed
annually or every yeare to the said Barrow or his heirs etc if Demanded Do by these presents bargaine and sell Lett and make over unto
Rich'd Jordan of the County of Essex his heirs or assigns the full and
Just Quantity of one hundred acres of Land lying and being on the (sc)
County of Richmond on the North side of Rappa River and part of that
Devident of Land formerly belonging to John Barrow being any part of
the said Land Except the Plantacon where the said John Barrow formerly
lived for the full of ninety and nine years to be Ended and expired
and also that the said Richard Jordan his heirs etc may have Privi-
ledge to make use of any Timber on the said Divident of Land during
the said terme of ninety and nine years. And do promise to make acknowledgment of this Deed in Richmond Court when Required or give the
said Jordan further assurance of the said Land as he shall Require or
be directed to of his Councell learned in the Law in the forfiting or
Penalty of foure thousand Pounds of Tobb To be Pd on all demands As
Witness my hand and seale this 26th day of Decemb'r 1692/3 (sic)
Teste

signed sealed and delivered   his
in the p'rsence of   Moses x Barrow
Humph Booth   mark
Geo: Loyde

Rec. 10 January 1692/3

Deed Book No.1

p.51. Deed. 26 Nov. 1692. Edward King and Eliz: King of Richmond Co.
to Wm Downman of same Co., 50 acres, "being part of a Devident of Land
lying on the North Side of Moraticon Creek which was given unto me the
said Eliz: King and my Brother Charles Cole by my Brother Nathan'll
Cole dec'd his will:". Adjs land of Wm Smyth.
Wit:
Tho: Glascock   signed   Edward King
Edwd. Jefferys   Eliz: x King
Thos x Cotton

Rec. 10 Jan 1692/3

p.52. Power of Atty. 26 Nov. 1692. Edward and Elizabeth King to Mr.
Tho. Glascock.

p.52. Bond. 26 Nov. 1692. Edwd and Eliz King to Wm Downman, 10000 lb
tobo for above.

p.53. Deed. 3 Jan'ry 1692/3. Alexander Fleming and Thomas Algar of
Richmond Co., to Tho: Baylis of same Co., "one Tract or parcell of
Land which wee the said Alexand'r Fleming and Tho: Alger have by the
Right of our wifes Sarah Fleming and Alitia Alger the which land was
left to our said wifes by the last will and Testament of Wm Kennedy
dec'd of the County of Rappa formerly so called but of late called
the County of Richmond That is to say the said Wm Kennedy by his last
Will and Testament did give and bequeathe after his death the said
Tract or parcell of Land unto the children then living of John Kennedy
and now become Co-heirs of the said Tract or parcell of Land the which
Land formerly was the dwelling Plantacon of the aforesaid Wm Kennedy
and is situate lying and being at or neere the head of Richardsons
Creek in the Parish of North Farnham in the above mencioned County and
Colony".
Wit:
Ja: Samford   signed   Alex'r Fleming
Isaac Wright   Tho Alger
Richd King
Sam'll Sanford

Rec. 10 Jan. 1692/3

p.54. Bond. 3 Jany 1692/3. Alexander Fleming and Tho Alger for above.

(see next page)

Deed Book No. 1

p.54. Deed. 2 Jan 1692/3. Edward Tayler of No. Farn. Par. Richmond
Co., Carpenter "with the Consent of my wife Eliz: Tayler" to Thomas
Baylis, Planter, "a Certaine Parcell of Land which was formerly bought
between Wm Kenney and Toby Stephens now dec'd the which land is neere
the head of Richardsons Creek and Joynes Plantacon where Wm Kenney
formerly lived in Richmond County"
Wit:
Richard King   signed   Edw'd x Tayler
Isaac Wright   Eliz x Tayler
Sam'll Samford
Tho Algar   Rec. 10 Jan 1692/3

p.55. Power of Atty. 2 Jan 1692/3. Eliz: Tayler to "my Trusty friend"
Sam'll Samford to ack above.

Note: See deed on p.16. The names Kennedy and Kenney appear to refer
to the same person.   B.F.

p.55. Deed. 5 May 1691. Mottrum Wright "of the Parish of Cittenburne
in the County of Rappa Gent and Sarah his wife" to John Babtist. (sic)
"That the said Mottrum Wright and Ruth his wife for and in Consideracon" (sic). Wright sells, for 10500 lb tobo, 210 acres "being in
the Parish and County aforesaid on the northwest side of Rappa Creek
part of the said Two hundred and Ten Acres of Land lying within the
bounds of a Patent formerly granted to Lieut Coln'll Hen: Fleet and
by the son and heir of the said Fleet sold and assigned unto the said
Mottrum Wright the residue lying in and being part of the Moyetie or
one half part of a Patent for Two thousand acres granted unto Walter
Granger by Patent dated the 25th day of March 1691 (?) and by the
said Granger sold and assigned unto Coln'll John Walker by assignment
of the said Grangers Patent dated the 20th of May 1662 and one
thousand the Moyetie of the said Two Thousand acres of Land given by
the Will of the said Coln'll John Walker unto his Daughter Sarah the
wife of Edwin Conway of whom the said Mottrum Wright purchased the
said Two hundred and Ten acres of Land". The land adjs the said John
Babtist's spring, the land of Mr. John Browne, land of John Coles,
the cow marsh swamp. This deed refers five times to "Mottrum Wright
and Ruth his wife".
Wit:
Fran: Wright   signed   Mottrum Wright
James Hall
                        Rec. 14 Feb. 1692/3

Note: The name 'Sarah' shown at the beginning of the deed is evidently
an error. Also the date 1691. Col. John Walker was dead before that.

Deed Book No. 1

p.57. Deed of Gift. 1 Feby 1692/3. "That I John Shurlock and Eliz:
my wife for the Love we beare to our Grandson Rich'd Evans" give "a
Certaine Heifer of foure years old Croped on both ears".
Wit:
Henry Seager   signed   John x Shurlock
Edwin Conway   Eliz: x Shurlock

Rec. 14 Feb. 1692/3

p.57. Power of Atty. 2 Nov.1692. Katherine Gladman wife of Tho:
Gladman to Angell Jacobus to ack sale of land to Evan Thomas.
Wit:
Shadrick Williams   signed   Katherine x Gladman
Wm Sisson
Rec. 14 Feb 1692/3

p.57. Fran: Williams marke: by crop and under keele on the Right Eare
the left eare whole: to be recorded
                                        Fran: Williams
                        Recor'd
                            Test
                                Wm Colston C.Cur.

p.57. Bond. 28 March 1693. Rees Evans of the County of Essex Gent to
John Loyd "of the County of Richmond also Gent". L 144. Current
English money. That Evans pay Loyd L 72. 3. 6 on 29th Sept following.
Wit:·
Rich'd Newsum   signed   Rees Evans
Isaac Webbe
Jno Taverner   Rec. 5 April 1693.

p.58. Mortgage. 20 March 1693 (actually 1692/3). Evans to Loyd, 6
negro slaves to guarantee payment of foregoing.

p.58. Deed. 1 April 1691. "Henry Goring late of the Colony of Virginia
now Resident in Calvert County in the Providence of Maryland" to

Deed Book No. 1

Antho Carnaby of Rappa River in the Colony of Virginia, for 2500
lb tobo, 50 acres in Rappa Co at the head of Papeto Creek, "which said
Land I bought of Wm Jennings", adj land of John Jennings and land of
Tho Erwin.
Wit: signed   Hen x Goaring
Tho x Smyth
Hen: Ferneley

p.59. Certificate. 21 June 1692. James Keith and Hen Mitchell, two
Justices of Peace for Calvert Co. in the Province of Maryland re. the
signature of Henry Goaring. Wit: Tho. Tasker.

Rec. 15 April 1693.

p.59. Deed. 3 June 16 -. Tho Arnold "of the County of Rappa and Grace
my wife" to Henry Goring of the same Co. 50 acres.
Wit:
Jos: Rutter   signed   Tho: Arnold
Wm x Tayler   Grace Arnold
                       Rec. 4 Nov 1689 in Rappa Co.

p.60. Assignment. 1 Apl 1691. Hen Goaring late of Rappa River in Va.,
now of Calvert County in prov. of Maryland, to Antho Carnaby, all right
and title to land in foregoing.
Wit: signed   Hen x Goaring
Thos x Smyth
Hen: Ferneley

p.60. Certificate 2 June 1692 re signatures.

p.60. Power of Atty. 1 Apl. 1691. Henry Goring of Calvert Co., Md. to
"my Loving friend Mr James Tayler of Rappa County" to ack sale of 2
pc land, each 50 acres, to Antho Carnaby. Signature and Wit: as above.
p.61. Certificate as above.

p.61. Deed of Gift, 6 Dec. 1692. Alexander Newman of the Co. of
Richmond "do give and grant unto my Goddaughter Easter Jeffery
youngest Daughter of Edward Gefery and Elizabeth his wife" a heifer.
Wit:
Benja x Evans   signed   Alexander Newman
Edwd Jeffery

Rec. 18 April 1693.

Deed Book No. 1

p. 62.

Mr Colston

Pray record my marke it is a Crop and a slitt a hole on the
Right Eare and a Crop and a slitt and bitt cutt out under the left
ear and this my noat shall make you satisfaction from Your friend

Tho: Scrivan

Date of record not shown but is 18 April 1693.

p. 62. Deed. 3 May 1693. "Alexand'r Doniphan of the County of Richmond
Gent and Margarett his wife Daughter and Co heir together with Eliza-
beth Ann and Ellen of George Mott of the County of Rappahannock" etc
to "Wm Colston of the said County of Richmond Clerke", for 18000 lb
tobo, 1246 acres, part of a patent formerly granted John and George
Mott, etc., for 15654 acres, adj land of Capt Glendening, land of John
Vickers, along Muddy Creek, etc.
Wit:

Tho: Taliaferro   signed   Alexand'r Doniphan
Josh Davis   Margarett x Doniphan
Abraham Blagg

Rec. 16 May 1693

p. 66. Bond for above.

p. 67. Deed. 3 May 1693. Richard Wood of Richmond Co to Thos. Reyly,
for a valuable consideration, a parcel of land "being on the side of
the Branch whereon the said Tho. Reyly now liveth", being part of 200
acres bought of Col. Wm. Loyd, adj land of said Loyd, Reyly, the land
of George Heuson.
Wit: signed   Rich'd x Wood
Jo: Fones   Mary x Wood
Charles Spee (or Spoo)
Martha x Stockford   Rec. 16 May 1693.

p. 67. Power of Atty. 25 April 1693. Mary Wood to Tho: Bradley "for
the acknowledging of a Parcel of Land which my husband Rich'd Wood
hath sold to Tho: Reyly".
Wit: signed   Mary x Wood
Charles Spee (or Spoo)
Jo: Fones   Rec. 16 May 1693.

Note: The name of this witness Spee or Spoo, which may be Shee or
Shea, is one of those minor matters that annoy the transcribers of
old records to bad language. I don't know what this obscure name is
and I'm sorry to say I don't care very much either.   B.F.

Deed Book No. 1

p.67. Agreement, 22 April 1693.
"Know all men by these Presents That whereas I Charles Snead of the
County of Richmond Planter Eldest Son of Charles Snead Sen'r decd late
of Rappa County Planter who by his Last will and Testament did give
and bequeath all his Estate both Reale and Personall unto me the subscriber my severall brothers and my sister Elizabeth now wife to
Frances Tayler allotting unto Every of us such Proporcons of Land as
he thought fitt as by his will may appeare And amongst the Rest gave
unto my above named Sister Elizabeth the part or parcell of her Broth.
in case any of them dyed without Issue. Now, so it is that for as much
as it hath Pleased God to take out of this world all my Brothers so
that what Land Remains unsold by them is vested in me and my above
named Sister Elizabeth wife to Fran: Tayler and for as much as some
differences have arose betwixt us relating to the aforesaid Land for
the prevention of any further Quarrells or dissentions betwixt us or
our Children hereafter Wee the said Charles Snead and Francis Tayler
have made a firme and Inviable agreement to keep and hold each of us
such Lands as wee have layed out by a Particoon line made by us with
a Joynt consent in presence of severall of the neighbours (Vizt)
William Griffin Tho Scrivan David Coleburn and John Britomwood, the
division Line beginning at the mouth of a great swamp by the River
Side which is betwixt us and Running up the said swamp to a marked
Poplar from thence Crossing the Road to a marked Gum Running along a
line of marked trees by the Path that heads to Tho: Scrivan to a
stake in the said Tho: Scrivan Line the above said Charles Snead to
hold keep and enjoy the upper part whereon he now lives and Fran:
Tayler to hold keep and enjoy the lower part whereon he now lives
also In Consideration of the premises wee the subscribers do for ourselves our heirs Executors and Administrators bind ourselves our or
either of our heirs Executors or administrators to each other upon
default made of the premises in the penall sum of one hundred
Thousand Pounds of good Tobb in Caske In witness we have hereunto
sett our hands and seales this 22'd day of Aprile 1693
Teste
James Harrison   signed   Charles Snead
Wm Davis   Frances x Tayler

Rec. 16 May 1693

p.63. Deed, 2 Nov.1691. William Yates of No. Farnham Par., Rappa Co.,
planter, to William Burnham of the County of Westmorland, shipwright,
for 4000 lb tobo in cask, 100 acres in N. Farn. Par. The following
item in this deed does not hold together but there is nothing to do
but give it as shown in the original record. So "part of a Devident
of Capt John Hull and by the said John Allaway sold to John Yates and

Deed Book No.1

by inheritance to the above said William Yeates son of the Jn'o Yates".
"The said land by these presents granted lying between the Two branches
comonly known or Called by the name of the Matchacomaeo branch and the
other Edward Lewis his branch".
Wit:

Edward x Newton   signed   Wm Yates
Edw'd Jones
Jno Battaile

Rec 27 Nov 1691

Note: These entries seem all wrong to me, but here they are nevertheless. Evidently I don't know everything. Newton and Jones all right
but what did Battaile have to do with it, not to mention Dew ?   B.F.

p.70. Assignment. 10 April 1693. William Burnham of the County of
Richmond, Carpenter, to Phillip Hunnings (again I question this name)
for 4000 lb tobo, all right in foregoing. "and do further declare that
my wife Ann Burnham hath given her free consent to this sale"
Wit:

Wm Barber   signed   Wm Burnham
Wm Barber Jun'r   Ann x Burnham
Tho Dew

Rec. 17 May 1693

p.70. This entry is also unbelievable. There is nothing to do but show
it as it is.
       Deed. 22 July 1672. John Byforest of the County of Rappa and
parish of Farnham, planter, to Dan'll Oneale of the same county,
planter, "the one halfe of a Dividert of Land which I have bought of
Thos. Madison lying and bounding upon the Land of Wm Mathews and
Thomas Maddison"
Wit:

Peter Calvin   signed   John Byforest
Arthur x Eatry

p.71. Assignment. 3 January 1677 (1677/8). Dan'll Oneale to George
Vinson all right and title in foregoing.
Wit:

Wm Brockonburrow   signed   Dan'll x Oneale
Hancock Were his mark

p.71. Assignment. 14 July 1691. Geo. Vinson to John Mills, all right
and title in foregoing.
Wit: signed   George Vinson
James x Gainer (or Gaines)
Charles Dodson

(see next page)

Deed Book No.1

p.71. Assignment. 12 Sept 1692. John Mills to William Richardson all right and title to foregoing.
Wit:

John x Hooper   signed   John x Mills
Charles Dodson
Tho: x Salsby   Rec. 17 May 1693
                                       Wm Colston CC

p.71. Power of Atty. 1 May 1693. Easter Mills of Richmond Co., to Mr Edward Read of same Co to ack sale of foregoing "made by my husband John Mills and myself unto William Richardson of the abovesaid County of Richmond".
Wit: signed   Easter x Mills
Ann Dodson her mark:
Charles x Dodson Jun'r
Charles Dodson Sen'r   Rec. 17 May 1693.

p.71. "This is to satisfie you that Richard Tompkins having swapped a Cow with his Daughter in Law Eliz: Palmer for a younge Horse the cow being Red marked with a Crop and two slitts on the left eare and a hole in the Right with half her increase to be Recorded for the said Palmer which bargaine being with the said Elizabeth and her Mothers consent
and in the presence of   Tho: x Hughes
                                    Rowland Thornton
To the Worship'll Justices of Peace

p.72. Deed. 10 Feby 1692/3. "Know all men by these Presents That I John Browne of Richmond County do hereby Alienate bargaine sell enfooffe and confirm unto my Brother William Browne x x a certain small Tract or parcell of Land Conteyning thirty acres more or less being my part of a larger quantity purchased by my father Wm Browne from Adam Woffendall and John Phillips lying upon the maine branch of Chingateague and binding upon the Line of my father Browne"
Wit:

James Tayler   signed   John (B) Browne
Sarah x Berry
                          Rec. 7 June 1693

p.72. Power of Atty. 2 May 1693. John Browne to Joshua Davis to ack above. Witnessed by Wm Mills and Wm x Whithorn.

Deed Book No.1

p.72. "The Gift of John Hughes to his God:son John Wells which is foure head of cattle and all the Increase of the females and the marke as followeth with a Crop on the Right Eare with a slitt in the Crop and three nicks under the left eare And if it Please God to take him out of this life before he come to age that the said Cattle and their increase be Equally divided amongst the Children of Jno Garten"

Rec. 17 June 1693

p.73. Power of Atty. 2 May 1693. Ann Burnham wife of Wm Burnham of Richmond Co., to Mr Jno Taverner of same Co., to ack sale of land "which my husband bought of Wm Yates of the aforesaid County Joyning upon Totoskey Creek unto Phillip Hunnings"
Wit:
Wm x Hoskins   signed   Ann x Burnham
Marg'tt x Hoskins
                       Rec. 17 June 1693

p.73. Lease. 17 April 1693. John Landman "of the County of Essex and Parish of Sittenburns" to Wm Puckford "of the County of Richmond and Parish of Richmond", for valuable considerations "all that point peice or parcell of Land That the said John Landman had demised unto him by Jonathan Barrow situate lying and being in the freshes of Rappa and in the County and parish of Richmond aforesaid comonly Called or knowne by the name of Cabbin Point and Conteyning by Estimation fifty acres", running down the River and adj land of Peter Faxon. This deed includes "for and during the Naturall Life of him the said John Landman and after for and during the naturall Life of Jane Landman his wife the Remainder thereof for and during The Landmans naturall Life son of the aforesaid John and Jane Landman".
Wit:
Ro: Brook   signed   John Landman
Katherine Brook   Jane x Landman

Rec. 23 June 1693.

p.74. Power of Atty. 2 May 1693. Jane Landman of Essex Co. to John Nicholls of Richmond Co., to ack above.
Wit:
Rob't Brook   signed   Jane Landman
Kat: Brook
                       Rec. 23 June 1693

Deed Book No.1

p.74.

Mr Colston

This is to Request to do me the favour to Record a Sorrell
Mare that I have for my son Wm: Shea she is branded with R:E on the
Buttock and with an :S: on the shoulder with all her increase Excepting the first foal she brings for myself As witness my hand the
24:th of February 1692.

Margery x Ieagoe

Note: I am none too positive about that name. It may possibly be
Jagoe or even Jaque.   B.F.

p.74. Deed. 2 June 1693. Clement Hill of St Marys County in the
Province of Maryland, Gent., to Eliz: Gardiner "widow and Relict of
Richard Gardiner late of St Marys County in the Province of Maryland
Gent deceased", 2502 acres, "being on the North Side of Richmond
River als Rappa River", this land "granted unto Maj'r John Werle
formerly of the said County of Richmond als Rappa and Parish of Sittenburne by Patent bearing date the sixth day of June in the yeare of
our Lord God one Thousand six hundred sixty and six x x x all which
Plantacon lands tenem'ts: buildings and appurtenances was by him the
said Clement Hill of late purchased by Deed Indented and enrolled at
James City of the aforesaid Rich'd Gardiner and Eliz: his wife as by
a certaine Indenture of bargains and sale bearing date this Ninth day
of Aprile in the yeare of our Lord God 1686".

Clement Hill, in the body of the deed, appoints "his trusty and
well beloved friends Capt Geo: Tayler and Mr James Harrison both of
Richmond County in the Colony of Virginia his true and lawful
attorneys x x to Expell and put out all other Person and Persons" and
give peaceful possession of the property to Eliz: Gardiner.
Wit:

Clement Hill Junr   signed   Clement Hill
Mary x Werkes
Ann Goodman   Rec. 27 June 1693

p.77. Certificate. 7 June 1693. Of peaceable possession of the above
property by George Tayler and James Harrison, attorneys to Elizabeth
Gardiner

signed   Wm Barber
Alex'r Swan
Den: McCarty

p.77. Deed. 6 June 1693. Elizabeth Gardiner, widow, of St. Marys Co.,
Maryland to James Shippie, planter, of Richmond County, for 4000 lb.

Deed Book No. 1

tobo, a parcel of land, 100 acres, "being in Richmond County about a
mile from Richmond River als Rappa River it being part of a Tract of
Land formerly belonging unto Maj'r John Weire", adj land of Wm Davis.
Shippie's name also appears in the deed as James Shipway.
Wit:
Den: McCarty   signed   Eliz: Gardiner
Wm Colston
                        Rec. 27 June 1693.

p.77. Deed. 6 June 1693. Eliz: Gardiner of St.M. Co. Md. to Wm Davis
planter, of Richmond Co., for 4000 lb tobo, 100 acres, part of land
formerly belonging to Maj'r John Weire. Signed and witnessed as above.
Recorded 27 June 1693.

p.83. Acknowledgment. 26 April 1690. Francis Goare of Rappa County
acknowledges "to make even x a firme Deed of Sale of the said Land"
100 acres, to James Orchard.
Wit: signed   Francis Goare
Ralph Rymer
Ang'll Jacobus   Rec. 28 June 1693.

p.83. Surveyors plat. 13 Nov. 1690. "Surveyed for Mr James Orchard
124 acres of Land in Rappa County above Rappa Creeke being part of a
Patent formerly granted unto Mr George Jones and Mr. Henry Clarke and
since purchased by Mr James Orchard of Mr Francis Gowre"
Plat shows Orchard's 124 acres with house. Adj Robt Wood's land and
"Mr Goures Land". Beyond Goare's a two story house is shown marked
"Jno Fenners"

p.84. Deed. 31 July 1693. Charles Dodson to his son Tho. Dodson a
cow "being in Exchange with him my said Son Thomas for one Sow shoat
given him by his God father Peter Elmore"
Wit:
Wm Wood   signed   Charles Dodson
Wm Colston
                        Rec. 31 July 1693.

Deed Book No. 1

p.84

Wm Colston
    I desire you will Record the ear mark of my Hogs and
Cattle which is a Crop and under keel and hole one the Right ear the
left eare a piece taken out from the Root both over and under and
stands peaked with a hole

                                    I am your friend
                                       Wm Wood

p.84. Deed of Gift. 22 July 1693.

                        Virginia Richmond County
    Be it known unto all Persons to whom these presents shall come
I John Willis of the aforesaid County for love and affection I have
unto Matilda Thacker whom I desire to make my wife do give and bequeath unto the aforesaid Matilda Thacker her heirs Executors administrators or assigns forever One bed and furniture which she shall
make choice of and foure breeding Cattle nott under three years nor
above six years old and one young mare not under three years old and
not above six years old and all her Cloathes And in Case I the said
John Willis should out live my said Intended wife Matilda Thacker
shee to dispose of the aforesaid Goods and cattle according as she
pleases And in case I should die before her then these goods and
cattle to be first taken out of my Estate and delivered my wife and
she to have her proporcon of my Estate according to law over and
above the goods and chattels aforemencioned as Witness my hand and
Seale this 22d day of July 1693
                                    John x Willis   (seale)
Wit:
Joshua Davis
Charles Minthorn   Rec. 11 Aug. 1693

p.85   Rich Ss
    I the subscriber do here authorize and Impower Joshua
Davis my attorney to acknowledge a Deed of Gift unto Matilda Thacker
in the aforesaid County bearing date the 22'd day of July 1693 And
this shall be his warrant for so doing as Witness my hand and seale
this 23d day of July 1693
Wit: his mark
Rebecca x Lowrey   John x Willis
James Tayler

Deed Book No. 1

p.85. Agreement. 2 August 1693. Morgan Williams and Wm Steward having
jointly purchased from Mr John Peirce and Hester his wife 267 acres
in Rappa on westward side of Rappa Creek"that wee are fully satisfied
with our proporconable parts layed out and divided by Mr Edwin Conway".
The line drawn from a stake in Jonah Wilson's line on 2 Febry 1692/3.
That part SW and W to Williams: that part SE to Steward.
Wit:
David x Janes   signed   Morgan Williams
Mary x Janes   Wm x Steward

Rec. 11 Aug. 1693

p.85.   Wm Colston
            Pray Record my Marke being a figure of three on the Right
Eare and a swallow Forke on the left
                                        Pithagoras x Powell

p.85. Power of Atty. 29 Nov. 1692. Mary Nicholls wife of Zacharia
Nicholls to "my friend Edward Jones" to ack sale of a mill by her
husband to Mr. John Newton.
Wit: signed   Mary Nicholls
John Trapley (sic)
Charles Barber
Jean Glascock   Rec. 24 Nov. 1693

p.86. Deed. No date shown. John Mewes "of Richmond County Planter and
Sinyere" (sic) sells to Arthur Notwell a cow calf.
Wit:
Wm x Powell   signed   John x Mews
Sam'll: Damounvill

p.86. Deed of Gift. No date. Arthur Notwell "do freely and voluntarily
give unto Cozin Catherine Mewes" the foregoing cow calf.
Wit:
Wm x Powell   signed   Arthur Notwell
Sam'll: Damounvill

Dates of record not shown.

Deed Book No.1

p.86. Deed. - September 1693. John Fosaker and Elizabeth his wife of
the par. of St Marys in Richmond Co., to Hugh French of same par. and
Co., for 2000 lb tobo, 146 acres "being the Remainding part of the
said Fosakers back Land which came by his said wife Elizabeth the
Daughter of Mr: Mott", adjs land sold to David Darnell
Wit:
Thos Parke   signed   John Fosaker
Antho Prosser   Eliz: Fosaker

Rec. 25 Oct 1693.

p.88. Power of Atty. 30 Sept 1693. Elizabeth Fosaker to Alexander
Doniphan to ack above.
Wit: signed   Elizabeth x Fosaker
Alexand'r Doniphan Junr
Benja x Harvey

p.89. Bond. John Fosaker for above.

p.90. Deed. - September 1693. John Fosaker and Elizabeth his wife to
Hugh French, for 3000 lb tobo, 100 acres adj land of Capt. Geo Mason,
land of Mr Wm Colston, land of Capt John Clendenen and land of John
Fosaker.
Wit: signed   John Fosaker
Alexan'r Doniphan   Eliz: x Fosaker
Fran: Thornton
Thos Parke
Antho: Prosser   Rec. 10 Oct. 1693

p.92. Deed. 21 Sept. 1693. David Darnell and Margarett his wife of
St Marys Par Richmond Co to Hugh French of sd Par and Co. for 7000 lb
tobo, 600 acres, adj land of Mr Wm Thornton, land of Coll: Wm Fitzhugh,
land of Mr Sampson Darnell, land of Rich'd Shipways and land of James
Orchard, "being part of a Patent for Land lying in Rappahannock and
Stafford Countys granted to Mr Motts".
Wit:
John Fosaker   signed   David Darnell
John Carter   Marg'tt x Darnell
Mauser x Hubbert
Rec. 10 Oct. 1693

p.93. Bond for above. Same signatures and witnesses.

Deed Book No.1

p.94. Power of Atty. 22 Sept 1693. David and Margaret Darnell to
Edward Jones to ack foregoing sale. Same signatures and witnesses.

p.94. Deed. 27 Sept. 1693. Arthur Spicer "of the County of Richmond
Gent and Elizaboth his wife" to George Tayler and John Tavener "of
the County aforesaid Gents", one half of 1150 acres, "being the
northernmost of the said Eleven hundred and fifty acres of Land
assigned by one Robert Hopkins unto Sam'll Nicholls and Edward Rowzee
and by them sold and conveyed to Tho Jones father of the said Eliza-
beth who claims the same as his only Heiress"
Wit:
Jno Parker   signed   Arthur Spicer
Edw'd x Newton   Eliz: Spicer
Dan: McCarty
Edward Bray

p.96. Arthur and Eliz: Spicer ack above sale. Recorded 11 Dec. 1693.

p.96. The mark of Matthew Peters is a Crope and hole in the Right
Eare and a slitt and a crope and a hole in the left Eare
No date of record shown, is doubtless December 1693.

p.96. Deed. 30 March 1693. Richard Brannham of Farnham Par. Richmond
Co., to Tho Gladman, for 2000 lb tobo, 100 acres of woodland. Adjs
land of Samuel Coggins and land of John Sherlock. "with consent of
Deborah my Lawfull wife".
Wit: signed   Richard Brannham
Wm Kissey   Debora BB Brannham
Robt x Thornton
                          Rec. 20 Dec. 1693

p.97. Deed. 3 January 1692/3. John Willis of Richmond Co, planter, to
Thos Kendall of the same Co., planter, for certain cattle, a parcel of
land in Richmond Co.,"being betweene the land of Indrein and Joseph
Mason"
Wit: signed   John x Willis
Tho Parke
Tho x Goffe   Rec. 20 Dec. 1693

Deed Book No. 1

p.99. Deed. 3 Jan. 1692 (1692/3). John Coombes of Richmond Co.,
planter, to Thos Kendall of the same Co., planter, "in Consideration
of a horse and a sow and pigs to him in hand Paid by the said Tho
Kendall", land, acerage not shown. Adjs land of John Willis and land
of sd John Coombes. Deed refers to "the said John Coombes and Ann his
wife".
Wit: signed   John x Coombes
Tho Parke
Tho x Goffe   Rec. 20 Dec 1693
                                       Teste
                                           Wm Colston Cl Cur

p.100. Robt: Palmers marke of hoggs and cattle is Two Cropps Two under
keels and a slitt in the Right Eare.
No date of record shown.

p.100. Robt Woods marke of hoggs and cattle is a crop and a hole in
the left Eare and a slitt in the Right eare
No date of record shown.

p.100. Deed of Gift. 7 December 1693. "Xpian Eastridge of the County
of Richmond widow do give assign and make over to my Daughter Ann
Eastridge one Cow and a Cow Calfe by her side and all the female increase"

                                  signed   Xpian x Eastridge

                    No date of record shown.

p.100. Deed. 21 Sept. 1693. "John Hill and Elizabeth his wife of the
County of Richmond in Virginia Plant'r" to John Creele of the same
Co., planter, for a valuable consideration, 60 acres in Farnham Par.,
Richmond Co., adj path going to Bartholomew Woods and a path going to
Walt'r Webb, a corner tree of Geo: Devenports and John Hill "thence
to the head of a small branch Issuing out of the maine branch of
Northumberland River and down the said branch till you come to the
maine swamp", also adj land of John Linkhorne. "which said sixty

Deed Book No. 1

acres of Land is part and parcell of a devident of Land Conteyning
Eight hundred acres of Land Patented by John Carpenter Charles Carpen-
ter and Wm West and part of it taken up by Jno: Hill"
Wit:
Gilbt Croswell   signed   John x Hill
Mary x Creel   Eliz x Hill
Charles Dodson
                        Rec. 20 Dec 1693
                            Wm Colston CC

p.102. Power of Atty. 4 Dec. 1693. "Elizabeth Hill the wife of John
Hill of Richmond County and the Parish of Farnham" to "my well beloved
and trusty friend John Rankin of the aforesaid County and parish" to
ack foregoing sale.
Wit: signed   Elizabeth x Hill
Charles x Vallen (or Valleu)
John x Davis
                        "Record'
                            Teste
                                Wm Colston Cl Cur"

Deed Book No. 2
20 Jany 1693/4 to 1696

page 1. The Ear Mark of Daniel Jacksons hogs and cattle is a half
spade and a nick in each Ear

page 1. The Ear Mark of Xpher Ascoughs hogs and cattle is a Crop and
three slitts in each Ear

page 1. The Ear Mark of Morris Hamletts Hogs and Cattle a Crop on
the Right Ear with an underkeel and overkeel and a Hole on the left
Ear a Crop, an underkeel and overkeel and a slitt

Deed Book No. 2

page 1.

Jurys Report
Partition of
Wm Moss' Land
int'r Wm Brown
and Jno Crask

In Obedience to an Order of Court bearing date
the 7th of December 1693 we being a Jury im-
pannelled and sworn did meet Capt Wm Moseley on
the 20th Day of December upon the Land of Mr Wm
Moss and there did equally devide the said Land
into two parts according to Quantity and Quality
having Regard to all Conveniences thereon (viz)
Two hundred acres of Land to the plantation where the said Wm Moss
dec'd lived for the one part and the Residue of high land being for
the other part. And after we had so done, the Choise according to the
within Order was given to Wm Brown as marrying the eldest Daughter of
the said Wm Moss dec'd which said Brown made Choise of the above said
Plantation with two hundred acres of Land, and the remaining part, the
Possession thereof given to John Craske as marrying the youngest
Daughter of the said Moss dec'd by the High Shoriff of the said County
according to Order as Witness our Hands and seals this 20th Day of
December 1693

Allen Monjoy	(s)	John x Ford	(s)
John Babtist	(s)	Avery x Naylor	(s)
Wm x Carter	(s)	Chas x Sneade	(s)
Humph Mallory	(s)	Wm x Bayly	(s)
Hen: Burditt	(s)	Thos x Newman	(s)
Hen: Chappel	(s)	Thos x Janes	(s)

Record'r int: Rotu' Cur: Com: Richmond 20°
die Jan'rii An'o: 1693.

Test: Wm Colston Cl:Cr

page 2. Surveyors Report. 29 December 1693. "Then in Obedience to an
Order of Richmond County Court x x have surveyed in the presence of a
Jury the patent granted to Wm Moss for one thousand and sixty acres of
Land and Marsh bearing date the 10th of September 1663 Between John
Craske Complt as marrying Elizabeth the youngest Daughter of the said
Wm Moss and Wm Browne as marrying Frances the eldest Daughter of the
said Moss x x x Have complyed therewith and surveying the same find to
be 639 acres x x

Your humble servant   Wm Moseley Survey'r
to command

Recorded 20 January 1693/4.

Deed Book No. 2

p.2. Deed. 14 Jan 1692/3. Simon Miller, planter, of Essex Co., to Tho.
Parke, schoolmaster, of Essex Co. "know ye that I the said Simon
Miller for several good considerations me hereunto moving and likewise
for the Love and affection that I the said Simon Miller bear unto Tho
Parke of the County of Essex schoolmaster", as much land as he shall
have use of during his (Parke's) life, in Richmond County, and at his
death to return to Miller's estate. This land "in the County of Rich-
mond on the North side of Rappahannock River on the back side of Mr
Hugh French his Plantation on the further side of a Marsh of Water
between the Line of Mr Antho: Savage and the Line of Robert Paine"
Wit:
Rees Evans   signed   Simon Miller
Samll: Jaques
                        Rec. 20 Jan 1693/4

p.4. Power of Atty. 9 Aug 1693. Symon Miller of the parish of St Marys
and County of Richmond to Mr James Orchard of same County to ack the
foregoing.
Wit: signed   Symon Miller
John Battaile

p.4. Deed. 2 January 1693/4. Samuel Travers and Frances his wife of
Richmond Co to Charles Dodson, for 10000 lb tobo and cask, 500 acres,
"being part of a patent granted to Mr Thomas Chitwood and George
Haselock bearing Date 9th Day of July 1663". This land lying on the
main branch of Totuskey Creek, adj land sold by said Travers to Dan'l
Everett. Entry includes "either of our Heirs in by from or under
Col'n William Travers Father of me the said Samuel Travers"
Wit:
Peter Hall   signed   Sam'l: Travers
Gilbert Hornby (or Fornby)   Fran: Travers
Mary x Wollard
                        Rec 22 January 1693/4

p.6. Power of Atty. 2 January 1693/4. Frances Travers to "my loving
and trusty Friend Mr John Taverner" to ack foregoing.
Wit:
Peter Hall   signed   Frances Travers
Gilb't Hornby (or Fornby)

p.6. Deed. 9 Dec. 1693. James Orchard, planter, of Richmond Co., to
Arthur Spicer, Gent., of the same Co., "by order of their Majesty's
Justices of the peace for the said County bearing Date the 7th Day

Deed Book No. 2

of July 1692 for a valuable consideration therein mentioned it was by
them agreed that the said James Orchard should by good and sufficient
conveyance to him made have conveyed and assured to him all that
Tract or parcell of Land containing by Estimation seventy acres be it
more or less whereon the then present Court House stood"
Wit:
Alex'r Chapple   signed   James Orchard
Jo: Taverner
                          Rec 22 January 1693/4

p.8. Deed. 7 March 1693/4. John Kenyon of St Marys par. in Richmond
Co., Gent., to John Jones of same par. and Co., blacksmith, for 5000
lb tobo, 200 acres, "as by a platt of the said Land under Mr Theodo-
rich Bland his Hand bearing Date the 7th Day of December 1693 survey-
or being part of a Devidend containing sixteen hundred sixty eight
acres sold by Mr John and Geo Motts to Mr Wm Moseley and by Mr Wm
Moseley sold to Mr Andrew Buckner and by him sold to Mr Abraham Kenyon"
this 200 acres adj a tract "being the lowermost corner in the Woods
of a Tract of four hundred fifty six acres sold by Mr John Kenyon out
of the said whole Tract of sixteen hundred acres to Wm Yates".
Wit:
Adam Woffendall   signed   John Kenyon
James Woffendall
Richd x Berry   Rec. 20 March 1693/4

p.10. Bond. 7 March 1693/4. John Kenyon for above. Wit: Joshua Davis,
Adam Woffendall.

p.10. "Mrs Mary Lewis her mark is two Crops and one whole in the left
Ear".

p.11. Deed. 10 Oct. 1691. "John Kenyon and Jabes his Brother of the
County of Rappaha'h" to William Yates of same Co., for a valuable
consideration, 456 acres, part of a parcel of land bought of Mr John
and Geo Mott and from them sold to Mr Wm Moseley and by him to Mr
Andrew Buckner and by him "to Mr Abraham Konyon the Father of the
said John and Jabes". This land "on the River side opposite to

Deed Book No. 2

Massiponey Creek's mouth" and adj. land of Wm Yates.
Wit:
Thomas Park   signed   John Kenyon
Charles Magan   Jabes Kenyon
Richd Hofton
                         Rec. 20 March 1693/4

p.12. Deed. 29 Dec. 1692. Adam Woffendall of Richd Co to Wm. Powell
of same Co, for 2000 lb tobo, 50 acres, adj main Branch of Chingoe-
teague above John Easters Plantation, the line of William Marshall,
the line of Mr. Fran. Sloughter, along the path to William Brown's
corner tree.
Wit: signed   Adam Woffendall
James Tayler
John x Brown   Rec. 20 March 1693/4

p.14. Bond on above. Same date, signature and witnesses.

p.15. Deed. 5 February 1693/4. John Landman of Northfarnham Par.,
Richmond Co., planter, to William Smyth of same par. and Co.,planter,
for a valuable consideration, 101 acres, on W side Totuskey Creek,
adj. land of Mr Robt Sisson, land of John Morgan and land of Geo Eale
Wit:
Jos: Dike   signed   John Landman
David Barwick
                         Rec 20 March 1693/4

p.17. Deed. 12 Dec 1693. Wm Mothlen of Sittenburn Par. Richmond Co.,
planter, to Arthur Spicer of same Par. and Co., Gent., for a valuable
consideration, 100 acres, in Sittenburn Par. Richmond Co., beginning
at the first Branch of Poplar Neck Creek, adj land of John Deane, the
house of John Carpenter, the Rappa River.
Wit:
Edward Bray   signed   William Mathon
Jo: Taverner
Tho: Fairechild
                         Rec. 20 March 1693/4

Deed Book No. 2

p.18. Acknowledgement. 6 March 1693/4. Rebecca Griffin reling. dower right to land sold by Wm Griffin to Alexander Doniphan. No witnesses shown on record.

Rec. 20 March 1693/4

p.19. Power of Atty. 8 March 1693/4. Debora Bramham the wife of Richd Bramham to "my well beloved Friend William Sisson" to ack 100 acres sold to Thos Gladman.
Wit: signed   Debora x Bramham
Thomas x Freshwater
John x Hill   Rec. 20 March 1693/4

p.19. Assignment. 10 March 1693/4. John Burkett "for the satisfaction of the Assignment of a Deed of Sale for one hundred Acres of Land more or less bearing Date the twenty sixth Day of June 1691 by Edmond Maglentia and Honor his Wife have granted assigned and sett over all my Right Title and Interest of the present Deed of Sale x x from me x x unto the said Edmond Maglentia x x".
Test
Nabu: Jones   signed   John x Burkett
David Coleburne
                            Rec 20 March 1693/4

p.20. Deed. 6 March 1688. James Orchard and Mary his wife, both of the Co. of Rappa., to John Burkett, for 3600 lb tobo in cask and "also a gold Ring of ten shilling price", 185 acres, on S.E. side of Clift Creek, part of a patent of 300 acres granted to Capt John Weire "bearing Date the last Day of March 1655". Adj land "sold by me the said James Orchard to James Jackson".
Wit:
Wm: Moseley   signed   James Orchard
Jean Charle Corhay   Mary x Orchard

Rec. 12 April 1694

p.21. Deed. 1 June 1691. "Rowland Thornton of Rappa County in the Colony of Virginia planter and Elizabeth my wife" to Edmond Maglentia,

Deed Book No. 2

for 3000 lb tobo, 100 acres, in Rappa Co on N. side of river "being
part of a Tract of Land formerly belonging to Capt Alexander Fleming
dec'd and then bequeathed to his Daughter Elizabeth by will". Adjs
line of John Barrow "at the Head of Colemans Gutt so running along the
said Line till comes to the Main Swamp then binding up the South side
of the said Swamp till come to the devident Line betwixt John Washington and Rowland Thorntons, along the said Line till comes to the
River Side"

Wit: signed   Rowland Thornton
Nabu Jones   Eliz: x Thornton
Farmer Wheatley
                          Rec 16 April 1694.

p.23. Assignment. 10 March 1693/4. Edmond Maglinsha (sic) and Honor
his wife - "satisfaction of the assignment of a Deed of Sale" for 185
acres dated 6 March 1688 by John Burkett, all right etc to the said
John Burkett.

Wit: signed   Edmond x Maglentia
David Colburne   Onor x Maglentia
Nabu Jones
                          Rec. 24 April 1694

p.23. Deed. 7 June 1694. James Orchard of Richmond Co., to William
Barber, for L 101. 9. 6 Sterling money of England, 533 acres, on N.
side Rappa Creek, adj land of widow Stopford, the line of Laurance
Barker, Coleman's line, land of John Garton.

Wit:
Rich'd Leighton   signed   James Orchard
Abrey x Naylor
                          Rec. 28 June 1694

p.26. Deed. 13 Febry 1693/4. Edward Lewis of Richmond Co., and Mary
his wife to John Cralle of Northumberland Co., 100 acres, where the
now Dwelling Plantation of the said Edward Lewis is, for 6250 lb tobo.
"That whereas Thos Freshwater late of Rappa County dec'd by his Deed
of Sale bearing date the 5th Day of January 1673 did x sell x unto
Robert Wood a certain parcell of Land lying and being in the said
County of Rappa containing two hundred acres x x and whereas Robert
Wood by his Deed of Sale bearing Date the 21st of August 1678 did x

sell x unto the said Edward Lewis x x ". The 100 acres in this deed
being 1/2 of foregoing. "and reserving unto him the said Edward
Lewis all such young Trees of Apples or peaches as may be now growing
in a certain Nursery on the said Plantation with free Liberty to dig
up and carry away the said Trees at his free will and Pleasure without any Lett or Denial of him the said John Cralle or any by from or
under him".
Wit: signed   Edward x Lewis
Peter Flint   Mary x Lewis
Collumb Flint
Wm Parker   Rec. 28 June 1694

p.28. Power of Atty. 13 Feb 1693/4. Mary Lewis wife of Edwd Lewis to
Mr Edward Jones to ack above. Signed Mary x Lewis. Witnessed as above.

p.29. Deed. 20 May 1694. William Richardson and Elizabeth his wife
of Richmond Co., planter, to John Henly of Richmond Co., planter, for
a valuable consideration, 50 acres in Farnham Par., adj land of Thos.
Dusin. "which said fifty acres of Land is part and parcell of a
Devident of Land purchased of John Mills of the County of Richmond".
Wit:
Ann x Dodson   signed   William x Richardson
Cha: x Dodson Junr   Eliz: x Richardson
Cha: Dodson sen'r
                           Rec 20 June 1694.

p.30. Power of Atty. 28 May 1694. Elizabeth Richardson of Farnham
Par. Richmond Co., to "trusty and well beloved Friend Tho: Dusin" of
same Co. to ack above. Signature and witnesses as above.

p.31. Survey. "Surveyed for Henry Berry the 10th day of May 1671 in
Stafford County in the Forrest betwixt the two Rivers of Potomak and
Rappa", 550 acres, "beginning at a marked Wm Lips corner tree stand
near the said Berrys Line", adj line of Mr James Kaye, etc.
                        signed per me   John Alexander

p.31. Deed. 12 March 1693/4. Richd Berry of Richd. Co., to Ralph
Whitton of same Co., for a valuable consideration, 250 acres, part of
550 acres (above), adj land of Will Lipp, Simpson's land, land of
James Key, "and binding upon my Brother Henry Berry and Robert Peck"
Wit:
James Strothers   signed   Richd RB Berry
Wm Berry
                           Rec 28 June 1694

Deed Book No. 2

p.32. Power of Atty. 13 March 1693/4. Richard Berry of Richmond Co.,
to Joshua Davis "to acknowledge one conveyance of Land to Ralph
Whiting" . This name is shown as Ralph Whitton in the entry for the
deed.
Wit: signed   Richd RB Berry
Wm Berry
Richd x Grubs

p.32. Relinquishment. 12 March 1693/4. Henry Berry of Richmond Co.,
"do relinquish all my Right Title and Interest of one Tract of Land
formerly taken up by my Father to my Brother Richard Berry".
Wit: signed   Henry Berry
John Berry
Adam Woffendall

p.32. Deed. 1 June 1694. "Wm Norris and Elizabeth his Wife of the
County of Northumberland blacksmith" to "Samuel Jones of the county
of Northumberland Planter", for a valuable consideration, 50 acres in
Farnham Par. Richmond Co., being part of land purchased of Tho: Dusin
by abovesaid Norris. Adjs land of Tho. Dusin, land of Wm Norris, the
line of Mr John Oohley, land of Wm Richardson, etc.
Wit:
Henry x Hartly   signed   William x Norris
John x Hill   Elizabeth x Norris
John x Hendley
Charles Dodson
          94   Rec. 28 June 1694

p.34. Power of Atty. 1 June 1694. Elizabeth Norris of Northumberland
Co to Tho: Duzen of Richmond Co to ack above. Signed Eliz: x Norris.
Witnessed by Henry x Hartly, Charles Dodson and John x Hill.

p.35. Deed. 23 April 1694. Tho: Dusin and Susanna his Wife of Richmond
Co., to Wm Norris of Northumberland Co., blacksmith, 100 acres in
Richmond County on the branches of Totuskey. Adjs land said Dusin now
lives on, the line of Wm Mathews, the "Line of John Oakley formerly
belonging to Tho: Madison", the line of Wm Richardson, etc. The
consideration being "That the said Thomas Dusin and Susanna his wife
do for and in Consideration of two thousand pounds of Tobacco in Cask
to the said Tho: Dusin in hand by the said Wm Norris well and truly
paid and two hilling Hoes to be paid yearly by the said Wm Norris unto

Deed Book No. 2

the said Duzen so long as he and his Wife shall live and if either of
them should die that then the said Norris shall pay but one hilling
hoe a year and to give the said Dusen one falling Ax"
Wit:
Henry x Hartly   signed   Tho: x Dusin
John x Hill   Susan x Dusin
Charley Dodson
          94   Rec 28 June 1694

p.37. Power of Atty. 31 June 1694 (sic). Susan Duson of Richmond Co
to "my trusty and well beloved Friend Wm Richardson" to ack above.
Signature and witnesses as above.

p.37. Deed. 3 April 1694. Wm Browne of Richmond Co., to John Suttle
of the same Co., planter, for 8000 lb tobo, 165 acres in St Marys
Par., part of a tract of 744 acres "formerly granted to my Father
William Browne deceased and to Daniel White and William Balthrop as
by patent dated the third of March 1664 and the said Daniel White
sold and assigned his part unto my Father Wm Browne dated the 20th
of Aug't 1668 and the said 744 acres was patented by my Father Browne
and William Balthrop as by patent dated the 7th day of August 1669
The said Land being not divided betwixt my Father Wm Browne and Wm
Balthrop and the said Wm Balthrop taking not the advantage of Survivorship the said Balthrop acknowledged four hundred ninety five
acres of the said Tract of 744 unto me the aforesaid Wm Browne and
my Brother John Browne and my Brother Maxfield Browne The aforesaid
one hundred sixty five acres being my proportional share which said
Land I formerly seated on the East side of Chingateague Swamp in the
parish and county aforesaid". Deed refers to William Browne's wife
but her name is not shown.
Wit: signed   William Browne
James Tayler
Adam Woffendall   Rec. 28 June 1694

p.40. Land Grant. 14 Dec. 1692. Phillip Ludwell to the Justices of
Richmond County. That 142 acres in Richmond Co., lately Rappa. Co.,
formerly belonging to Mr James Sandford, who sold it to Michael
Hugill deed who died and left a son who also d.s.p. The land thereupon escheated, and "Hezechia Turner of said County who intermarried
with the Widow and Relict of the said Hugill petitioning the Right
Hon'ble Sr Wm Berkley Knight Governour etc for the preference of
Escheat of the said Land as being in possession of the same his petition was accordingly granted under the Hand of the Governour dated

Deed Book No. 2

the 28th Day of February 1676/7 which said Land accordingly escheated
as appears by the Verdict of a Jury of Inquest dated the 7th of May
1677 and the said Turner after the escheating of the said Land dying
also did by his last Will x x appoint the abovesaid Court his
Executors". The land to be disposed of at the discretion of the Court.
                              signed   Phillip Ludwell
Record'd per Richd Whitehead Clk of the proprietors Office

p.41. Deed. 6 June 1694. Justices of Richmond County, late Rappa Co.,
to James Sanford, planter, 142 acres shown above. "according to the
true Intent and meaning of the last Will and Testament of Hezechia
Turner decd".
Wit: signed   Wm Colston Cl Cur
Joshua Davis
John Tarpley   Rec. 28 June 1694.

p.41. Bond. 3 May 1694. Henry Fleet of the County of Lancaster, Gent.,
to Col'o John Stone of the County of Richmond, Gent., L 600. Sterling,
not to disturb peaceable possession of "nine hundred Acres lying on
the Eastward side of Rappa Creek formerly in the Possession of Mr
Bryan Hodgson dec'd and also of one other Devident of Land containing
seven hundred and thirty Acres of Land lying on the Head of Rappa
Creek now in the possession of the said Coln'l John Stone both which
Devidents of Land was granted to Coln'o John Walker by patent bearing
Date 16th Day of April 1668"
Wit: signed   Henry Fleet
Tho: Lawson
John Montague   Rec. 20 June 1694

p.43. Power of Atty. 3 April 1694. Henry Fleet of Lancaster Co., to
Henry Seager to ack foregoing bond.
Wit: signed   Henry Fleet
John Monjoy
Tho: Lawson   Date of record not shown.

p.43. Power of Atty. 5 June 1694. Honoria Woffendall to James Tayler
to ack "my Thirds of a parcell of Land unto William Powell"
Wit:
Wm Reynolds   her mark
John x Spiller   signed   Honoria x Woffendall

                Date of record not shown.

Deed Book No. 2

p.43. "The Mark of Evan Thomas Hogs and cattle a staple fork on each Eare". Date of record not shown.

p.43. Deed. 1 May 1694. George Mason of the County of Stafford in Virginia, Gent., to Edward Smyth of the same Co., for the use and account of Mr Martin Scarlett, for 12000 lb tobo, 357 acres in freshes of Rappa river, which land was sold by Mr John Fosaker to said Mason 28th March 1692.
Wit: signed Geo: Mason
Edward Smyth
Jos: Green   Rec. 22 August 1694

p.45. Power of Atty. 9 May 1694. George Mason and Mary his wife to "our trusty Friend Mr Alexander Doniphan" to ack foregoing.
Wit:
Theoderick Bland   signed   Geo: Mason
Jos: Green   Mary Mason

p.45. Deed. 1 Aug 1694. John Morgan of Farnham Par, Richmond Co., blacksmith, to John Pound of same Par and Co., for L 17.10.- Sterling, 100 acres in same Par. and Co., on W side of Totuskey Creek, formerly purchased of Wm Landman by Wm Clayton and by several means and conveyances made lawfully came to the possession of said Morgan.
Wit: signed   John x Morgan
Sam'l Travers
Tho: Lloyd
John Taverner   Rec 24 Aug 1694

p.47. Power of Atty. No date shown. John Morgan and Barbary his wife to John Taverner to ack foregoing
Wit: signed   John x Morgan
Sam'l Travers   Barbery x Morgan
Tho: Lloyd

p.47. Deed. 3 July 1693. Wm Griffin of Rich'd Co., planter, to Edward Price, for 475 lb tobo, 10 acres adj land of sd Wm Griffin.
Wit:
Alex'r Doniphan   signed   Wm Griffin
Anne x Doniphan
                         Rec 24 Aug. 1694.

Deed Book No.2

p.48. Deed. 4 May 1694. John Powell of Farnham par. Richmond Co.,
planter, and Michall his wife to John Woollard of same par. and Co.,
for 4000 lb tobo. 100 acres in same par., "being part of a greater
Tract of Land situate in the Woods formerly given by Hezechia Turner
to his Children by a will bearing Date the 25th Day of December 1677
being near the Land of John Peck on the one side and Richard King on
the other bounded as followeth, to begin where the Land of Ann
Chissell (given unto her by the abovesaid Turner in the Will aforesaid", etc "said one hundred acres of Land belonging to my wife"
Wit:
Saml Travers   signed   John Powell
Teage x MacDonals   Micall x Powell
Ann x Hawkins

Rec. 28 Aug. 1694

p.50. Power of Atty. 4 June 1694. John Powell to "my trusty and well
beloved Friend and Neighbour Mr John Baker" to ack above.
Wit:
Jane Baker   signed   John Powell
Ann Norsier (or Norpier)

Note: Dr. J. M. Hill made the memo to follow on my Mss notes. "The
will of Hezechia Turner is included in the records of Essex County
and names Ann Chissel specifically as his grand-daughter"   B.F.

p.50. "This Indenture Tripartite made the 4th Day of May in the year
of our Lord (according to the Computition of the Church of England)
one thousand six hundred ninety and four Between Sarah Suggitt of the
parish of Farnham in the County of Richmond widow of the first part
William Barber Sen'r of the county of Richmond and Rawleigh Travers
of Northumberland County Gent of the second Part and John Suggit and
Margarett his wife James Suggitt Edgcomb Suggitt and Thos Suggitt
sons of the said Sarah of the third Part Witnesseth That the said
Sarah Suggitt for the Love and affection she hath and beareth unto
her said children and for their better Preferment and advancement in
this World and for other good causes and considerations her thereunto
moving Hath given x x x unto the said Wm Barber and Rawleigh Travers
all that plantation x x being in the said parish of Farnham and
County aforesaid on the North side and adjoining to Rappa River containing according to antient bounds thereof five hundred and ninety
acres and surveyed by Wm Moseley by virtue of an order granted by the
general Court dated the seventeenth of October 1687 which said Land
was taken up by Patent dated the 18th of April 1650 by Anth'o Jackman
and by him sold and assigned by writing endorsed the 6th of October

Deed Book No. 2

1652 unto John Edgcomb father of the said Sarah Suggitt by whom she
claims the premises". 190 acres "thereof concluding the two long
Necks so called with Houses Buildings and orchards thereon" reserved
for life use of Sarah Suggitt, this home tract adjoining the land of
Edgcomb Suggitt. 190 acres lying next to the land of Thos Suggitt for
his use. "One other hundred acres parcell of the said Tract or
parcell of Land hereby granted at the upper End thereof including
forty acres sold to be taken up by John Suggitt the elder dec'd lying
next the Line parting the same and the Land late in the holding of
Robert Baylis sen'r" to use of John Suggitt and Margarett his wife
and his heirs. 75 acres adjoining the land of John Taverner and the
River and adjoining the land of James and John Suggitt to use of Tho.
Suggitt. 150 acres adjoining the land of Henry Lucas and the land
of John, Edgcomb and Thos Suggitt to use of James Suggitt. 75 acres
to use of Edgcomb Suggitt. etc.
Wit:
Isa: Webb   signed   Sarah Sugitt
Wm Thornbury   John Sugitt
Wm Fitzherbert   Marg't Sugitt
John Taverner   James Sugitt
Edward Jones   Edgcomb Sugitt
                                          Tho: Sugitt

Date of record not shown

p.55. Power of Atty. 4 May 1694. Sarah Suggitt to John Taverner to
ack above. Signed Sarah Suggitt and witnessed by Edwd Jones and Wm
Fitzherbert. Date of record not shown.

p.56. Deed. 1 June 1694. Thos Freshwater of Farnham parish, Richmond
County, to Dan'll Swillivant of same par and Co., for a valuable
consideration, 300 acres, on N side Totuskey Creek, adj tract of land
purchased by Dennis Swillivant dec'd of Thos Freshwater dec'd and adj
land of Edward Lewis.
Wit: signed   Thomas F Freshwater
Alex'r Swan
Wm Colston   Rec 14 Sept 1694

p.58. Bond. 1 June 1694. On above. Signed Thomas Freshwater. Witnessed
by John Tarpley and Wm Barber junr.

p.58. Assignment. 13 Aug. 1694. Wm Yates and Elizabeth his wife to Tho
Gill all right and title to Deed.
Wit: signed   Wm Yates
Joseph Dike   Eliz: Yates
Wm Smyth
                                Rec. 15 Sept 1694.

Deed Book No.2

p.59. Deed. 5 Sept 1694. Henry Fleet of the parish of Christ Church
in the County of Lancaster Gent to Edwin Conway of the same parish
and Co., Gent., for L 11. 6. - current money of England, 2000 acres
"being in the County of Richmond bounded on the south East with
falling Creek south and southwest upon the River of Rappa: Northwest
upon a small Creek there and near Warasquit Indian Town North East
upon the Hills there which said Land was formerly granted to one
Nich'las Meriwether by patent dated 13th of April 1655 and by him
sold and assigned by Indorsment on the said patent dated the 8th Day
of September 1656 unto Cap't Henry Fleet Father of the said Henry
Fleet partie to these Presents by whom he claims the said Tract of
Land as his Son and Heir apparent". Excepting 200 acres of the said
tract granted to Joshua Mason, 100 acres to Peter Butler and 300
acres to Malachi Peale by the said Henry Fleet party to these parts.
Deed refers to Henry Fleet and Elizabeth his wife.
Wit:
John Stone   signed   Henry Fleet
Jn'o Taverner
                    Rec. 15 Sept. 1694.

Note: Mrs. Elizabeth Fleet was Elizabeth the daughter of Wm. Wildey
of Fairfield, Northumberland County. Col. John Stone, who appears as
a witness was the 4th husband of this Henry Fleet's mother.   B.F.

p.61. Deed. 4 June 1693/4 (shown thus in records). "James White of
Northumberland County in faire field parish and Colony of Virginia
planter with the Consent of my Wife patience" to Richard Smyth of
same par. and Co., planter, for 20000 lb tobo and Cask, 350 acres in
Richmond Co. formerly Rappa., adj land of Col.Travers and the land of
Richard Rout.
Wit: signed   James x White
Henry x Ridder (or Kidder ?)
James x Garse
                    Rec. 15 Sept 1694,

p.65. Power of Atty. 3 March 1693/4 (Note error in date of deed shown
above) Patience White to "my everloving Husband James White of faire-
field Parish in Northumberland County planter" to ack foregoing deed.
Wit:
Joseph x White   signed   Patience x White
James Rogers
                    Date of record not shown

Deed Book No.2

p.63. Deed. 20 Feb 1694 (in 5th year of W. and M), meaning in the
manner these records are written 1693/4. John Ownes (sic) of Richmond
Co., Tayler, to Stephen Fewell, for 1000 lb tobo, 50 acres in Richmond
Co., being part of a tract of 1300 acres bought of Capt Wm Hubbart
by Fran: Hales "and after patented in the said Hales own Name and by
the Decease of the said Hales fallen to the aforesaid John Owens",
adj land of Mr Hugh Williams, land of sd Jno Owens, the line of James
Lamb, etc. "And I the said John Owens with the consent of Rebecca my
Wife".
Wit: signed   John x Ownes   (sic)
Rich'd Bryan
Jn'o Williams
Edw'd Virgin his mark   Rec. 22 Nov 1694.

p.66. Power of Atty. 5 Oct. 1694. John and Rebecca Owens to "well
beloved Friend Mr John Nichols" to ack above. Witnessed by Wm Allen.

p.66. Deed. 7 Sept. 1694. "x x Thomas Freshwater of the County of
Richmond being seized and possessed in a certain Tract of Land in
Right of my Father Thomas Freshwater dec'd as by patent bearing Date
the 24th of Augst 1664", containing 7221 acres granted to "my Father
Tho: Freshwater as aforesaid Mr Richard Webley and Mr Robert Davis"
by Gov. Berkeley. This land now being sold to Daniel Swillivant, for
15000 lb tobo, excepting land already sold out of the patent as
follows: "sold by my Father and myself to Coln'll Hull one thousand
acres Wm Hamock three hundred Robert Wood two hundred Denis
Swillevant two hundred and fifty William Davis one thous'd John
Crutcher one hundred Dan'll Swillivant three hundred and fourty".
Wit:
Willoughby Allerton   signed   Tho: x Freshwater
Charles Barber
                                Rec. 22 Nov. 1694

p68. Deed. 1 Oct. 1694. George Tomlin of Richmond Co. Gent., to
Humphrey Mallery of same Co., planter, for 3000 lb tobo, 50 acres
known by name as Sandy Bay. Adjs land of Capt George Tayler, Robert
Evans' corn field, Geo Tomlin's old field, line of Mr Wm Moss dec'd.
Deed refers to "Hanna Tomlin wife of the said George Tomlin"
Wit:
John Weale   signed   Geo. Tomlin his mark
Tho: Reylee his mark   Hanna Tomlin her mark

                    Rec 25 Sept 1694

Deed Book No.2

p.71. Deed. 5 Sept 1694. 5 Sept 1694. Dan'll Swillivant of Richmond
Co., to John Cralle of Northumberland Co., for 9500 lb tobo, 250 acres.
"Whereas Thomas Freshwater dec'd by his Deed of Sale bearing Date the
first Day of December 1673 did for ever bargain sell alien and make
over unto Denis Swillivant the Father of the said Daniel" 250 acres
in Richmond Co., formerly Rappahannock, adj land of Wm Tufley (or
Tusley ?) and Wm Hamock, etc.
Wit: signed   Dan'll Swillevant
Tho: Hobson
Wm Parker   Rec 25 Nov 1694.

p.72. Deed. 4 Sept 1694. James Orchard of Westmorland Co., planter
and Rebecca his wife to John Morton of Northumberland Co., planter,
for 7000 lb tobo, 157 acres in Richmond Co. "and was taken out of
Harman Skeldermans seat or Tract of Land and by the said Harman sold
unto Patrick Norton and was twice sold by the said Patrick to William
Moss and by the said William Moss in and by his last Will and Testa-
ment given and bequeathed unto his Daughter Elizabeth which by the
said Elizabeth and her Husband John Craske sold x x to the said James
Orchard". Adjs main Run of Rappa Creek and land of Harman Skelderman.
Wit:
David Connier   signed   James Orchard
William Greenstead his mark   Rebecca Orchard

Rec 25 Nov. 1694

p.75. Power of Atty. 3 Oct. 1694. Rebecca Orchard wife of James
Orchard to "my loving Freind Nebuchodonozor Jones" to ack above.
Wit: signed   Rebecca Orchard
John More his mark
Stephen Beaman his mark   No date of record shown.

p.75. Deed. 6 Nov. 1694. "Belliner Pursell Executrix of the last Will
and Testament of David Pursell late of the County of Richmond" to
Tho Parker of same Co., planter, for 10000 lb tobo, 250 acres, where
said Belliner now lives for term of 99 years, "one pepper Corn by
way of Acknowledgement on every the five and twentieth day of December
during the said Term if the same be lawfully demanded"
Wit:
Rich'd x Jasper   signed   Billenor x Pursell
Edw'd Geffery
Nich'o x Liscom   Rec 14 Dec 1694

Deed Book No. 2

p. 78. Deed. 12 Nov. 1690. "John Bartlemew and Charles Fleming of the
County of Rappaha'k have sold and demised unto Capt Malachi Peale",
for 5500 lb tobo, 350 acres. And by these presents confirm unto the
aforesaid Capt Peale of Stafford Co., the afsd Land in the Freshes of
Rappa, this land formerly sold by Mr John and Geo. Mott to Peter
Gallon "and by the said Gallen demised unto Tho: Chapman and by the
said Chapman sold and made over unto John Fosaker and made over from
the said Fosaker unto the above named John Bartlemew and Fleming".
Adjs land of Mr John Creed, being surveyed by Mr Geo Morris.
Wit:
Samp: Dorrell   signed   John x Bartholomew
Joshua Davis   Charles x Fleming
Theodorick Bland

p.80. No date. "Know all men by these presents that Wee Sarah
Bartholomew wife to John Bartholomew and Elizabeth Fleming wife to
Charles Fleming do acknowledge and for ever relinquish our Thirds
Right and Title of Dower to the within mentioned premises as Witness
our Hands"
Test   signed   Sarah x Bartholomew
James Hearse   Eliz: Fleming
Rich'd Bryor

p.80. Statement that above papers were acknowledged in the County
Court of Stafford on 12th Day of November. Signed by James Hearse,
Deputy Clerk.

p.80. 15 Nov. 1694. Assignment of foregoing by Malachi Peale to
Joshua Davis of Richmond Co.
Wit: signed   Malachi Peale
Josias Long John Pike
John Linton   Rec. 14 Dec. 1694.

p.81. Power of Atty. 15 Nov 1694. Malachi Peale to Mr Samuel Sandford
of Richmond Co. to ack foregoing. Signed by Malachi Peale and witnessed by Josias Long and John Pike

p.81. Deed of Gift. 1 December 1694. "x x That I the said John Willis
sen'r of the County of Richmond in St Marys parish in Virginia Planter
for divers good Causes and Considerations me hereunto moving especially
for the natural Love and affection I bear unto my loving Son John
Willis Jun'r of the County and parish aforesaid" gives a parcel of
land "taken up between myself and John Powers sen'r late of this
County dec'd as per patent will appear bearing Date the 27th Day of
February 1690/1 under the Hand of Philip Ludwell Deputy to the

Deed Book No. 2

Proprietors in England".
 Also 100 acres more to be laid out next and adj foregoing, being
part of a patent of 261 acres granted to said Willis Sen'r by Sir Wm
Berkeley dated 21 Oct 1669.
Wit: signed   John x Willis Senr
Nath'l Pople (Nathaniel Pope)
Wm x Willis

p.83. "Know all men by these presents That I Matilda Willis true and
lawfull Wife of John Willis sen'r do assign over all my Right of my
Thirds and Dower of the abovementioned Land unto John Willis jun'r
as abovesaid Witness my hand seal this 1st Day of December 1694"
Wit:
Nath'll Pope   signed   Matilda x Willis
Willm: Willis

                    Rec 14 Dec 1694

p.83. Power of Atty. 1 Dec 1694. John and Matilda Willis to Nathan'l
Pope to ack above deed of gift.
Wit: signed   John Willis his mark
Wm Willis his mark   Matilda Willis her mark
John Willis junr his mark

p.84. Deed. 2 Nov. 1694. "James Jackson of the Parish and County of
Richmond planter"   to   John King of same par. and Co., for 4500 lb
tobo, 30 acres, "the plantation whereon I now live", 20 acres bought
of Wm Griffin and 10 acres bought of James Orchard.
Wit:
James Harrison   signed   James Jackson
John Banks
                    Rec 27 Dec 1694.

p.85. Power of Atty. 1 Dec 1694. Susanna Jackson wife of James Jackson,
to "my trusty Friend" Mr James Harrison to ack above.
Wit:
Ja: Harrison   signed   Susanna x Harrison
Tho: x Scriven

p.85. Agreement. 2 Nov. 1694. John King and wife (her name not shown)
with James Jackson re above sale.
Wit: signed   John x King
James Harrison
Tho: x Scrivan

Deed Book No. 2

p.86.   Sale of Land. 9 Nov 1691. John Crutcher of Youcomaco, Planter,
to John Kerby of Rappa Co. Planter, for 15000 lb tobo, tract of land,
acerage not shown, formerly purchased of Mr John Sampson. Payments
as follows: 2500 lb tobo Now
                    6250 "   "   After 10 Oct next (1692)
                    6250 "   "   After 10 Oct 1693
Wit:
John Jadwin   signed   John Crutcher his mark
Sam'll Warcupp   John Kirby

                    Date of record not shown.

p.87.   "Sir
            Peter Ollans woud desire you to record his Mark being an
upper keel and an underkeel and a Slitt on the Right Ear and an underkeel and a Slitt on the left"

Note: There is a name 'Olin' still in use in Virginia in a family
that originated in this section. Particularly Mr. Olin Blincoe of
Ashland, Virginia. I have known this gentleman since I was a small
child. Ashland, formerly Slash Cottage, will just have to change
it's name again when there is no more Miss Nita Blincoe. Or Mr. Olin
Blincoe.   B.F.

p.87. Deed of Gift. 12 Janry 1694/5. X'pian Williams (Mrs. Christian
Williams) of St. Marys Par. Richmond Co. gives "unto my Grandson
James Elkins the son of Rich'd Elkins and Mary" 5 cows, a good feather
bed and furniture and 2 brass kettles one to hold about 13 gallons,
2 Iron pots, 1 bell metal spice mortar and pestle, 5 pewter dishes,
and 2000 lb tobo in cask "to be paid for my aforesaid Grandchilds
schooling". All to be delivered when he comes to age of 23 years.
Wit:
Nebu Jones   Xpian Williams
mark of Charles Snead   her mark

                    Rec. 14 Feb 1694/5

p.88. Deed. 4 Dec. 1694. John Wakeman and Mary his wife to Leonard
Robinson, for a valuable consideration, a parcel of land, acerage not

Deed Book No. 2

shown, adj land of Mr Thomas Loyd, land of John and Mary Wakeman, Mr
Hogsons plantation.
Wit: signed   John x Wakeman
Jos: Dike   Mary x Wakeman
Sam'll Bayly
                              Rec 10 May 1695

p.90. 17 Nov. 1694. Martin Sherman of Richmond Co., planter, to Henry
Tillery the elder, of same Co., planter. For 2000 lb tobo, 50 acres,
"being part of a Devident of Land formerly granted Mr James Samford
by patent bearing Date the 20th of March 1665/6 the whole being eight
hundred acres". The land transferred by his deed to Quintan Sherman
"and by the said Quintan Shermans last Will devised and given unto me
the aforesaid Martin Sherman as by Mr Samfords Deed and my Fathers
Will doth fully appear". Adjs Capt Barbers land, a marked hickory
near Totuskey Ferry Road, etc.
Wit:
John Newton   signed   Martin Sherman mark
Rich'd Dudley mark
Xpher Coleburne mark   Rec. 16 May 1695

p.92. Deed. 29 Aug 1694. "Sam'll Griffin of the County of Northumberland Gent: and Sarah his Wife" to Thomas Mallard of same Co., for
2500 lb tobo, 100 acres, in Richmond Co., at "Head of Totuskey Creek,
standing in a certain place known by the name of Hogg Town", adj land
of Hugh Harris.
Wit: signed   Sam'll: Griffin
Wm Parker
W.F by Wm Fantleroy
Mary Caine   Rec. 17 May 1695

p.94. Power of Atty. 25 Nov. 1694. Sam'll Griffin to "my loving friend"
Mr Edward Jones of Co of Richmond, to ack above.
Wit:
Wm Parker   signed   Sam'll Griffin
Mary Caine

p.94. Power of Atty. 29 Aug 1694. Thos Mallard of Northumberland Co.,
planter, to "my good Freind Sam'll Samford" to accept foregoing.
Signed Tho Mallard his mark. Witnessed by Jeffery Adamson and Phill
Drake.

Deed Book No. 2

p.95. Lease and Release. (Is this not the first of this form that appears in these records ?). 15th and 16th of March 1694/5. John Landman of the Parish of Farnham in Richmond Co., to John Browne of same Par. and Co., for 18570 lb tobo, 464 acres in the same Par. and Co. Known by the name of long Neck "in a fork between two great branches issueing into the Head of Totuskey Creek", adj land of Wm Hasle Dec'd being part of said Neck, also adj land of Mr John Hull dec'd, "and upon a place called Jenkinses Mobby Tubb", being part of a Devident formerly granted unto Thos Robinson and Edw'd Lewis by patent dated Febry 20th 1662 (1662/3) and by them transferred unto Sam'll Man and Wm Landman father of the said John Landman by a Deed bearing Date the six of September An'o Dom: 1664".
Wit:
Alex'r Spence   signed   John Landman
John Hindmer
                          Rec. 22 May 1695

p.101. Deed. 9 Janry 1694/5. John Powell and Michal his wife of the County of Richmond to Wm Hill of the County of Northumberland, 150 acres in Farnham Par. Richmond Co., adj "on the side where Martin Ham'ond and Job Hamond lives on and running the whole Breath of Hezechia Turners Land"
Wit: signed   John Powell
Mark of Michalls Connell   Michal x Powell
Mark of Rich'd Doudy
David Conner   Rec 22 May 1695

p.103. Assignment. 30 April 1695. Wm Hill and Ann "my wife" of the Co. of Northumberland, assign to Richard Flint all right and title to above.
Test   Signed   Wm Hill
Geo: Hill his mark   Ann Hill her mark

p.103. Power of Atty. 30 April 1695. John Powell of No. Farn. Par., Richmond Co., to "my Neighbour John Partridge" to ack 150 acres "which was given by Hezechia Turner to Ann Chissell the Land bounding upon Martin Hamond and Job Hammond As Witness my Hand and Seal April the 30th 1695"
Wit: signed   John Powell
Rich'd Sables his mark
Thos Garrat his mark

Deed Book No. 2

p.103. Deed. 13 April 1695. "To all Xp'ian People to whom these
presents shall come I William Hill of the County of Northumberland
planter and Ann my Wife send greeting etc   That whereas Hezechia
Turner late of Rappa: County dec'd did by last Will and Testament
give and bequeath unto Ann Chissell the now wife of the said William
Hill one hundred and fifty acres of Land x x and whereas the said
Land after the decease of the said Ann Chissell the now wife of the
said William Hill doth devoule unto John Powell and Michall his Wife
both of the County of Richmond as she the said Michall was the
Daughter and only heires of the said Hezechia Turner the said John
Powell and Michall his Wife did by their Deed of sale bearing Date
the ninth Day of Jan'ry in the year of our Lord 1694 grant bargain
sell and alein unto the said William Hill x x all that their Right
of Reversion of the said one hundred and fifty Acres of Land before
devised by the said Hezechia Turner unto the said Ann Chissell".
Wm and Ann Hill now sell to Richard Flint, for 4200 lb tobo, the
above 150 acres of Land.
Wit: signed   Wm Hill
Geo Hill his mark   Ann Hill her mark
Rich'd Hill Junr

                              Rec 22 May 1695

p.103. Power of Atty. 30 April 1695. Rich'd Flint of Northumberland
CO, Va. "do hereby depute and appoint my son Rich'd Flint my lawfull
Attorney" to ack 150 acres from Wm Hill and Ann his wife in Richmond
County Court.
Wit: signed   Rich'd Flint
Christopher Dawson
Mary Flint her mark

p. 106. Gift in Tail. 8 Nov. 1694. George Tayler, of Sittenburn Par.
Richmond Co., Gent., to Geo Tomlin of same Par. and Co. Gent., and
planter, for 5 shillings, 140 acres, all that plantation now in
occupation of sd Geo: Tomlin, on the eastermost of a creek there
called Taylers Creek in Par. and Co. aforesaid. And is part of a
greater quantity of land held by sd Geo Tayler by patent.
Wit:
Wm Tayloe   signed   Geo: Tayler
Sam'll Peachey
Edw'd Jones
Jn'o Taverner

                              Rec. 20 June 1695.

Deed Book No. 2

p.107. Deed. 1 June 1695. Wm Barber of Totuskey Creek in Richmond Co.
To Richd Dudley Senr, "for a consideration in Tobacco", a parcel of
land, adj land bought of Roger Williams, etc., "The Path intended is
the old path that leads over the Swamp to John Chapmans".
Wit:
Charles Barber   signed   Wm Barber

Rec. 21 June 1695

p.108. Deed. 5 April 1695. Richard Dudley, Sr. of Farnham Par, Rich'd
Co., to Richard Jasper, for 1600 lb tobo, 50 acres, on S side of
Totuskey Creek, adj land of sd Richd Jasper "to a marked beech that
stands over against a branch which was formerly called Quintilian
Shermans branch"
Wit: signed   Richard Dudley
John Chapman
Geo: Madox his mark
Wm Tillere: his mark   Rec 21 June 1695

p.109. Grant. 14 Dec 1692. Phillip Ludwell Esq etc. "unto the worship-
full their Majesties Justices of the Peace for the County of Richmond
lately Rappa County", 711 acres in Richmond Co., All that remained of
853 acres, upon a resurvey "as appears by a Verdict of a Jury of Inquest dated May the 7th 1677". Said land formerly belonging to
Michael Hugill dec'd who died and left Issue a son who also died
without heir, whereupon the land became escheatable, and "one Hezechia
Turner of the said County who intermarried with the Widow and Relict
of the said Hugill" petitioning Sir Wm Berkeley for the escheat by
preference as being in possession of same and was accordingly granted
28th Febry 1676/7, the said Turner after the escheating of the land,
dying, by his will, appointed the Court Executors and ordered his
lands disposed of at the Courts discretion.
                              signed   Phill: Ludwell

p.110. Deed. 7 August 1695. Justices of County of Richmond to John
Powell of said Co., planter, and Michall his wife. "according to the
true Intent and meaning of the last Will and Testament of Hezechia
Turner of the said County dec'd", land in foregoing entry.
Wit: Robt Brent   signed   Wm Colston Cl Cur
     Joshua Davis
                         Rec. 22 Aug. 1695

Deed Book No. 2

p.111. Grant. 14 Dec. 1692. Phillip Ludwell for the proprietors, to
Joane Loyd, widow and administratrix of Lewis Loyd, late of Rappa Co.,
dec'd and parish of Northfarnham, 159 acres in above par. and Co.,
"formerly surveyed and taken up by her dec'd husband Lewis Loyd as by
Survey dated February the 6th 1681 under the hand of Mr Edwin Conway
x x x the which survey and benefitt thereof the said Loyd gave to his
Wife by his last Will", adjs land of Roger Williams.
                                        signed   Phill: Ludwell

p.112. Assignment. 1 Aug 1695. Joan Loyd to Wm Phillips all right
and and title in above 159 acres "excepting my widowhood"
Wit:
Grace x Rider   signed   Joane x Loyd
Hen Shalter
                        Rec 29 Aug 1695

p.113. Power of Atty. 1 Aug 1695. Joan Loyd to "my trusty and faith-
full Freind Wm Davis" to ack above. Sig and wit as above.

Note: Please do not forget my frequent notes that this name was pronounced, and frequently appears under the phonetic spelling as Lyde.
                                                              B.F.

p.113. "Know all men by these presents that I the withinmentioned
King doth hereby assign over all my Right Title and Interest of the
within mentioned Land housen plantation and fencen to Martin Fisher
or his heirs or Assigns forever Witness my hand and seal the 29th
day of July An'o 1695"
Wit: signed   John x King
John Jenings   Mary x King
Wm: Jenings
                        Rec. 29 Aug 1695

p.113. Assignment of Lease. 3 March 1694/5. "Nich'o: Smyth of the par
of Sittenburne in the County of Richmond planter and Agatha his Wife"
to Richard Jordan of same par and Co., 200 acres in exchange for 150
acres (see following entry). "whereas Moses Barrow late of the parish
and County aforesaid dec'd did in his life Time by one Indenture of
Lease bearing date the seventh Day of December x 1692 x lett unto x
Nich'o: Smith Agatha his Wife and Ann her Daughter for their lives
two hundred acres of Land x x"
Wit: signed   Nich'o: Smyth
Arthur Spicer   Agatha x Smyth
Robt: Clarke
                        Rec 29 Aug 1695

p.115. Deed. 4 March 1694/5. Richard Jordan of Richmond Co., planter,
and "Cisley my wife" to Nicho: Smyth, 150 acres, for 2000 lb tobo and
an assignment of a lease for 200 acres "granted by Moses Barrow to
Nich'o Smyth for three Lives bearing Date the 7th Day of December 1692".
The 150 acres being in Richmond Co and "being part of a Devident or
Tract of Land that did formerly belong to John Barrow dec'd" adjoins
"at a red Oak at the head of the Race Ground", the line of Wm Richard-
son, the line of Mr James Scott, the line of Rowland Thornton.
Wit:
Wm Moseley   signed   Rich'd: Jordan
Rich'd Wharton   Cisley x Jordan
James Scott
                        Rec 30 Aug 1695

p.117. Assignment. 20 June 1695. Tho: Gladman assigns all right and
title in a certain deed (Vide p 47 former Book) to John Wilcocks
Wit:
Tho: Lewis   signed   Tho: x Gladman
Henry Shalter   Catherine x Gladman
                        Rec 30 Aug 1695

p.118. Power of Atty. 6 Aug 1695. Catherine Gladman to Wm Sisson Junr
to ack sale to John Wilcocks. Signed Catherine x Gladman. Witnessed
by Henry Shalter and John Wilcocks.

p.118. Deed. 2 Feb 1694/5. John Henly of Richmond Co., planter, and
Ruth his wife to Tho: Rout of Northumberland Co., planter, for a
valuable consideration, 50 acres in Farnham Parish. Adjs land of
Richard Williamson. Said 50 acres was purchased of Wm Richardson,
being part of land that said Richardson purchased of John Mills of
Richmond Co., and being upon a main Branch of Totuskey Creek.
Wit:
Christopher Patty   signed   John Henly his mark
Owen Mackdaniell his mark   Ruth Henly her mark
Ann Petty her mark
                        Rec 30 Aug 1695

p.120. Power of Atty. 2 Feb 1694/5. Ruth Henly of Farnham Par. Rd. Co.,
to "my trusty and well beloved Freind" Domonick Beneham to ack above
Wit: signed   Ruth Henly her mark
X'pher Patty
Owen MacDaniell his mark

Deed Book No. 2

p.121. Deed. 26 June 1695. Shedrick Williams of Northfarnham Par. Rd.
Co., planter, toCornelius Chenshello of the same Par. and Co., planter,
for a valuable consideration, 100 acres on W side of Totuskey Creek,
adj land of Wm Smyth and land of abovesaid Chenshello.
Wit:
Henry Shalter   signed   Shedrick Williams his mark
John Rider his mark
                    Rec 30 Aug 1695

p.123. Deed of Gift. "Mr Colston Sr Please to Record a two year
old heifer marked on the right Ear Crop and underkeel, the left Crop
and overkeel unto Mary Jordan from me Nich'o Smyth".

p.123. Deed. 4 May 1695. William Woodbridge of Northfarnham Parish,
Richmond Co., to William Hanks and Sarah his wife of same Co., for
5000 lb Tobo, "all that part and parcell of Land lying on the north
side of a Branch called or known by the name of the Dunsman's branch
or by some (the Indian Town branch) situate lying and being in the
County of Richmond containing one hundred Acres be it more or less".
Adjs land of Thomas Wilson, land of Robert Palmer, land of Edward
Geffery, land of William Hanks and the land of William Woodbridge.
Wit:
Wm Mishell   signed   William Woodbridge
Rob't Palmer his mark
Edward Geffery   Rec. 12 Oct. 1695.

p.127. 18 June 1695. George Woodbridge of No. Farnham Par., Richmond
Co., to Wm Woodbridge of same Co., for 3000 lb tobo, a parcell of land
"comonly called the Indian Town lying in the said County of Richmond
x x which said Land came to my x Inheritance of my Father Mr Paul
Woodbridge late of this County dec'd".
Wit:
Fran: Fowler   signed   Geo: Woodbridge
Ed: Jeffery
Jno. Bonnovoll his mark
                    Rec. 22 Oct. 1695

Deed Book No. 2

p.129. Deed. 2 Oct. 1695. James Shippie of Richmond Co., to John Dod
of same Co., planter, for 2000 lb tobo, 40 acres, part of 100 acres
purchased of Mrs Eliza: Gardner, widow, of Maryland, 6 June 1693.
Wit:
James Harrison   signed   James Shippie
Richd Shippie
                        Rec. 22 Oct. 1695

p.130. Deed of Gift. 30 Aug 1695. John Alloway of Northfarnham Par.
in Richmond Co., "in Consideration of the natural affection and
fatherly Love which I have and bear unto my well beloved Daughter
Priscilla Tillery now Wife of Thomas Tillery of the County and
Parish aforesaid" gives a parcell of land, "being Part of the Devident
of Land I now live on and com'only known or called by the name of
the Indian Town beginning on Totuskey Creek side at the mouth of a
Branch com'only known or called by the name of Flax patch branch
running up the said Branch to a marked Gum thence over the County
Road". Adjs land of John Howell, the line of Edward Lewis, land "I
formerly sold John Yeats", along the courses to the "Head of the
Matchycomicoe branch".
Wit: signed   John x Allaway
Gabriell Allaway
John x Morgan   Rec. 30 Oct. 1695.

p.132. Statement of above gift. Signed John x Allaway. Witnessed by
Gabriell Allaway, John x Morgan and Edward Jones.

p.132. Power of Atty. 30 Aug. 1695. Dorothy Allaway wife of John
Allaway of Northfarnham Par. Richmond Co., planter, to Edward Jones
to ack "a Deed to my well beloved Daughter Priscilla Tillery".
Signed Dorothy x Allaway. Witnessed by Gabriell Allaway, John x Morgan
and Edward Jones.

p.133. Deed. 4 March 1695. Francis James of Richmond Co., planter
and "Mary my Wife", to Edward Lamby of Westmorland Co., Carpenter,
for 1000 lb tobo, 50 acres, being in Co. of Westmorland and Parish
of Washington. Adj land of Wm Jetts, Mr Blagg's dam, Barrows Bridge.
Wit:
Peter Rawlls   signed   Fran: James mark
Rose Thomas her mark   Mary James mark

                        Rec. 30 Oct. 1695.

p.135. Power of Atty. No date. Mary James wife of Francis James to John Burkett to ack foregoing deed.
Wit: signed Mary James her mark
Edward Roberts his mark
James Rosser his mark

p.135. Deed. 1 Oct. 1695. John and Michall Powell of Richmond Co., and Farnham Par. to John Patridge of Richmond Co., for 600 lb tobo, 10 acres in Co. and Par. above, at head of Richardsons Creek, along line of said Patridge formerly purchased of John Peck, a branch called "Webbs Beaver dam Branch", the line of John Wollard, etc.
Wit:
Wm: Barber Jun'r   signed   John Powell
Jno: Woollard   Michall Powell her mark

Rec 30 Oct. 1695

p.137. Power of Atty. 1 Oct 1695. Michall Powell wife of John Powell to Wm Barber Jun'r to ack above. Signed Michall Powell her mark. Wit. by John Woollard.

p.137. Deed. 1 Oct 1695. John and Mary Woollard of Farnham Par. Rd. Co. to John Patridge of same Co., for 1000 lb tobo, 13 acres, adjoins Totuskoy Creek, the land of said Patridge, "to a Hickory by the Church Road", to "a stake in a small indian Field".
Wit:
Wm Barber Junr   signed   John Woollard
John Powell   Mary Woolard

Rec 30 Oct 1695

p.138. Power of Atty. 1 Oct 1695. Mary the wife of John Woollard to Wm Barber Junr to ack above. Signed Mary Woollard her mark. Witnessed by John Powell.

p.139. Deed. 14 Aug 1695. Richard Shippie of Richmond Co., and Ellinor his wife one of the Daughters and co-heirs of Geo: Mott late of Rappa. Co., doo'd, and one of the neices and co-heirs of John Mott late of Rappa, dec'd., to William Fitzhugh of Stafford Co., for 15000 lb tobo, 1246 acres, in the forest betw N side of Rappa and S side of Potomack

Deed Book No. 2

Creek part of a greater tract granted by patent 1670 to Jno and Geo
Mott, etc. Adjs land of John Vicars, line of Mr Wm Thornton, etc.
Wit:
Alex'r Doniphan   signed   Rich'd Shippie
Wm Fitzhugh   Elenor x Shippie
Ame x Doniphan

p.141. Power of Atty. 4 Nov. 1695. Richard and Ellinor Shippie to Mr
Wm Colston to ack above.
Wit: signed   Richard Shippie
Alex'r Doniphan   Ellinor x Shippie
Wm Fitzhugh Jun'r

                    Rec. 19 Nov. 1695

p.142. Deed. 1 March 1694/5. Adam Woffendall of Richmond Co.,
planter, to Thomas Arnold of same Co., planter, for 2000 lb tobo,
100 acres. In freshes of Rappa River, adj land of Mr Anthony Savage.
Refers to "Adam Woffendall and Honoria his Wife".
Wit:
X'pher Edrington   signed   Adam Woffendall
James Woffendall   Honoria x Woffendall

                    Rec. 20 Nov. 1695

p.144. Deed. 26 Feb 1694/5. Thomas Dusin and Susanna his wife of
Richmond Co., to Thomas Southerne of same Co., for 1600 lb tobo, 30
acres, part of a patent granted to Tho Dusin dated 21 Sept 1687. Adjs
land of Dan'll Oneale, land of Mr Spencer, land formerly belonging
to Wm Mathews, land of Thos Dusin and land formerly belonging to
John Henly.
Wit: signed   Tho: x Dusin
Wm Norris mark   Susanna x Dusin
Eliz: Norris mark
Cha's Dodson   Rec. 20 Nov. 1695

p.146. Power of Atty. 26 Feb 1694/5. Susanna Dusin to "my loving and
trusty Freind" William Norris of Richmond Co., to ack above.
Wit:
Charles Dodson   signed   Susanna x Dusin
Wm: Brokenburrow

Deed Book No. 2

p.146. Deed, 23 Dec. 1695. Alexander Swan of Lancaster Co. to John
Newton of Westmorland Co., for 10000 lb tobo, 1000 acres in freshes
of Rappa River and near the falls. Adjs land late of Col. Clayburne.
This land granted by patent 26 Oct 1666 to Tho: Colley and Jno Noble.
"the sole Right whereof discended unto the said Colly by Right of
survivorship and by the said Colley conveyed by Deed to me the said
Alexander Swan x x the 29th day of August An'o Dom: 1685".
Wit:
Wm Payne   signed   Alexand'r Swan
Jn'o Baker

Rec 6 Feb 1695/6

p.149. Bond for above dated 23 Dec 1695, signed and wit. as above.

p.150. Deed of Gift. "the last Day of November" 1695. Richd Peacock
of Northfarnham Par., Richmond Co., Gent. "whereas the said Richard
Peacock hath lately married and taken to Wife Mary Glascock the
Relict and Administratrix of Geo: Glascock late of this County dec'd
Now for the Love and natural affection which I have and bear unto my
loving Wife and her Children and for their better and further
advancement" etc., "give and grant unto her children the Sum of ten
thousand pounds of Tobacco after my Decease".
Wit:
Wm Woodbridge   signed   Richard x Peacock
Edward Jeffery

Rec 14 Feb 1695/6

p.151. Power of Atty. "this last Day of December an'o Dom: 1695".
Richard Peacock to "my trusty and well beloved friend" Edward Jeffery
of Richmond Co. to ack above.
Wit: signed
Wm Woodbridge   The mark of x Rich'd Peacock
Ann Glascock

p.152. Deed, 24 April 1694. John Pratt of Westmorland Co., Gent., to
Saml Lucas, in exchange for land in Stafford Co, 165 acres in Richmond
Co. on upper side of Chingateague Run and adj land of Joshua Davis
and land of Wm Brown. "surveyed by Mr William Moseley Surveyor of
Richmond County on the 10th of December 1684 for Henry Arkhill of
Richmond County x and by the said Arkhill bought x of Adam Woffendall
and Honoria his wife x the 2d day of June 1685 x acknowledged x in x

Deed Book No. 2

County Court of Rappahannock on the 3d day of March An'o Dom 1685
and now since by the said Henry Arkhill sold x unto me the said John
Pratt on the sixth of July Anno Dom: 1685". Recorded 3 March 1685/6.
Wit:
James Hearse   signed   John Pratt
Jn'o Brenton
                        Rec. 21 Jan 1695/6.

p.156. Power of Atty. 31 Dec 1695. John Pratt to Alexander Spence to
ack above. Signed by John Pratt. Witnessed by Jos: Davis and Wm x
Jackson.

p.157. Power of Atty. Stafford Co. 28 Sept 1695. Sam'll Lucas to
Joshua Davis to ack above. Signed 'marke of x Sam'll Lucas'. Witnessed
by John Brenton. Recorded by Wm Colston Cl Cur Richmond Co.

p.157. Deed of Gift. 1 Jan'ry 1695/6. James Taylor to his God-son
William Browne Jun'r and God Daughter Bridgett Browne, an ewe each.
"and also one Ewe lamb to Elizabeth Browne with Increase Daughter to
my Son in Law William Browne sen'r". The sheep "now running on
William Brownes Plantation sen'r". "also one young heifer named
Star all with their Increase William Browne Jun'r abovesaid"
    "Sr Please to make Record of this and William Browne will make
you pay for the same. I am y'r servant Jan'ry the first 1695/6"
                        signed   James Tayler

p.157. Deed. 1 April 1696. Angell Jacobus of Farnham Par. Richmond Co
to Thomas Redley, for 5000 lb tobo, 127 acres. Adjs land formerly
granted James Williamson and the land of Sherlock.
Wit:
Rich'd Eltonhed   signed   Angell Jacobus
Humph: Mallery   Ann Jacobus
                        Rec 30 April 1696.

p.160. Deed of Gift. 4 March 1695/6. Geo: Hopkins of Richmond Co gives
a young mare to Mary Babtist of the same county.
Wit:
Willoughby Allerton   signed   Geo: x Hopkins
John Craske
                        Rec 4 March 1695/6.

Deed Book No. 2

p.161. Power of Atty. 1 Oct 1695. Ann Jacobus to "my well and trusty Freind" Mr Willoughby Allerton to ack sale of 127 acres by her husband. See page 63.
Wit: signed   Ann Jacobus
Ang'll Jacobus
Jo: Stevenson
Jane x Richards

p.162. Deed. 1 Apl 1695. James Orchard of Westmorland Co., Gent., to Arthur Spicer of Richmond Co., Gent., for 12000 lb tobo, 343 acres, "all that the Plantation or Tract of Land now commonly known or called by the name of the new Court House situate lying and being in the Parish of Sittenburne and County of Richmond aforesaid and now in the Tenure or Occupation of Richard Hill". Adj "main Branch of Chonamun", land of Major John Weire. 120 acres of this land bought of Mr Francis Gowre of Richmond Co. The other part granted to the said Jas. Orchard.
Wit:
Tho: Lloyd   signed   James Orchard
John Scott
                          Rec. 30 April 1696

p.165. Bond for above.

p.166. Assignment. 24 Jan. 1695/6. William Richardson of Farnham Par. Richmond Co., planter, all right and title to land (vide page 35 former book) to John Mills of same Par. and Co.
Wit:
Richd x White   signed   Wm x Richardson
Tho: Dawson, mark
Tho: Southerne, mark   Entered as recorded 30 April 1698.
John Rankin   We presume this should be 1696.

p.166. Deed. 13 October 1664. "James Samford of the county of Rappa-hannock plant'r and Mary my Wife" to Quintilian Sherman of same Co., for 1400 lb tobo, 200 acres, near Totuskey Creek. Adjs land "now seated by Edward Lewis and also upon an other parcell sold by William Barber unto Roger Williams"
Wit: signed   James Samford
Fran: Suttle   Mary Samford
Tho: Freshwater
                          Rec. Rappa Co. 30 Jan 1664

Deed Book No. 2

p.168. Assignment. 24 Feb 1695/6. Quintillian Sherman of Richmond Co.,
planter, to Decemia Dalton of the same Co., cooper, for 3000 lb tobo,
right and title "unto the within Deed and the land therein mentioned.
See foregoing entry.
Wit: signed   Quint: Sherman
Nich'o White
Samuel Travers
Edm'd Sheale mark   Rec. 30 April 1696.

p.169. Bond on above. 24 Feb 1695/6. Signature and Wit: as above.

p. 170. Deed. 2 May 1696. Angell and Ann ~~Jackson~~ Jacobus to Henry
How of Farnham Par. Richmond Co., for a valuable consideration, 100
acres, part of a tract and entered at the Proprietors Office with
Col. Fitzhugh, surveyed by Capt Alexander Spence surveyor, part of
455 acres formerly called Cogwells Land, said 100 acres adj land of
John Sherlock's swamp, land of John Crutcher dec'd, standing in back
line of James Williamson dec'd, land of Thos Ridley, all in parish
of Farnham.
Wit: signed   Angell Jacobus
John Herridge   Ann Jacobus
James Stevenson
                         Rec. 15 June 1696.

p.172. Power of Atty. 3 June 1696. Ann Jacobus of Farnham Par. To
"trusty and welbeloved Freind" David Berwick to ack above.
Wit:
Henry Lucas   signed   Ann Jacobus
Jane x Lucas

p.173. Deed. 3 March 1695/6. William Jennings and Mary Jennings his
wife of Richmond Co., to Nathaniel Hall and John Mothlon of same Co.,
for 6000 lb tobo, 130 acres, whereon said William and Mary now live,
being part of land bought by Wm. Jennings from Martin Fisher.
Wit:
John Jennings   signed   Wm Jennings
James Strothers   Mary Jennings mark

                         Rec. 15 June 1696.

p. 174. Agreement. 4 March 1695/6. Nath'll Hall and John Mothlin in
agreement with Wm Jennings concerning land. That the land be bounded
with trees marked by John Jennings and Martin Fisher and adjoins
land bought by John Jennings from Tobias Butler.
Wit:
John Jennings   signed   Nath'll x Hall
James Strothers   John x Mothlin

p.175. Deed. 17 March 1695/6. Martin Fisher of Richmond Co., planter,
to Wm Jennings of same Co., planter, for 2500 lb tobo, 100 acres, adj
John Butler's line, land of Jno Jennings and line of Nath Hall and
Jno Mothlin.
Wit: signed   Martin Fisher his mark
Nich'o Smyth
Francis Sterne his mark   Rec 17 June 1696

p.177. Deed. 9 April 1696. Martin Fisher of Richmond Co., planter, to
Christopher Pritchett of same Co., planter, for 4500 lb tobo, 150
acres in Richmond Co. Adjs land of Wm Jennings, "running along down
Mattox path", also adjs line of "Robert Varses binding upon his Line
to John Butlers line", Cattail branch, etc.
Wit:
John Jennings   signed   The mark of Martin Fisher
James x Kitchen
                          Rec 18 June 1696

p.178. Deed. 2 Nov 1691. Wm Yates of Northfarnham Par, Rappa Co.,
planter, to "Wm Burnham of the said County of the County of Westmorland shipwright", for 4000 lb tobo in Cask, 100 acres, in sd Par and
Co., part of a tract formerly bought by John Alloway of Capt John Hull
and by said Alloway "sold to John Yates and by Inheritance to the
abovesaid William Yates son of the said John Yates", "lying between
two Branches com'only known or called by the name of the Matchacomaco
branch the other Edw'd Lewis his Branch"
Wit:
Edward Newton his mark   signed   William Yates
Edward Jones
John Battaile   Rec. Rappa Co. 27 Nov 1691.

Deed Book No. 2

p.180. Assignment. 10 April 1693. Wm Burnham of Richmond Co. Carpenter
to Philip Hunnings, for 4000 lb tobo, land contained in within men-
tioned deed of sale. Meaning the foregoing entry on p 66. This entry
refers to "my Wife Ann Burnham".
Wit: signed   William Burnham
Wm Barber   mark of Ann Burnham
Wm Barber junr
Tho: Dew   Rec 17 May 1693 in Richmond Co.

p.181. Assignment. 22 Oct 1695. Philip Hunning and Eliz: his wife to
John Morgan, for 5000 lb tobo, land contained within this bill of sale.
(land in two foregoing entries)
Wit: signed   Philip Hunnings
Charles Barber   Eliz Hunnings her mark
Walt'r Wright
                       Rec 18 June 1696
                           Wm Colston Cl Cur

p.182. Power of Atty. 2 June 1696. Eliz Hunnings wife of Philip
Hunnings of Richmond Co., to James Caward (sic) to ack above.
Wit:
the mark of Tho Yates   signed The mark of Eliz Hunings

End of Deed Book No. 2

Memo: re Richmond Co. records.
Deed Book No.2 and Deed Book No.14 are bound together.
Deed Book No. 3 - missing from records.
Deed Book No. 4 and Court Order Book No. 4 are bound together.

Mr. E. Carter Delano, Warsaw, Virginia, knows these records better,
far better, than any other living person.   B.F.

Richmond County
Miscollaneous Records.

Title page of this Record Book marked:

From October 1699 to September 1724

There is Recorded in this book   )
Deposicons, Severall sorts of bonds Deeds)
for personall matters, Letters of Attorney)
Jurys Reports, and some other odd things)

Clerks Office

office of Delinquishment

p.1.   "Know all men by these presents That wee Sarah Suggett Rawleigh
Travers and Thomas Beal of the County of Richmond do and are justly
indebted unto his Majesties Justices for the said County the full sume
of sixty thousand pounds of every way well Conditioned Tobacco in Cask
To be paid unto the said Justices their Executors Administrators or
assigns   To the which payment well and truly to be made and performed
wee do bind us our heirs Executors and administrators Joynth and sev-
erally firmly by these presents sealed with our seals Dated this 4th
day of October in the Eleventh yeare of the Reigne of our Sovereigne
Lord William of England Scot- etc Ano'q Dom 1699
       The Condicon of this Obligacon is such That if the above bound
Sara Sugget Rawleigh Travers and Tho: Beal or any of them or any of
their heirs Executors or administrators do or shall from time and at
all times for ever hereafter save defend keep harmless and indemnified
the above named Justices their heirs Executors or administrators of
and from all actions suits Controversies deb- Pleas Judgments Execu-
tions and demands whatsoever concerning the Estate of Tho: Baylis of
this County late dec'd And if the said Sarah shall and will upon all
times Render a Just and true Account of the said Estate and surrender
the same and every part thereof unto the executorship of the Court of
the said County or to whom it shall more properly belonge when thereunto Lawfully Required That then this Obligation to be voyd and of
none Effect otherwyse to stand in full force and Virtue
Sealed and delivered
in presence of   Sarah Baylis   (seal)
Wm Brokenbrough   Raw: Travers   (seal)
Wm Colston   Tho Beall   (seal)

                    Record'dd Tes't Wm Colston Cl Cur

Misc. Records.

p.1. Bond. 4 Oct. 1699. "Know all men by these presents That I Sarah
Suggitt of the County of Richmond Widow do stand Justly indebted unto
Rawleigh Travers and Thos Beall of the said County of Richmond in the
full Just Sum of One hundred and twenty thousand pounds of every way
well Conditioned Tobacco in Caske to be paid unto the said Rawleigh
Travers and Thos Beall their Execut'rs Admst'rs or order To the which
Paym't well and truly to be made and performed I bind me my heirs
Execut'rs and admst'rs firmly by these presents Sealed with my seale
Dated this 4th day of Octob'r in the Eleventh yeare of the Reign of
our Sovereign Lord Wms of England Scotland etc King Ano'q Dom 1699
        The Condi00n of this Obligacon is such That if the above bound
Sarah Suggitt her heirs Execut'rs and admst'rs shall from time to time
and at all times hereafter save defend discharge keep harmless and
indemnifyed the above named Rawleigh Travers and Thos Beall their
Execut'rs and admst'rs for or by reason of their being herein bound
with the said Sarah Suggitt for their saving harmless and indemnified
his Mag'ties Justices of this County their heirs Execut'rs and
admst'rs from all manner of persons whatsoever pretending any Claims
Right title or interest of in or unto the Estate of Thomas Baylis of
the said County late dec'd or of in or unto any part or parcell thereof That then this Obligacon be voyd otherwise to stand and remaine
in full force and Virtue"
Sealed and delivered   signed   Sarah Baylis (seal)
in the presence of
Wm Brokenbrough
Wm Colston   Record'd Tes't Wm Colston Cl Cur

p.1 - A. Bond. 1699 (Month and day of month not shown on record)
Thos Richardson, 20000 lb tobo., to Justices of Richmond Co. "concern-
ing the Estate of Wm Puckford of this County late dec'd"
Wit:
Wm Colston   signed   Tho: Richardson
                                               Geo: Phillips
                                               Silvest'r Thatcher

p.2. Bond. 1699. (Month and day of month not shown on record). Tho:
Richardson, 40000 lb tobo, to keep harmless, etc., Silvester Thatcher
and George Phillips, who have signed preceeding bond.
Wit:
Wm Colston   signed   Tho: Richardson

p. 2 - A. "Attachm't Issued to Tho: Mackey Merch't against the Estate
of Phillip Hunnings for 1320 lb of Tobacco. Returned executed the

2'd day of December 1699 in the hands of Charles Barber upon 1125 lb
of Tobacco. Also Decem'r the 4th 1699 upon one Gray colored mare w'ch
was appraised at 700 lb of Tobacco by M'r Wm: Woodbridge M'r Tho
Ascough M'r Tho: Bryant Sen'r and M'r John Mills appraisers Sumoned
for that purpose

Per

LeRoy George   Sub Sh   "

p.2 - A. "Attachm't Issued to Nich'o Smyth against the Estate of
John Jones for 3225 lb of good Tobacco Returned Executed the 22'd day
of Decemb'r 1699 upon a parcell of Tobacco hanging in a Tobacco house
(one Levey Excepted) and a parcell of Indian Corne lying in a Dwelling
house which said Tobacco and Indian Corne were appraised by M'r John
Burkett Mr: Wm Pannell M'r Richard Jordan and M'r Silvester Thacker
(sic) appraisers sumoned for the purpose as followeth (Viz't)

LeRoy George   Sub Sh

A parcell of Tobacco hanging)
in a Tobacco house at   )   1200

A parcell of Indian Corne lying)
in a dwelling house at   )   1000
                                      - -- -- -
                                         2200   "

p.2 - A. "Attachm't Issued to Wm Robinson Gen't against the Estate of
Jeremia Smyth for 600 lb of good Tobacco in Caske upon bill and Acc.
Returned Executed the 10th day of 9'br 1699 upon Tob that is hanging
in the said Jeremiah Smyths Tobacco house to satisfie the within
men'coned debt

per James Phillips Sub Sheriff   "

p. 2 - A. "An Attachm't Issued to David Gwin and Wm Colston as impowered to Collect the Goods and Creditts of Mr. Tho: Loyd dec'd in
Right of M'r John Loyd against the Estate of Phillip Hunu- Hunings
for 634 of Tobacco by Acc
Also Attachment Issued to David Gwin and Wm Colston as impowered etc:
against the Estate of Phillip Hunings for 550 lb of good Tobacco upon
a bill assigned by Walt'r Pavey Both Executed the 20th of Novemb'r
1699 . . upon the body of one Patrick Macgarr servant to the said

Misc. Records.

Phillip Hunings and was valued at 1200 lb of Tobacco by Geo: Glascook
Jno: Suggitt Fran: Lewoas Jno Battin (? - bottom of page worn
away) "

signed   John Tarpley Jr Sheriff

p.3. "Attachm't Issued to John Smith Merch't against the Estate of
John Bennett for 1423 lb of Tobacco by ac'ct: Returned executed the
2'd of 9'br 1699 upon a parcell of Tobacco hanging in an old house
per Leroy George Sub Sherif "

p. 3. "Attachm't Issued to John Chartres Merch't against the Estate
of Phillip Hunnings for 1200 lb of good Tobacco by bill Returned
Executed the 14th day of 9'br 1699 upon Tobacco in the house of
Thomas Lewis

John Tarpley Sheriff "

p.3. "Attachm't Issued to Edmond Aglsonby Merch't: against the
Estate of Phillip Hunnings for 968 lb of Tobacco. Returned Executed
the 10th of 9'ber 1699 upon Tobacco in the house of Tho: Lewis
per John Tarpley Sheriff "

p.3. "Attachm't issued to Andrew Crumwell assignee of Wm Clarke and
Company of Bristoll Mercht's against the Estate of Dommsick Benneham
for 1125 lb of Tobacco by bill. Returned Executed the 5th of 10'br
1699 upon

One long Gun	200	
One large Couch	120	
One Tobo	150	
One old Chane	12	
One feather bed bolster)		
Red Rug one blankett one)		
Course sheet on pillow and)		
Course pillowber)	900	1382

which said Goods were appraised by Rob't Palmer Wm Miskill Tho:
Bryant Jun'r and Tho: Bryant Sen'r who were Lawfully summoned and
sworn before Mr: Wm: Doleman
Test: Leroy George Sub: Sheriff

Misc. Records.

p.3. "Attachment issued to John Hughes Merch't against the Estate of Phillip Hunnings for 544 lb of good Tobacco in Caske. Returned Executed the 7th of 9'ber 1699 upon a sorrell horse with a flaxen Mayne and tayle branded on the neare buttock with H and one Iron pott and potthooks which are appraised by M'r John Battin M'r John Suggitt M'r Henry Hay and M'r Francis Lewcas appraisers as followeth (Viz:)

One Sorrell Colored horse   600
One Iron pott and pothooks   50

                               650

                                    Leroy George   Sub Sheriff

p. 3 - A. "Attachm't issued to Sam'll Nockolls Merch't of London against the Estate of John Bennet for 919 lb of Tobacco by Bill. Returned attached in the hands of John Henderson 772 of Tobacco being the proper Estate of John Bennett this 10th day of 10'br 1699
                                    per Jams Phillips "

p. 3 - A. "Attachm't issued to Jn'o Reynolds against the Estate of Jeremiah Smyth for 7 1/2 yd's of kersey and 65 lb of Tobacco. Returned Executed the 10th day of Novemb'r 1699 upon a parcell of Corne in the house of the said Jeremiah Smyth to satisfie the within Debt
                                    per James Phillips "

p. 3 - A.

The Estate of M'r William
Clapham jr D'br to Tho
Richardson Viz't

To worke don by me in his life time Virt
        To Building a 60 foot house   1500
        To building a 30 foot house   700
        To building a 50 foot ditto   500
        To putting in a - (illegible)   400
        To making a Cart   150
        To making 3 Axle fells   090
        To making a long latter   050
        To making a great Gate   080
        To 3 little gates   090
        To a Shed at the end of the house   350

                    (continued)

Miso. Records.

Thomas Richardson in a/c with the estate of Mr. Wm. Clapham, jr. Decd.
(continued)

Goods Lent
    To a bush'le of Salt   150
    To 2 Ells of Dowlas at 30 per ell   060
    To a bush'll of Salt   080
    To making his Coffin   300
                                                 -- -- -- --
                        The sum is   4500

To Sundry Debts paid by me Contracted in his life time
    To John Hasl'r   630
    To John Spencer   570
    To N.buck Jones   500
    To Doct'r Chappell   1500
    To Jn'o Franklin   869
    To Mr Booker Minister   550
    To Jn'o Manning   310

per Contra Cr
    By Tobacco Rec'd by me in his life time   1800

By Debts due to him in his life time rec't per me
    By Tobacco of Nich'o Smyth   1530
    By Tobacco of Ja: Bourne   0500
    By Tobb of Tho Genstree   0800
    By Tobacco of Rich'd Hill   1200
                                                 -- -- -- --
                                                   4030
                                                   1800
                                                 -- -- -- --
                                                   5830

    To Mr Spicer   544
    To James Orchard   270
    To Mr Walters   170
    To Edward Scrimshaw   170
    To John Spencer   310
    To 5 Tithables at 91 per poll   455
    To Doct'r Micou   600
    To Leveys and Quitrents Essex   616
    To Clerks fees   714
                                                 -- -- -- --
                                                   8779
                                                   4500
                                                 -- -- -- --
            The whole sum   13279
                I D   5830
                                                 -- -- -- --
                                                   7993
                    (continued)

Thomas Richardson in a/c with the estate of Mr. Wm. Clapham, jr. Decd.
(continued)

The said Thomas did present unto us an acc't of three thousand pounds
of Tobacco for a boy appraised as the said Claphams Estate which in
our Judgm't he should have &c for
  In Obedience to an order of Court bearing date the first of 9'br
  1699 Wee the subscribers did meet at the house of Capt: Arthur
  Spicer and then and there did adjust the acc't of Thomas Richardson concerning the Estate of Wm Clapham dec'd and find the
  Ballance merited
        John Deane
        Wm Robinson

     Recorded 2 Jan 1699 (1699/1700)

p.4. "The Deposition of Charles Dodson Sen'r aged fifty years or
thereabouts sayeth that about the 16th day of April last past being
on board of the Dublin Merch't in Company with John Macgill late
dec'd did in presence heare the said John Macgill agree with M'r
Francis Moore Merch't of the said ship for a man Servant named John
Connor which had six years to Serve by Indenture and that I the said
Dodson read the said Indenture and further saith not
       Charles Dodson "
Sworn in Richmond Co. Court 6 March 1699/1700.

p. 4-A. "Attachm't issued to Charles - - (faded out) - - Estate of
Tho: Gaines for Eight hundred pounds of Tobacco by bill. Returned
Executed the 9th of 9'ber 1699 in these words Then attached two
parcells of Tobacco hanging in two severall houses, One Levey Sixty
Seven and a halfe being 1st paid for the use of the within menooned
       Test Leroy George Sub Sh "

p. 4-A. "Attachm't Issued to Roderick Jones against the Estate of
John Lovett for three hundred and fifty pounds of Tobacco Returned
January the 9th 1699. The within attachm't was Leveyed upon a black
and white colored cow marked with a Crop and a slitt on the Right
Eare and an underkeil on the left oare and a black yearling bull
Calfe unmarked which were appraised by Peter Ellis Edward Pryor Richd
Dowdan and Ralph Bartlett Appraisors summoned for that purpose as
followeth (Vizt) for the use of Roderick Jones
One black and white cow marked as abovesaid   420 1.Tob
One black yearling bull Calfe unmarked   080
            - - -
      in all 500
    Test: Leroy George Sub Sh.

p. 4-A. March Court. 1699. (1699/1700) Attachm't Issued to Geo: Glascock, against the Estate of Phillip Hunnings, for 275 lb of good Tobacco. Returned December the 2d 1699. The within attachment was served in the hands of Mr. Charles Barber.
Tobacco in Mr. Barbers hands 275   Signed Leroy George Sub Sh

p. 4-A. Attachmen't Issued to Mr. John Waugh against the Estate of Cap't Thomas Baker for 3000 lb of Tobacco in Caske.
    Returned Executed this Attachm't in the hands of John Lee
                    Signed   James Phillips

p. 4-A. "Execution Issued upon an Order of this County Court dated the 2d of Mar An'o 1698/9 to Robert Payne against John Browne for 845 lb of good Tobacco in Caske and Costs sixty three pounds of Tobacco
    Returned Executed on the body of the within named John Browne the 8th day of 9'ber 1699
                      per Jams Phillips
    Rec'd of John Browne the full Contents of the within order together with all Charges incident thereunto
                    James Phillips "

p. 4-A. "Execution issued upon an Order of this County Court dated the 7th of June 1699 granted to Tho: Ascough against Jn'o Pitman for 500 lb of Tobacco with Costs of suit
    Returned Executed the 18th of February 1699 (1699/1700) upon the Body of the within men'cooned John Pitman, and for Redemption of his Body produced the -- timo the value of the said debt And after appraism't according to Law made -- of a horse on tho behalfs of pl't being appraised at 500 lb of Tobacco by us
John x Willis   James Phillips   )
John x Coomes   did choos for the plt)
                    John x Tarkington
                    Will Willis   "

p. 5. Execution Issued upon an Order of this County Court dated the 1st of June an'o 1699 granted to Susanna Gose Admst'a of John Stampson dec'd against John Tarkington for 514 lb of Tobacco in Caske upon bill together with Cost of suit. Returned Executed the 14th of Decemb'r 1699 upon a horse appraised to eight hundred forty seaven pounds of Tobacco
By   Nath'll Pope   James Phillips Sub Sh
    Rob't Payne

p. 5.   "Execution Issued upon an Order of this County Court dated the
2'd of March 1698/9 Granted to John Size and Thomasin Whiting Exeut'rs
of Ralph Whiting dec'd against John Henderkin for 3000 lb of Tobacco
and Caske together with Costs etc.
        Returned Executed on the body of the within named John Henderkin
the 19th day of Octo'br 1699
                                            per me James Phillips   Sub Sh
9'br the 2'd day 1699
Rec'd of John Henderkin the full contents of the within Order together
with all charges incidental hereunto
                                            per me   James Phillips "

p.5.   Apr'll Court
                                 1700
Attachm't Issued to Capt John Miller of Bristol mariner against the
Effects of Girard Newton for 490 lb of Tobacco   Returned Executed the
25th of March 1699/1700 on one hogshead of Tobacco weight Gross 562 lb
Tare: 40: Nett 482 Caske 90: 512: 22: weight 534"

p.5. Exors Bond. 6 May 1700. Joshua Lawson Exor of Thos. Parker of
Richmond Co. 20000 lb tobo.
Wit: signed   Joshua Lawson
James Byard   Jos Dike
Wm Colston   Tho: Lewis

p. 5. Bond. 6 May 1700. Joshua Lawson, Exor of Thos. Parker to Jos.
Dike and Tho. Lewis, 40000 lb tobo, to save them harmless in having
signed foregoing bond.
Wit: signed   Joshua Lawson
James Byard
Wm Colston

p.6. Bond. 15th June 1700. Sam'll Peachey, Sheriff of Richmond County,
100000 lb Tobo.
        "The Condicon of this Obligation is such That whereas his most
Sacred Majestie William the third by his Letters Patent under the seal
of this Colony of Virginia and Tes'te of his Excellency Fran Nicholson
Esq: his said Majesties Lieut: and Govern'r Genr'll of the same Bearing date the 8th day of April An'o Dom 1700. Hath Commissioned ordered
and appointed the abovenamed Sam'll Peachey Sheriff of the said County
of Richmond during his pleasure. If therefore the said Sam'll Peachey
shall Render unto Mr Auditor Bird or such other as shall be appointed
to Receive the same a particular perfect and full account of all his

Misc. Records.

Majesties Revenues and dues in the said County during the time of his
Sherifalty as also due payment made of all such Publick dues as shall
be Leveyed in the said County unto the severall persons that shall be
appointed to Receive the same and full performance made of all things
belonging to the said office of Sherif That then this obligation be
voyd otherwise to stand in full force and virtue"
Sealed and delivered
in presence of   signed   Sam'll Peachey
Leroy George   Wm Tayloe
Wm Colston   John Baker
                         Record'd Tes't Wm Colston Cl Cur

p.6-A. Bond. 5 June 1700. Samll Peachey to Wm Tayloe and John Baker,
200000 lb Tobo., to keep them harmless in having signed above bond.
Wit:
Leroy George   signed   Sam'll Peachey
Wm Colston

p.7. "Attachm't issued to John Molton against the Estate of Geo Luke
gen't for 500 lb of Tobacco   Returned Executed the 3d of Feby 1699
(1699/1700) in the hands of Cap't Alvin Mountjoy upon all the
Tobacco due from the said Mountjoy unto Mr. Geo Luke (Quantitie of
which said Tobacco is unknown) for the use of the said John Molton
                              Leroy George Sub Sh "

p.7. Power of Atty. 28 May 1700. Augustine Woodward to Mr George
Glascock, to transact certain business.
Wit:
John Tarpley   signed   Augustine Woodward
Wm Donhman
                         Rec. 5 June 1700

p.7. Power of Atty. 23 May 1700. George Foxcroft of Liverpool,
merchant, to Mr. George Glascock to transact business in his name
Wit:
Cha: Barber   signed   Geo: Foxcroft
Zaold: Nicholls
Jno. Tarpley   Rec. 5 June 1700.

p. 7-A. Bond. 17 August 1700. Hanna Hughes as executrix of Jno Hughes
of Richmond Co.   signed Hanna x Hughes
Wit: Geo: Payne
Edward Jones   Jn'o Kelley
Nath'll Pope

p. 7-A "Attachm't Issued to Wm Colston against the Estate of Richard Smyth Camand'r of the Benjamin and Mary of London but on the River of Rappahannock for 19: 3: 0: upon a protested bill of Exchange together with Cost of the protest and damage according to Act of Assembly

Returned Executed July the 5th 1700 the within Process on the Estate of Richard Smyth in the hands of Mr Nich'o Smyth who acknowledged he hath Estate of the said Richard Smyth in his Custody to the value of the within - "

Wm Brockenbrough Sub Sh

p. 8. Power of Atty. Dated Virginia, 15 March 1699/1700. Francis Linch to "my trusty and well beloved friend and kinsman Mr Stephen Linch" to collect accounts in Virginia.
Wit: signed   Fran: Linch
Wm Griffin
Rich'd Coleman his marke
Edward Fitzegerbelt his marke
                    Rec. 7 August 1700

p. 8-A.
"Septemb'r 24th 1700
Jane Baker 34 years of age or thereabouts being Examined and sworne saith That some time before Mr Robert Baylis Sen'r died he sent for me (and) James Samford and desired him to take Notice that those two feather beds he lay on was not in his will and that his desire was that after he was dead That Wm Baylis his grand son should have one of the feather beds and his Grandaughter Amadine Baylis should have the other bed And after Mr Baylis decease that his Estate came to be divided amongst his children those two beds was first given by the Execut'rs to me one bed for my son Will Baylis and the other bed to Mr Thomas Baylis for his Daughter Amadine before any division and further saith not

                         Jane Baker
Jane Baker was sworn to the
within Deposition this 29th
of 7'br 1700
        John Baker
        Law: Travers   Record't Test
                             Wm Colston Cl Cr   "

Note: The following indicates the descent of one of our old families from the persons appearing in the foregoing entry. It is from Richmond County Court Order Book No. 3, p. 351. 3rd August 1704. "The action brought by Job Hamond Jun'r and Amadine his wife adm'rs de bonis non

Misc. Records.

of Thomas Baylis Late of this County dec'ed x x" etc.
And also the same book, the same date, page 354. "the said Job and
Amadine by Virtue of the said Qualification to the said Amadine Grant-
ed humbly prayes order for against the said James Suggett Ex'r of the
said Sarah Baylis".
There is more of this in confirmation to follow.   B.F.

p. 8-A. "James Samford aged Seaventy six years or thereabouts being
sworn saith
        That some short time before Mr: Rob't Baylis Sen'r departed this
life he sent for me your Deponent and desired me to take Notice that
the two feather beds he then lay on was not mentioned in his will and
that he gave them to William Baylis Grandson to the said Robert and
to Amadine Baylis Grandaughter to the said Robert Baylis and desired
me this and desired me this deponent to take care that the said beds
should be delivered to his said Grandchildren (that is to say) each
of them to have one and further this Deponent saith that after the
decease of the said Robert Baylis the aforesaid bed with bolster and
rugg and sheets were delivered before the said Baylis Estate was
divided by the Mutuall Consent of the Execut'rs or persons interest
one to Jane Baylis for the use of her son Wm Baylis the other to Mr
Thos Baylis for the use of his Daughter Amadine and further saith not
                                                James Samford

Mr James Samford was sworne
before us to the above Deposition
this 24th day of 7'br 1700
(Signatures omitted here)
                                Record' Tes't Wm Colston C "

p. 9. "Attachm't Continued to Wm Colston against the Estate of Phillip
Hunnings for 863 lb of Tobacco with cask of suit Returnable
        Returned Executed 7'br the 30th 1700 upon 665 lb of Tobacco in
the hands of John Bartlemew
                                per James James Phillips Sub Sh

p. 9. Execution Issued against the Estate of Richard Smyth mariner
upon an Order of Richmond County Court Dated the 7th of August 1700
Granted to Wm Colston for 4440 lb of Tobacco in Caske with costs of
suit   Returned Executed the 19th day of August 1700 on the Body of
Nich'o Smyth in whose hands so much of the Estate of the said Richard
Smyth then was and Rec'd the full Contents and all Costs
                                James Phillips Sub Sh

p. 9. "Know all men by these Presents That I William Fitzhugh Jun'r
the attorney of my father Wm Fitzhugh in his Qualification as he is
Attorney of the Right Hon'ble Margarett Lady Culpeper The Lord Fairfax
and Catherine his wife do by these presents fully authorize and give
power to Mr Geo: Glascock and Mr Charles Barber to Receive Collect
demand and when Received to give discharges for all the Quitrents and
arrerages of Quitrents due to the said Proprietors in the Parish of
Farnham from each and every Respective Land holder therein when Received And in Case any Land holder or Land holders in the said Parish
Refuse payment then to distraine as the law directs in like cases
always provided they demand of no Land holder in said Parish aforesaid payment for no longer time then till Michelmass last past being
the 29th day of September of the said Proprietors dues, and for or by
Lawfully acting in the abovesaid premises this shall be their sufficient warrant given under my hand and seale this 2'd day of October
1700
                              Wm Fitzhugh   (seal)
Sealed and delivered   Jun'r
in the presence of
James Jameson
Ann x Lewis   "   Rec. 5 March 1700/01

p. 9-A. Executors Bond. 6 May 1701. Elizabeth Thornton of Richmond
Co., Extx of Estate of Rowland Thornton of Rd. Co., late deceased.
60000 lb tobo. Also issued in names of Tho: Pacie and Geo Payne
whose names do not appear in the record as signing the bond.
Wit:
Wm Underwood   signed   Elizabeth Thornton her mark.
John Tarpley

p. 9-A. Bond. 6 May 1701. Elizabeth Thornton to Thos Pacie and George
Payne, 12000 lb tobo, to hold them harmless in above. Signed and
witnessed as in foregoing entry.

p. 10. Bond. John Tarpley as Sheriff of Richmond Co. Dated 26 May 1701
for 100000 lb tobo. Appointment by Gov. Francis Nicholson dated 25th
April 1701.
Wit: signed   John Tarpley
James Suggitt   Wm Downman
Tho: Suggitt   Wm Colston
(Note: The name Wm Downman also appears as Wm Doleman in this entry)

p. 10-A. Bond. 26 May 1701. John Tarpley, to Wm Dolman and Wm Colston
120000 lb tobo, to keep them harmless in foregoing. Signed by Tarpley
and witnessed as above.

p.11
                        May the 3rd 1701
Account of Goods attached of James Holladay for to satisfie a Debt of
Cornelius MaCarty as followeth
                                                            1 Tob

A Bed Rugg and paire of blanketts   650
17 ps of Earthen Ware and old Tin pan   70
a Washing Tubb a Smll Tubb a Can a piggon and)
     a frypan and ladle   )   10
4 Chaires   40
2 Sowes throe piggs   300
                                                             -- -- --
                                                            1170

The above goods appraised by us the subscribers
Frans Sloughter   Alex'r Spence
                                     Jno Reynolds his mark
                                     Cha: Tibbo his mark

p.11-A.

Att MaCarty   )   May the 3'd 1701
    vs   ) Attached to satisfie the within process an old
Holladay for 926) Iron pott an old Chest a yearling calfe
                             per Jas Phillips

The above goods appraised as followeth
     An old Chest and old pott   50   (1b tobo)
     a yearling Calfe   100   "
                        By us the subscribers
                        Alex'r Spence
                        John Reynolds his mark
                        Cha: Tibbo his mark

p. 11-A. Power of Atty. Dated Virginia 9th June 1701. Geo Foxcroft
of Liverpool Morcht., to Capt John Tarpley to collect debts in Va.
Wit:
Charles Barber   signed   Geo: Foxcroft
Geo: Glascock
Raw. Doleman
                        Rec. 2 July 1701.

Note: Now I never before ever heard of the good old Virginia name
Downman as having been either pronounced or spelled Dolman or Doleman.
But here we are. Of course there is an evident connection between the
words down and dole.   B.F.

p 11-A. Power of Atty. 1 July 1701. John Bowley to Nathaniel Pope of
Richmond Co., to transact all business in Richmond Co. that he is
concerned in.

                          signed   John Bowley his mark.

p.12. Indenture. 6 Nov. 1700. "John Summervile of Edinborough in the
Kingdom of Scotland Merchant of the one part and John Smyth of Murray
in the said Kingdom Labourer of the other part Witnesseth That the
said John Smyth hath and by these presents doth bind and put himselfe
an apprentice and servant to the said John Summervile to serve him or
his assignes in the Plantation of Virginia beyond the seas for the
space of foure years next ensuing the arrivall of the said Servant in
the said Plantation x x according to the Laws and Customs of the said
Plantacon x x"
Wit: signed   John Somervile (seal)
Robert Griggs.

p.12-A. "These are to Certifie That the above named John Smyth came
before me Wm Parson of Whithaven the day and yeare above written and
declared himselfe x x to be of the age of thirty two years x x "
                          Wm Parson D Register

                     Recorded in Rich'd Co. 21 July 1701.
                     Wm Colston CC

p.12-A.   "To his Excellency Francis Nicholson Esqr his Maj'ties
Lieut and Govern'r Gen'll of Virginia
          The Humble pet'n of William Smoote
          Humbly sheweth that your pet'r haveing behaved himselfe in
all Respects a Loyall Subject ought to do notwithstanding Cap't John
Tarpley high Sheriff of the County of Richmond did come to the house
of your pet'r in your pet'rs absence upon the twenty sixth day of
March Last past and there under pretence of seizing for publick dues
which your pet'r had already paid but having no receipt the said
Tarpley did beat your pet'rs wife very much and abuse her after a
very Grievous manner and wounded her in severall places and threaten
her so much that whee is afraid to stay att home in your pet'rs absence and further May itt please your Ex'cy The said Tarpley did
afterwards breake open a doore of your pet'rs house that was fast
nailed and itt was Gods great mercy that the said Tarpley had not
killed a young Child that was behind the doore your Pet'r have (sic)
Applied himselfe to the County Court to for to Come to an account
with the said Tarpley and he altogether Refuses to Come to an account
and further may it please your Ex'cy the said Tarpley have retained
all the attorneys that belong to the County Court thinking to Justifie

his unlawfull doeings so that your pet'r being a poore man and haveing
a great Charge of small Children and haveing no reliefe if not relieved by your Ex'cy therefore your pet'r humbly Implores your Ex'cys
Relief and your pet'r as in duty shall ever pray for your Exc'es
Conservation
                      Recordat: 9 die May 1702 Test
                        James Sherlook Cl Cur

p.13.

        May itt please your Ex'cy
        I have Read the petition of William Smoot agt Capt John
Tarpley Shorriff of the County of Richmond and have also Inquired
into the Subject matter of the said petition and humbly Conceive that
itt may be Expedient for your Ex'cy to reforr the same to the County
Court of Richm'd with Directions to Examine into the truth of the
fact by Evidences upon oath and make returne thereof together with
theire Opinions therein to your Ex'cy to the end that such further
proceedings may Be had thereupon as shall be agreeable to Law
April 7th 1702
                            B: Harrison

                         James Sherlook   Cl Cur

p.13

Virginia Sct
            Aprill the 7th 1702
I do hereby In his Maj'ties name Will and require to Justices of his
Maj'tes County of Richmond to do according to the proposition of M'r
Benjamin Harrison his Maj'ties Councill att Law and they are so soone
as Possible to send theire proceedings therein to
                            Fr Nicholson

                         James Sherlook   Cl Cur

Note: Just wait one moment. Before the descendants of Mr. and Mrs.
Smoot (and there are many) rise in indignation at the treatment of
their ancestors - just a moment. All this may never have happened at
all. It looks very much as though it were one of the old Governor's
petty little traps to catch the County Officials. It bears all the
hall marks of his technique. First the cooked up disturbance. Then
the noble Governor with much noise and damnation to the rescue. The
offending officials put out in disgrace, only to be immediately re-
placed with the Governor's friends, or others of whom he knew why, if
we do not. The sham became so evident and was so universal throughout
the colony that the profane old gentleman had to be removed from the
Governorship by Queen Anne within two or three years of this episode.
Personally I would hesitate to shed one single tear, no not even for
the child nailed up in the room to save it's life.   B.F.

p.13-A.

Decemb'r the 3rd 1701

William Marke aged fifty two or thereabouts Deposeth and saith
that your depon't being att the house of Mrs Anne Ascough the seventh
day of Sept'r Last past where Thomas Ascough son of the said Anne
Ascough then Lay Sick, the said Thomas Ascough Called your depo't to
the bedside and desired your depo't to take notice of what he was
going to say (to witt) in these words that what his mother was then
possest withall she should Enjoy without any molestation and further
your depo't Saith not to the best of his knowledge

William Marks

Sworne to in Court

Recordat   Test

James Sherlock   Cl Cur

p. 13-A. "Mary Pinkett aged twenty yeares or thereabouts deposeth
and saith that her master Thomas Ascough being sick att the house of
his mother Mrs Anne Ascough on the seventh of Sept' Last past her
said master called her to him and desired your depo't to take notice
of what he was then goeing to say (to witt) in these words (to the
best of your depo'ts knowledge that what his mother was then Possest
withall she should Quietly Enjoy without any molestation and further
your depo't saith not

her
Mary x Pinckett
Sworne to in Court   mark   "

Note: Oftentimes in these records only the first round bracket "("
of a parenthesis, the second ")" omitted. At first I thought this in
error. But later I came to know that it was not an omission in error.
It was a form of the period (I mean by period as of that time)
having somewhat the use of the modern comma.   B.F.

p.13-A

Richmond Ss

The 30th of March Last past att the plantation of Mr James Keys
then by the river side a man being found dead named John Newdell after
notice given a Jury of Inquest and the Jur'ys oppinion was by severall
Cutts in his head came by his death by whome could not tell It seems
this man which is now dead wont on board a shipe and his wife with
him and a man which Lives in the house with them which by all reports
keeps company with the said mans wife and the seamen gave them
Lyckrs but not out of Reason the seamen put them a shore all together
well att this same place whore this man is found dead noe other person

with them and not a Gunne shott from the house where she live this
being Saturday and Sunday notys to me that a man was there dead which
do realy believe that these two persons his wife and Abraham Harrison
(or Hannison) her mate is guilty of the above said mans death as also
severale persons has heard both these threaten his Life William
Stone for one as emformed by Henry Gollop hearing nothing of these
passages when the Jury of Inquest was on him but all Contrary to what
now have sifted out Thomas Porter saith that the man sometime before
his death was att said Porters house the man declared there the first
time was drunk that she should heare he was murthered by that man and
his wife

These are therefore in his Maj'ties name to Comand you William
Bronaugh Constable forthwith to goe with good strength to the house
of Mr James Keys now Martha Newdalls and there to seize the bodies
of Abraham Harrison (or Hannison) and Martha Newdall one suspistion
of being guilty of murther of the abovesaid John Newdall and when
seized to secure them with good aid and assistance and carry them
to the next Constable and there to take receipt of your delivery and
so the next to the next Constable and so from Constable to Constable
untill come unto Capt John Tarpleys high sherriff of Richmond there
to take receipt of Delivery faile not as youle answer the Contrary
att your Perile Given under my hand this 15th of Aprill an'o Dom 1702

                                        Alex'r Doniphan

This for Wm Bronaugh   )
Constable and all other Constables)
betweene this and the high sherr)
of Richmond   )

                          Reeordat: Test
                          James Sherlock Cl Cur

p.14

Richmond Ss: March 30th an'o 1702
A man being found dead att the River banke of Mr: James Keyes plantation his name John Newdell a Jury of Inquest pannell'd and sworne
after notice given and we of the Jury find by severall cutts in the
forehead was the occasions of his death by whome we cannot Give any
account supposing

James Phillips	Thomas x Pilpin	Charles Steward
Tho x Porter	John Rowley	Mark Rymor
Robert x Engeles	John x Clay	Robt x Gollop
Wm x Bridges	John x Corbin	James x Richardson

All the Jurors above has given theire opinion and itt is mine he came
by his death supposing a hamer was the cause by reason of the dent in

his forehead and but small cutt

                             Alex'r Doniphan   Corron'r

Recordat'r Test

            James Sherlock   Cl Cur

Note: It is impossible for me to decide as to whether the name of the
murderer was Abraham Hannison or Abraham Harrison. It appears many
times in the entries to follow. In the originals, at times it is
plainly Hannison. At other times just as plainly Harrison. I don't
think anybody wants him as an ancestor very much. Either family can
easily put it on the other if they care to step out from the shadow
of the gallows. But give the Devil his due. This man did protect and
feed this woman. He brought her out of what they called Marry Land.
He fought for her. He murdered for her (that is if she did'ent do
it herself) and we presume he died for her. In this day a divorce
can be bought for a small sum of money, That was impossible then.
Events are at times greater than we. And human nature, love and the
law do not always agree. Perhaps you or I would have murdered that
drunken pest under the same circumstances.   B.F.
          Yes, I rather think we would.

p. 14-A "Jane Porter aged twenty nine yeares or thereabouts being
duely sworne and Examined saith that sometime in Feb'ry Last John
Newdall came to the house of your depo't to pale in a yard and your
Depo'ts husband being from home and in dyscourse the said Newdale
told your depo't that Abraham and his the said Newdalls wife came
out of Mary Land together and Left him there and the said Newdall
followed them and when he overtooke them his wife told him that she
would not live with him without the said Abraham did too, and your
depo't asked the said Newdall whether he was not afraid to Live with
them for feare they should murther him and the said Newdall made
answer and said that it was a thing that he did not foare but did
Expect the first time as he was drunk then they (meaning the said
Abraham Hannison and the said Newdalls wife) would murther him to
the best of your depo'ts knowledge and further she saith not

                        her
                    Jane x Porter
                    mark

Sworne in open Court
            Recordat Test
                  James Sherlock   Cl Cur

(see next page)

p. 14-A

Richmond Ss
John Corbin aged thirty years or thereabouts being duly sworne and
Examined saith that sometime in Feb'ry Last past John Newdall being
att the house of Thomas Philpin where your Depo't then was the said
Newdall tooke this depon't by the hand and told your depo't that he
had a heartbreaking in his breast and said that Abraham (meaning
as this depo't believes) Abraham Hannison and his the said Newdals
wife wer so Impudent together that he the said Newdall was In danger
of his life in so much that as soone as Syder came he the said
Newdall and this depo't should be merry together if they did not
End his dayes before to the best of your depo'ts knowledge and
further saith not

his
John x Corbin
mark

p.15.

May the 6th 1702

Richmond Ss:
James Richison aged 30 yeares or thereabouts being duely sworne and
Examined sayes that he went to the house of John Newdall and there
saw that the said John and Abraham Hannison had beene a fighting and
heard John Newdall say that if the drink had not workt out of his
head he would have beene murdered betwixt his wife and the said
Abraham but being come to himself was too many for them to the best
of your depo'ts knowledge and further saith not

his
James x Richisson
marke

p.15.

Richm'd SS
Wm Bowlin aged 27 yeares or thereabouts being duely sworne and
Examined sayes that when his sister was buried that the murdered
nam was a little in drink and that the said John Newdall the
murthered person had a mind to Quarrele with Abraham Hannison the
prisoner and the said John went home after him and fought and this
said Abraham was too strong for John that was murthered and flung
him in the fire and burnt his Coate and that John Newdall came from
his owne home for an (?) Evidence Wm Bowlin to Tho Philpins but I
would not go and when this Abraham and Johns wife came out of Marry
Land together but John followed them into Virg'a and when he over

tooke them his wife tooke a knife and struck att him but mist him
to the best of your dept's knowledge and further saith not

his
Wm x Bowlin
mark

Sworne in Court

p.15

Richmond Ss.
William Stone aged twenty three years or thereabouts being duely
sworne and Examined sayes that he came a Sunday morning some time in
March and Wanted to go over to Church and so went downe to the Hop
yard Landing and there he see Jn'o Newdall lye not dead as the depo't
thinks and the wife of John Newdall came downe after me but he cant
tell whether the said wife touched him or no I went back againe up
to the said John Newdalls house (the Cannoa not being there) and
borrowed Abraham Hannisons Mare and went to one Wm Berrys when he had
beene there about the space of three hours a messenger came and told
me that the said John Newdall was dead and so ssnt the mans mare to
go to Mr Doniphans he being Coronor to the best of the Depo'ts
Knowledge and further sayth not but that when your depo't went by the
said Newdalls house there was no body in the house but the said
Newdalls wife and the said Abraham Hannison

Wm Stone

Sworne in open Court

p.15-A

Richmond Ss
Mark Rymer of the said County aged fifty years or thereabouts being
duely Sworne and Examined saith that on the Sabbath day in the morning sometime in March Last past being on the same day that John
Newdall dyed your depo't being at the house of the said John and did
then see the said Johns wife bring a broad axe and a hatt from the
said John and your depo't asking the said Johns wife where her husband
was she told your depo't that he came from aboard a sloop that night
before being a Saturday night about Cook Crow and that he Lay att the
Hop yard all night after and your depo't did heare the said John
Newdall say that he was alwayes Affraid of being murthered by the said
Abraham Hannison and her the said Newdalls wife when once Syder time
came to the best of your depo'ts Knowledge and further sayeth not

Mark Rymer

Sworne in Court

p.16.

Richmond Ss.

Thomas Philpin aged fourty nine yeares or thereabouts being duely
sworne and Examined Saith that sometime in Jan'ry last to the best
of your depo'ts knowledge Martha Newdall came to the house of your
depo't late in the night and said father Philpin are you a sleep to
which your Depo't made answer and said no and bid her open the doore
and your depo't heareing the said Martha Crying asked her what was
the matter and she told your depo't that her husband had beene beating
of her and your depo't told her that she ledd a bad Course of Life to
keep Company with another man and the said Martha told your depo't
that she did never Love her husband nor never would Love him and that
shee had more reason to Love Abraham Hannison than him for he had
found her Victuals and other things when John Newdall would not and
sometime in Feb'ry last John Newdall Came to the house of your depo't
late in the night and told your depo't that he had been fighting with
Abraham Hannison and that the said Abraham was too strong for him and
threw him on the fire and burnt his Cloathes and his Skinn and the
said John Newdall desired William Bolin to go along with him and see
fair play but he denied and would not go along with him and then the
said John Newdall went homewards and your depo't did heare Martha
Newdall the wife of the said John say after her husband was dead that
shee was not sorry for his death but that he dyed out of doors to the
best of your depo'ts knowledge and further saith not

his

Thomas x Philpin

mark

Sworn in open Court

p. 16. Joseph Vaines a sayler and Gunn'r of the Shipp Gloster Cap't
Edward Ellis Commander aged thirty yeares or thereabouts being sworne
and Examined saith that on Saturday before the death of John Newdall
being in a sloop bound up the Rappa River with severall other saylers
in the Sloop did stopp against the Landing where the said Newdall then
Lived and the said Newdall and his wife Martha now standing att that
barr Came on board the sloop in Curnew and very soon after Abraham
now prisoner att the barr soone after a hollow from the said Newdall
Came on board the Sloop wher your Depo't with the said John Newdall
and Martha his wife now prisoner at the barr as aforesaid and the said
Abraham now prisoner as aforesaid and three other saylers then be-
longin to the said sloop did drink about 1 pt and 1/2 punch in all
amongst the said seven persons and likewise about a pt and half of
rumm more then the said John Newdall and Martha his wife now prisoner and Abraham Hannison now prisoner as aforesaid being minded to go

on shore your Depo't and one Sayler more named Rich'd Ingram about 6
or 7 of the Clock in the Evening went into the boate out of the Sloope
and the said John Newdall and the said Martha came downs into the
boat without Injury and goeing on shore the said Newdall satt downe
upon the fore thwart of the boate and in goeing shore from said Sloop
when we came on shore tooke up the said Newdall out of the boate the
said Newdall being in drink carryed him on shore and Laid him downe
not being any aummage (image) or sign of any damage he had received
by any thing received in the said boate or Sloope and the said Newdall
being in drink your depo't did order or desire the said Martha his
wife to Cover him with a Rugg

And further your depo't Sayth the said Abraham as aforesaid did
not come with your depo't with the said John Newdall and Martha his
wife but came att the same time in a Curnew with a Sayler and to the
same Landing and the said Abraham went away up to the house and your
depo't and the rest of the saylers went on board the Sloop and went
up the River and on Munday next this being Saturday we heard the said
Newdall was dead, the morning before being Sunday Looking into the
boate saw about a spoonfull or thereabouts of Water and blood in the
boate and further saith that he see no other person upon the plantation but the prisoners att the barr and the said John Newdall
                          Joseph Vanis

p. 16-A. Richard Ingram Sailer and Cooke of the ship Gloster Cap't
Edward Ellis Comander aged fourty three yeares or thereabouts being
duely Sworne and Examined saith that on Saturday being the day before
the death of John Newdall your depo't being in a Sloop with other
Saylers bound up Rapp'a River did Stopp against or neare the Landing
where the said John Newdall Lived and your Depo't with the rest of
the Saylers seeing the said John Newdall and Martha his wife now
prisoner att the barr att work on shoar did hollow to them to come on
board theire sloop and after twice hollowing they x x came on board
the Sloop in a Connoa and after drinking about a pint and a halfe of
Punch and a pint and a half of Rumm or thereabouts amongst seven
persons (Vizt) your depo't and three Saylers more and the said John
Newdall and Martha his wife x x and Abraham Hannison x x who Afterwards Came on board the Sloop in a Cannoe the said John Nowdall being
minded to go ashore your depo't and another sayler did about 6 or 7
of the Clock in the Evening sett the said John Newdall and Martha his
wife prisoner as aforesaid ashore in the flatt belonging to the sloop
and the said John Newdall being in the flatt satt downe a Cross a
thwart att the head of the boat and in goeing a Shoare he fell of the
thwart being about a foote from the botthome of the boate into the
bottom of the boate but received no hurt by the fall to the best of
your depo'ts knowledge and when the boat came to the Landing your
depo't and another sayler Lifted the said John Newdall out of the

boate and told him that they would carry him up to the house but the
said John Newdall would not lett them and therefore your dep't and
the other sayler left him att the Landing Cleare of any hurt save
that he was in drink to the best of your depo'ts knowledge but your
depo't further saith that the next morning your depo't looking into
the boate and where the said John Newdall fell downe to the best of
your depo'ts knowledge did see a small Quantity of blood and water to
the value of a Spoonfull or thereabouts and further your depo't saith
not to the best of his knowledge but that your depo't saw no other
person upon the plantation but the prisoners att the barr and the said
John Newdall

                              his
                       Richd x Ingram
                            marke

                  James Sherlock Cl Cur

p.17-A. Power of Atty. 26 July 1702. Thomas Paise of Sittingburne Par.
Richmond Co., to "my Loveing Wife Jane Paise" to collect debts.
Wit:
George White   signed Thomas Paise
Dan'll White

                  Rec. 11 Nov. 1702.

p.17-A. Power of Atty. 6 March 1702/3. Wm Fitzhugh Junr, the Atty of
Col. Wm Fitzhugh agt and Atty for the Proprietors of the Northernneck
of Virginia, to Mr James Phillips of Richmond Co., to collect rents
and arrearages in St Marys Parish in Richmond Co. Also rents in
Sittenburne Parish "that is to say from Gravelly Runne or Perpetua
Creek upwards in said Parish of Sittenburne".
Wit:
Samll Peachey   signed Will Fitzhugh Junr
James Jameson

p.18. Power of Atty. 11 May 1700. Bryan Blundell of Liverpoole,
marriner, to "my Trusty Friend Edgecomb Suggitt of Richmond County" to
collect debts in or about the Rappahannock River.
Wit:
James Suggitt   signed Bryan Blundell
Thos Suggitt
                  Rec. 2 June 1703.

p.18-A

"The Estate of Cap't Lawrence Washington dr
March sixteene hundred ninety six

To 120 Gallons of Sider att 9 1 per Gal'o   1080

Sworn in Court   his
                                        Francis x Williams
                                              marke

                              Recordat' Test
                                        James Sherlock Cl Cur "

p. 18-A. Power of Atty. 21 June 1703. William Braithwait of the port
of Whitehaven in England, to "my well beloved Friend John Craske of
the County of Richmond in Virginia" to collect debts in Virginia.
Wit:
John x Mackmillion   signed Will Braithw't
James Ingo

Note: Pronounce Braithwaite 'Brevet'. As for our well known name
Macmillan, it's too bad the clerk did'ent slip a little further and
spell it Makemillions.
Also the name Hodgkins in the following entry is 'Hoskins'. In fact
the family use the phonetic spelling now. Hoskins' Creek, etc.

p.19.

In Obediance to an order of Court dated the 7th of July 1703 we whose
names are hereto Subscribed being mett att the house of Mr Sam'll
Peachey hath proposed these Interrogations following

Imp'rs Mrs Phoebr Slaughter, whether or no the said Mr Sam'll Peachey
        was not owned and acknowledged by your first husband Mr Wm Hodg-
        kins to be his owne Sisters Son by father and Mother and that you
        are fully satisfied of the truth thereof

Answered That he used to Call him Cousin but she never heard him say
        that he was his owne Sisters Son but Doe believe that he was so

2'dly Whether or no when your said husband M'r William Hodgkins
        careyed you for England in Company with your Brother Mr Henry
        Smith you did not see there the said Mr Peacheys mother Anne

Misc. Records.

Peachey and that she personally Requested of your husband M'r
William Hodgkin and your self that if att your Returne to Virginia
the said Peachey were living to lay her Comands on him to pay
her a personall Visitt and that accordingly you did

Answered that she see Anne Peachey who the said M'r Hodgkin Called
    his sister

3'dly whether or no you were not perfectly satisfied when you were
    in England with your husband Mr Wm Hodgskin that his brother
    M'r Martin Hodgkins was then dead without Issue and that your
    husband Mr William Hodgkins disposed of his Estate as descend-
    ing to him as the next heire and further that the said M'r Sam'll
    Peachey Mother M'rs Anne Peachey was theire Eldest Sister and
    the said M'r Sam'll Peachey is her Eldest Son and that you have
    been Certainly Informed of the truth of the aforesaid premise
    in Every Article

Answered That the said Martin Hodgskins was then dec'ed and that her
    husband Mr Wm Hodgkins disposed of his Estate and that the said
    Mr Wm Hodgkins owned the said Mrs Peachey to be his sister

                            Phoebe Slaughter

Sworne to in Richmond County Court the first of Sep'tr 1703 and
Recordat
        Test
            James Sherlock Cl Cur

Mr Richard Peacock
First Whether or no you being a liver here in this parish of Farnham
    when Mr William Hodgkins bought of Coll'o Fantleroy the planta-
    tion called Haines and that when he came to live upon itt he
    brought M'r Sam'll Peachey along with him as his kinsman, and
    that he the said Hodgkins alwayes acknowledged him to yourselfe
    and all others so to the best of your knowledge and Rememberance
    and that you Ever lookt upon him to be

Answer Yes I did.

Mr Daniell Dobbins
    Whether or no you have not heard your Late wife M'rs Eliz'a
    Dobbins In discourse by your selves as also the demandant M'r
    Sam'll Peachey was present att other times owne and declare that
    the said M'rs Elizabeth Dobbins and the aforesaid Sam'll Peachey

were first Couzins that is that their mothers were owne Sisters
and that M'r Wm Hodgskins dec'ed was theire owne Brother and to
the best of your Rememberance you were fully satisfied in the
premises

Answer. Yes I did

Mr Edw'd Adcock
    Whether or no you M'r Edward Adcock and M'r Wm Hodgkins dec'ed
    marrying two sisters have not often heard the said Hodgkin
    owne the demandant M'r Sam'll Peachey to be his kinsman

Answer Yes to the best of my Rememberance I did

2'dly whether or no you did not Remember that you have heard the
    said Hodgkins your Brother in Law declare in your heareing that
    the said M'r Sam'll Peachey was his owne Sisters Son

Answer I do not remember itt

3'dly whether or no you have not heard M'rs Elizabeth Dobbins say
    that her mother and the demandant M'r Sam'll Peacheys mother was
    owne sisters and that M'r Wm Hodgkins was theire Brother

Answer Yes I have

Mr James Samford
    Whether or no you being a Liver in this parish when M'r Wm
    Hodgkins came to live on the plantation called Haines which the
    said Hodgkins bought of Collo Fantleroy that the said Hodgkins
    then brought the Demandant M'r Sam'll Peachey along with him
    and that he upon all occasions owned him the said Mr Peachey to
    be his kinsman to your Certaine Rememberance

Answer Yes I did

2'dly Whether or no you did ever to the best of your memory heare
    him the said Hodgkin say in your heareing that the said Sam'll
    Peachey was his owne Sisters son

Answer I know nothing of itt

The above Interrogatories was Sworne to before us this 16th of August
1703   John Tarpley
                                  Charles Barber

                                  James Sherlock Cl Cur

Misc. Records.

p. 20-A

In obedience to an order of Court dated the 7th of July 1703 we whose
names are hereto subscribed being mett att the house of Wm Brockenbrough dec'ed hath there audited and stated all and singular the
account of John Dalton and Mary his wife adm'rs of the said dec'ed
as they were presented to us per the sd Dalton

Imp'rs
to pd Doct'r Clarke per ord'r   624
To pd Mr Jesper   240
To pd Mr Colstone   205
To Josh'a Lawson ord'r   303
To George Glascock   204
to paid Col'o Geo Taylor   721
to Edward Jefferys   2266
to Mr Tho Gregson   L   s   d   1000
to M'r John Suggitt: 10: 16: 10   3760
to paid Capt Tarpley   729
to John Muse   62
to pd M'r Travers   133
to M'r Stephen Lynch   2400
to pd Th'o Suggett for clks and sherriffs fees   0859
To pd James Phillips   1204
to pd Mr Loyd   1547
to M'r Sherlock   -
to Doct'r Belfield   460
to M'r Mackey   400
to M'r Th'o Lewis   900
to Jam's Parsons   705
to Mr Crumwell   1332
to Mr Peachey   493
to Sim Cox   500
to M'r George Eskridge   500
to M'r Henry Jenings   210
to Jn'o Linsey   500
to M'r Jones   1000
to Funerall charges   1200
                                                      -- -- -- --
                                                            23613

Per Contra   Cr
by Inventory   22622
By tobbo Rec'ed of James Biddlecomb   741
By John Batten   500
By Tho Taylor   110
by John Alloway   230
By Robt Benford   15

Estato of Wm. Brockenbrough (continued)

By Roderick Jones	74
By Martin Fisher	976
By Simon Taylor	47
By James Phillips	4000

$$\begin{array}{r} - - - - \\ 28715 \\ 23613 \\ - - - - \\ 5102 \end{array}$$

Given under our hands this 30th of August 1703
                                     John Tarpley
                                     Charles Barber

                    Recordat Test
                              James Sherlock Cl Cur

p.21. Power of Atty. 14 Oct. 1703. Augustine Woodward of the Kingdome
of England to John Tarpley to transact business.
Wit:
Raw Downeman   signed Augustine Woodward
Henry Robinson
                    Rec. 3 Nov. 1703

p.21. Power of Atty. 20 April 1703. John Tarkenton of Richmond Co. to
"my trusty friend Thomas Kendall" to transact business.
Wit:
Sam'll Samford   signed John x Tarkenton
Margrett Harper
"Marg'a Harper did this day come before me and Testafie upon oath
that she did see John Tarkenton signe and seale the above Letter of
Attorney"
Feb'ry the 1st 1703
Sworne before me
        Wm Underwood
             Test James Sherlock Cl Cur

p. 21-A
Richmond County in Virginia July the 17th 1699
Gent'men
Thirty days after Sight of this my third of Exchange my first and
second not, pay to Mr Stephen Lynch merchant or order five pounds

Miso. Records.

seven shillings and ten pence Curent money of England being for the
like value here rec'ed
Att time make Good payment and place it to the acoo't of
Gen'tmen
Your humble Serv't to Comand
To Mr Clemt Nicholson   Raw Travers
and M'r George Ribton merchts
in
Whitehaven
present   Recordat Test
James Sherlock Cl Cur

p.21.
Stafford Ss
I doe by these presents appoynt Daniell Maccarty attorney att Law my
attorney in all Suites wherein I am Concerned in Richmond County and
for soe doeing this shall be his Warrant
Novemb'r 17th 1703   G. Mason
Recordat
Test
James Sherlock Cl Cur

p.21-A.

Sr
   I have now agreed my Difference with the Execut'rs of Capt Spicers
Estate Coll'o Carter hath payd me Seven Thousand Eight Hundred pounds
Tobbacco and Caske and I have given him a full dyscharge. It is
further agreed between us that att your next Court Judgment should
pass against the said Execut'r for the sayd summe and I am Immediate-
ly to acknowledge satisfaction on the Judgment and having no person
so much in my acquaintance as your selfe, desire you will favour me
so Far as in my name upon passing of the sayd Judgment to acknowledge
satisfaction thereon and to Cause this my Letter to be put upon
Record for Which this shall be your Warrent Wittnesse my hand and
seale this seventeenth day of Feb'ry 1703
Ralph Bowker
To Mr Wm Robinson
Richmond County
These
Signed and Sealed in presence
of us
John Spicer
John - illegible - (Appears to be John Babe, possibly Bebe)

p.22.   Power of Atty. 29 Feb. 1703/4. Henry Hayes of Richmond Co.,
Labourer, to Mr. James Suggitt.
No witnesses   signed
shown on record.   Hen Hayes

p.22.   Power of Atty. 6 Oct 1703. Sim: Coxe to Nath'll Pope to act
in suits in Richmond Co. Courts.
No witnesses   signed
shown on record.   Sim: Coxe

p.22-A.   We the Subscribers in obedience to an order of Court Dated
the first of March 1703 (1703/4) for the division of the Estate of
Henry Williams Late of this County dec'ed have according to the best
of our Judgments devided the Estate of the said Williams into five
Equal parts as his will directs
Then follow lists containing considerable personal possessions. The
heirs are shown:
Lettice Williams her Choice (this list includes "A Servant man named
     Jno Palmer") x x x.
Sarah Williams her Choice x x x.
Jane Williams her Choice x x x.
John Williams two parts (his list includes "A Serv't man named Wm
     Harrow") x x x.
                                          signed
                                          Will Woodbridge
                                          Jos: Deeke
                                          Andrew Dew
                                          Tho Dew

p. 23-A. Power of Atty. 3rd of 8'ber (Oct.) 1704. "Margaret Cary of
the parish of Kingston in the County of Gloucester Adm'r of my dec'ed
husband Richd Cary have named and Constituted and by these presents
do name Ordaine appoint and make my Trusty and well beloved Brother
David Bronaugh of the County of Richmond my True and Lawfull attorney"
to collect debts.
Wit: signed
Alex'r Doniphan   Margarett x Cary
John x - illegible appears to
          be John Tidee

Att a Court held for Gloucester County on wednesday the 16th day of
Feb'ry 1703
Margarett Cary Widdow of Richard Cary Deced upon her petition hath

order granted for administration of all and singular the Estate of
the said Richard Cary giveing Security according to Law.
        Whereupon Jeremiah Bronaugh and Lawrence Parrott haveing Entered
into bond of foure hundred pounds Sterl with the said Margarett Cary
for her due administration Came into Court and acknowledged the same
                        A True Copy Test
                                    P Beverley Cl Cur
                        Recordat Test
                                James Sherlook Cl Cur

p.24. Power of Atty. 24 May 1704. "John Charteris of Liverpoole in the
County of Lancaster merchant" to Capt John Craske of Sittenburne Par.
Richmond Co. to transact business.
Wit: signed John Charteris
Francis x Mathes
Andrew Howmes   Rec. 4 Oct 1704

p.24.

Mr Garrard Lynch
        These are to authorise and Impower you to Confess Judgment for
me to Avery Naylor in two actions of Debt the one to him as assignee
of Robt Cole for five hundred 30 pounds of tobbo the other to himselfe
in his owne Capacity for Seven hundred pounds of tobbo the sd action
being now depending in Richmond County Court and for your so doeing
this shall be your Warrant from
                        Sr your humble Ser't
                                her
                        Anne A Walker
7: the 5th 1704   mark
To Mr Garrard Lynch
        these

p. 24-A. Power of Atty. 20 May 1704. Henry Robinson of Liverpoole,
mercht., to Mr William Woodbridge, to collect debts.
Wit:
Charles Barber   signed Henry Robinson
Dom' Bennehan
                        Rec. 1 Nov. 1704

p.24-A. "A Crop on the Left Ear and two Slitts and the Right Ear an
under keel
                        Joseph Russell
                        Rec. 3 Nov. 1704.

p.24-A

Nicholas Lowis Dr to Charles Speer (or Charles Spoor)   lb
                                                                 --
For a hilling hoe and weeding hoe   54
For 3 Ells of fine Linnen att 36 per Ell   108
For 2 Ells Canvis att 14 per Ell   28
For 4 yards of shefting Linen att 14 per ele   56
For a paire of Stockins   60
For a vest   250
For a pair of Leather Breeches   250
For Shirt Buttons   12
For silk and thred   30
For a paire of shoos   60
For 3 Ells Shofting Linen att 24   42
For a Grubbing hoe   40
For an ax   40
for an hileing hoe   30
for his Levy   55
Paid to Gyles Mathres on his accot   55
Paid to Edward Jeffreys   50
For a knife   12
                                                         - - - -
                                                             1232

To his Funerall Expenses what this Hon'ble Court thinks fitt
More to this yeares Levy
                              Rec. 3 Nov. 1704.

INDEX

Coleman, Riohd. 78
Coleman's Gut 38
Coleman's line 38
Coles, John 17
Colley, Tho. 14, 62
Colston, Wm. 29, 70
                (officially) 2, 3
                4, 9, 10, 18, 20
                25, 26, 27, 31, 32
                33, 42, 45, 55, 58
                61, 63, 68, 69, 70
                76, 77, 78, 79, 80
                82, 95
Comens, Philip 12
Comer, Tho. 10
Connell, Michalla 53
Conner, Jno. 74
Connier, David 48, 53
Conway, Edwin 6, 11, 13, 14, 17
                18, 28, 46, 56
        Mrs. Sarah 17
Coombes, Ann 31
        Mrs. Eliza: 2
        John 2, 31, 75
Coumbs, Wm. 2
Corbin, John 4, 85, 87
Corhay, Jean Charle 37
Cotton, Thos. 16
Court House 64
Cox, Sim: 95, 98
Cralle, John 38, 48
Craske, Eliz: 13, 48, 33
        John 3, 13, 33, 48, 63
                92, 99
Creed, John 49
        Mary 3
Creed's land 3
Creele, Jno. 31
        Mary 32
Cromwell see Crumwell
Croswell, Gilbt. 32
Crumwell, Mr. 95
        Andrew 71
Crutcher, Jno. 47, 51, 65
Culpeper, Alexander 14
        Hon. Mrs. Catherine 14
        Lady Margaret 30
        Tho: Lord 14

Dalton, Deoemia 65
        John 95
        Mary 95
Damounville, Saml. 28
Darnell, David 5, 29, 30
        Margaret 29, 30
        Sampson 29
Daenell see Darrell
Darrell, Sampson 6
Davenport see Devenport
Davis, Jno. 32
        Jos. 63
        Joshua 20, 23, 27, 35, 40
                42, 49, 55, 62
        Robt. 47
        Wm. 21, 26, 47, 56
Dawson, Christopher 54
        Tho. 64
Deane, Jno. 3, 12, 13, 14, 36,
                74
Deeke, Jos. 98
Deeke see Dike
Delano, Mr. E. Carter
Derry, Barbary 8
        John 8
Devenport, Geo: 31
Dew, Andrew 96
        Tho. 22, 67, 98
Dike, Jos. 4, 36, 45, 52, 76
Dike see Deeke
Dobbins, Danl. 93
        Mrs. Eliz: 93, 94
Dod, Jno. 59
Dodson, Ann 23, 39
        Charles 22, 23, 26, 32
                34, 40, 41, 61
        Charles Jr. 23, 39
        Charles Sr. 23, 39, 74
        Tho. 26
Doleman, Raw: 81
        Wm. 71, 80
Doleman see Downman
Doniphan, Alex. 2, 3, 6, 7, 9,
                11, 20, 29, 37, 43
                61, 85, 86, 88, 98
        Alex. Jr. 3, 6, 11,
                29
        Ame 61

VIRGINIA COLONIAL ABSTRACTS

Vol. XVII
Richmond County Records
1704 - 1724

Abstracted by
Beverley Fleet

PREFACE

A man from this section introduced himself as knowing less about more things than anyone.

We hope that wise gentleman never catches us napping.

In reverse, this volume has more about lesser things than any other in the series. It is in continuation of Volume 16. The records from which these abstracts were taken are a gold-mine for students of social history and genealogists. We find here whether our ancestors were honest, sober and law abiding, or if they were interesting.

Beverley Fleet.

January 1st 1943.

Richmond County
Miscellaneous Records

Book 1. page 25. "In obedience to the within order the Subscribers
mett at the place appointed by Mr Dan'll McCarty and then and there
to the best of our Judgements Layed out an acre of Land on the East
and opposite side of his mill Dam beginning att the rumn on the Lower
side of the Dam x x x and Valued the said acre of Land to be worth
twenty shillings given under our hands this 21st of Octob'r 1704
                                        Giles Webb
                                        James Suggitt
                                        Edward Jones
                                        Job x Hamon   "

                    Rec. 3 Nov. 1704.

p.25. "In obedience to the Within order we the Subscribers have mett
(and have to the best of our Judgement Layd out an acre of Land) on
the within mentioned Land on the South Side of the Rumn within mentioned beginning att a beach by the swamp side thence down the swamp
x x which said acre of Land we have Valued to two hundred pounds of
tobbo witness our hands this 30th Day of Octob'r 1704
                                        Will Barber
                                        James Tarpley
                                        Edward Jones

                    Rec. 3 Nov. 1704.

Note: Richmond County Order Book No.3. p.367. 4th October 1704.
George Glascock petitions that he might be admitted to build a mill
according to above. Also on the same page Capt. John Tarpley ditto.

p. 25-A. Power of Atty. 26 Sept. 1704. Thomas Cressey of the Island
of Nevis to John Harper to collect debts in Virginia.
Wit:
David Crosse   Signed   Tho: Cressey
Dom: Bonnehan
                    Rec. 1 Nov. 1704

p. 25-A. Indenture. Made in Richmond Co., 1 Nov. 1704, betw. William
Stephenson on the one part and John Harper of Richmond Co., of the
other part. Stephenson agrees to serve Harper for 6 years, according
to Law and custom.   Signed William Stephenson
                                      John Harper

                    Rec. 1st November 1704.

p.26. "Thomas Longdale aged 24 yeares or thereabouts being Examined
saith that a jeare and a halfe before James Gilberts death John Mills
came over to James Gilberts, where your depo't then Lived and when
the said John Mills went away, the said John Mills told your depo't
that James would make his will, meaneing your depo'ts master to the
best his knowledge and sometime after that John Mills Junr came to
your Depo'ts masters house and your Depo'ts master, James Gilbert
went along with the said John Mills Jun'r, and when the said James
Gilbert came back againe your Dep't: asked him whether he had finish-
ed his Business and the said James Gilbert answered, yes, and some
time after that your depo't asked John Mills Junr who your Depots
master had left his Estate to, and the said John Mills Jun'r answered
that he had left it all to him onely twenty shillings and that he
left to his wife, and sometime after that your depo't: mett with Tho:
White and he told your depo't that his master had Sett him Free when
he dyed

                                                his
                                        Tho   V   Longdale
                                              mark

Jurat in Cur 2'd die 9'br 1704
                        Recordat Test
                                James Sherlock Cl Cur. "

p.26-A. "Anne Kelly aged 20 yeares or thereabouts saith that on new
yeares Day Last, Thomas Dierham your depo'ts master sent her to James
Gilbert to desire him to Come Downe to pipe it and your depo't and
the said James Gilbert were coming back, by John Mills his plantation,
James Gilbert asked your depo't whether his old woman was att your
depo'ts masters house, and your depo't answered, yes she was, and the
said James Gilbert hold up his two hands and said, God's Curse Light
upon that Family nameing John Mills, and all his Familly, and said
that if it was not for John Mills and his wife, he and his wife would
never have lived att Variance as they did, and your depo't told him
the said James Gilbert that it was his own Fault living so and asked
him why he had not saught away his Chest and Confound that will which
he made, and the said James Gilbert said that John Mills and his
Family had Robbed his Chest so that they would not agree upon any
meanes that he should Fetch it away, and that they were ashamed of It,
and the said James Gilbert said that there was a will made but Swore
by God, that he knew not what was in it no more then I did, and your
Depo't asked the said James Gilbert whether he was sent for to signe
his will, but the said James Gilbert answered sweareing by his God,
that he did not signe it, and told your depo't that he had not the
sense, to make a will, and that John Mills was a Rogue for makeing
a false Will, and that that made him and his wife live so discontent-
edly and further your depo't saith that she see the said James Gilbert

in Feb'ry Last to the best of your Depo'ts knowledge, Count 15 head
of Cattle for fourty

her
Anne x Kelly
mark

Jurat in Cur 2'd die 9'ber 1704

Recordat Test

James Sherlock Cl Cur "

p.27. "Lawrence Callahan aged 21 yeares or thereabouts being Examined saith, that your depo't being att John Simons his house on a
Sabbath Day sometime the Last Summer he heard John Mills and Tho's
Landale Talking together, and Thomas Langdale told John Mills that
he did not know that he was to be sett Free by his masters will till
he had mett Tho White coming From Moratico Mill, and the said John
Mills said that It was his mistake not to putt it in but that he
should be Free nevertheless
    And further your depo't saith not

his
Lawrence x Callahan
mark

Sworne to in Cur
2'd Nov'r 1704 "

p.27. "Dorothy Durham aged 41 yeares or thereabouts saith that
sometime before James Gilberts death being in Company of the said
James Gilbert and William Smoote amongst others Discourse she heard
the said James Gilbert say, to the said William Smoote that he did
not know that there was any Resurrection or not and that he had made
a will to John Mills, but that It signified nothing and that your
depon't did severall times heare the said James Gilbert say that John
Mills was a rogue, and that he nor any of his should ever be the
better for what he had
    And Further your depo't saith not

her
Dorothy x Durham
mark

Jurat in Cur 2'd 9'br 1704

Recordat Test

James Sherlock Cl Cur "

p.27-A. "John Ingo aged twenty nine yeares doth give upon oath that
James Gilbert a small time before his death was att his house and did

declare to him that he did Intend to Fetch away his Chest from John
Mills house for he said it lay in such nasty condition with hen dung
and such like nastiness that he could not well come at his Chest for
it and that he was afraid that the Chest and Goods, both would be
damnifyed with nastiness and that he did Intend to Fetch the Chest
home to his owne house and did sweare bitterly that John Mills nor
none of his Family should ever be the better for any thing of his
Estate and that the will that he made did signifye nothing and the
said John Ingo further saith that a little before James Gilbert was
burnt he asked him whether he was not perswaded to make a will or
made Drunk when he did make it, and the said James Gilbert answered
that he was not, but was as sober as he was att that time, and then
the said James Gilbert was sober to the best of your depo'ts knowledge

                                                      Jno Ingo
Jurat in Cur 2'd 9'br 1704. "

p.28. "Martha Ingo being sworne and Examined saith that some small
time before James Gilberts Death the aforesaid James Gilbert being
att your Depo'ts house she did aske the said James Gilbert why he did
not alter his will, and the same James Gilbert confessed that he would
and att the same time your depo't did heare the said James Gilbert
sweare, (by God or Gods Blood) that John Mills nor any of his family
should ever be the better for any thing that he had, for he was a Very
Rascall or a Rogue which of them your depo't cannot well say, and
further the said Martha Ingo saith that a small time before the said
James Gilbert was Burnt, she heard her husband John Ingo aske the said
James Gilbert whether he was not perswaded to make a will or made
Drunk when he did make it and that the said James Gilbert answer'd
him and said that he was not Drunk but that he was sober
                                                      her
                                             Martha O Ingo
Jurat in Cur 2'd Nov'r 1704   mark
                    Recordat Test
                              James Sherlock Cl Cur

p.28. "Will: Smoot saith that to the best of his Judgment that James
Gilbert was not in his perfect sences by Reason of fitts which had
followed him for severall yeares, and I having some discourse with
him about a will which he had made to John Mills For to had him alter-
ed it and he said he had made a will to John Mills but it signifyed
not for it was good for nothing and I advising him to prepare for his

Misc. Records.

End and to make his peace with God and to be reconciled with his wife
and he giving very foolish and cross answers, I told him that if he
had a mind to have the Sacram't given to him that no minister would
give it to him if he did not change his mind and likewise I asked him
if he thought there was a Resurrection or not and he said he did not
know, and that he did not goe to Church nor would not yeild to have
any reading to him in his sickness nor att other times did not care
for it as ever I could understand but it was his delight to be in the
woods with his Gunn on the Sabbath Day

                                             Will Smoot
Jurat in Cur 2'd 9'br 1704
                          Recordat Test
                                  James Sherlock Cl Cur

p.28-A. "John Rankin aged thirty Eight yeares or thereabouts being
examined and sworne saith that about three years ago or thereabouts
saith that your depon't being in the woods with Mr George Davenport
neare unto your depo'ts plantation, John Mills Sen'r nett there with
your depo't and said to your depo't that James Gilbert late dec'ed
was goeing to live up in Stafford, and the said Mills did request your
depo't to perswade the aforesaid Gilbert not to go. Imediately while
the said Mills was in your depo'ts Company the said Gilbert came into
the aforesaid Company and your depo't did by his advice att that time
perswade the said Gilbert not to go nor did the said Gilbert ever go
and further your depo't did some short time after meet with the said
Mills and the said Mills said that the aforesaid Gilbert did Intend
to gett your depo't to write the said Gilberts Will, but your depo't
never did, some considerable time after your depo't mett with the
said Gilbert and after some discourse the said Gilbert said to your
depon't that that will that he had made to young Mills signifyed
nothing and some time before the said Gilberts death about ten days,
your depon't went to see the said Gilbert att his house and amongst
some other Discourse the said Gilbert told your Depo't that the aforesaid Will signefyed nothing and further your Depo't sayeth not

                                             Jn'o Rankin
Jurat in Cur 2'd 9'ber 1704
                          Recordat Test
                                  James Sherlock Cl Cur   "

Note: 'depo't' appears in the above entry 14 times.   B.F.

```
            8'ber 31    Thomas Richardson   Dr
            1704        to Geo Purvis merchant
Vizt                                                            lb
to tobbo rec'ed of M'r Fran: Stone                            1400
to tobbo rec'ed of John Franklin                              2000
to tobbo rec'ed of James Scott being for a man   )
     servant sent to the said Richardsons house  )            1500
to one man servant more sent to the said Richardsons )
     house not sould                             )            - -
To one woman Serv't sent to the said Richardsons )
     which was sick                              )            1600
                                                              - - - -
                                                              6500


                    Per Cont'r                                 lb
By tobbo paid Capt John Battle per Purvis ord'r              4312
By tobbo paid Simon Robins for attorneys fee against )
     John Franklin and Fra: Stone per d'r: ord'r     )       0530
By a servant woman dyett and lodging five moneths)
     in sickness per Capt Purvis order           )           0400
By one man Serv't which Runn away and was not found againe   - -
By Trouble in the business                                   500
By Trouble of keeping a man Serv't three months in )
     sickness per Purvis ord'r                   )           200
                                                             - - - -
                                                             5942
                                                              558
                                                             - - - -
                                                             6500
```

In Obedience to an Order of Court bearing date Octob'r 4th 1704
have stated the accounts of plt and defend't as above and do find the
Ballance due to the plt five hundred fifty and Eight pounds weight
of tobo

Edward Barrow
Tho: Beale
John Craske

Rec. 13 January 1704/5

Misc. Records.

p. 29-A.

Mr John Pound Dr   L   s   d

To Sundry Goods   25: 9: 4
to Cred Xto Predham 1340   (Christopher Predham)   6: 14: 0
to Cred Mr Sam'll Peachey 535   2: 13: 6
To Zach'ry Effords accot 799   3: 19: 10
                                                    - - - - - - -
                                                    38: 16: 8
                    Due to John Pound   2: 3: 9

Dr Cont'r is Cr.

By 3 1/2 months storage att 7: 10: per month   26: 5: 0
by two Stears att 1300   6: 10: 0
by one Hhd Tobbo att Robt Bannivells 500   2: 10: 0
by one hhd do att Robt Hopkins 582   2: 18: 2
by 1 hhdd att Zach'rys 454   2: 5. 3
by a Sick man two weeks   0: 12: 0
                                                    - - - - - - -
                                                    41. 5. 0

        In obedience to an order of Court Dated 4th of Octob'r 1704
have stated the acco'ts of plt and Defend't as above and do find
for the defend't two pounds three shillings and nine pence
                              Tho Beale
                              Geo: Heale
                              David Barrick
                              Edward Barrow

                Rec. 13 January 1704/5.

p.29-A.
        To the Worsp'll her Maj'ties Justices of the County of
Richmond holding a Court of Claymes the 6th day of March 1704/5

        Wm Tayloe Coll'll and Comander in Cheife of the said County
in the behalfe of himselfe and the militia within said County and
humbly sheweth that the severall charges and services hereafter
mentioned have bin preformed by himselfe and others therein mentioned as 'tis to your wors'pps very well knowne for the due satisfaction
of Which I desire you to recomend it to his Excellency and the
Hon'ble the Gen'll Assembly att theire next sitting.

                (see next page)

p.30.
Col. Wm. Tayloe's Account (continued)

1704 August 31	For an Express from Cap't Robinson with the news of the murd'r of the English being 30 mile 4 d per mile	0: 10: 0

To Do from Capt Slaughter fifty mile att 4d per
   mile   0: 16: 8

To Do from Cap't Doniphan fifty mile 4 d per
   mile   0: 16: 8

All which I answered by the same Express and
sent Orders to march part of theire Troops and
Companys in search of the Enemy I sent Imediate
Notice to the two Lower troops to march

Sept'r the 1st	Another Express from Capt Robinsons with the particulars of the Murd'r Upon which I Ordered our Indians to	-: 10: -

be secured

Sept'r the 2'd	Another Express from Cap't Doniphan advising that he had secured nine of the Indians	-: 16: 8

to another Express from Cap't Robinson advising
   that he had secured the Rest of the Indians -: 10: -

1704 Sept'r the 2'd	two Squadrons of horse of 24 men went from my house being supplyed with powder and ball out of the Queens stores	

I then sent an Express to the president to
acquaint him with the mischeife for which I
paid Peter Evans for a hundred and foure miles 1: 14: 8

7'ber 3d	Cap't Robinson and Doniphon sent me ten Indians under a Guard of	

20 men which I maintained till I could Gett
the Indians secured for which I charge   2: -: -

to three Carpenters for makeing 9 pr stock   900

to three hundred of halfe Crowne nailes two
   knotts of bed Cords and two knotts of
   Drum Lines from Maj'r Gwyns   0: 10: 0

(continued)

Misc. Records.

p.30.
Col. Wm. Tayloe's Account (continued)

7'ber the	I sent another Express to the	
4th	president to acquaint him with the	
	takeing of the Murder's for which	
	I charge as before	1: 14: 8

The same day I had twelve men upon Guard
Relieved every 24 hours

7'ber the	I called a Court for the Examina-	
6th	tion of tho prisoners att my house.	

I also called a Councill of warr
where It was resolved to Fetch downe the rest
of the Indians for the Expense of all which I
charge   2000

7'br the	the Court haveing Considered the
7th	Insufficiency of our prison Order-
	ed me and Capt Barber to take care
	of tho prisoners

7'ber the	the Sherriff carryed away Eight
7th	Indians Capt Robinson sent me 35
	Indians, the same Day I rec'ed an

Express from the president acquainting me that
the Councill were to meet the 11th: 7'br
    I sent Back an Express the same Night
with the Examinations of the Prisoners for
which I Gave him one thousand pounds of tobbo   1000
to Ride day and night to be there before the
Councill broke up
    Capt Robinson brought four Indians more
to my house

7'br the	Capt Barbour Fetched away twelve
10th	Indians I likewise Ordered two
	Companyes to relieve one another

att Capt Barbers for the Security of the Indians

7'br the	I sent an Express to the president	
17th	to know what should be done with the	
	women and children theire towne	

being destroyed by the English the president
being gone up to the Falls the Express was
forced to Goe 150 miles for which he rec'd   2: 10: 0

for keeping 14 Indians five dayes att five
pound tobbo per day   350

for keeping 41 two dayes   410

p.30.
Col. Wm. Tayloe's Account (continued)

for keeping 30 Indians the rest being Fetch-
ed away by Capt Barber from the 10th of 7'br
to the 5th of 8'br   3900

for keeping Cap't Barbers 20 Indians one day
and night as they were Goeing to Court   100

for a steere bought of Maj'r Gwyn for the
use of the Guards   3: 0: 0

for one Gallon of Rum in 24 hours for the
Guards as long as they stayd which was from
the 4th of 7'br to the 5th of 8'ber
32 gall att 5 s per Gall   3: 0: 0

p.31.

to 20 pr of Candles to Burn in the prison   0: 10: 0

for Extraordinary Charges for Buying of
Flower and two Beeves and Rum for the
Entertaineing Express souldiers coming and
goeing besides what the Constant Guards had
I charge   10: 0: 0
It is not halfe the Charge I have bin att

for my Extraordinary trouble the use of my
houses for the prisoners and getting wood
for the Guards to Burn I charge   5000

To Cap't Tho Beale to Cap't Jn'o Craske,
Capt Wm Barber Cap't Brereton theire foure
Companyes have bin upon duty twelve att a
time att my house and as many att Cap't
Barbers 33 dayes which Comes to 792 dayes
and as many nights for which the Clayme
theire pay according to Law
Cap't John Tarpley and Capt CharlesBarber
sent out two Squadrons of 12 men each under
Quarter Mester Andrew dew and Corp'll Will'm
Smoote being 14 dayes make theire Clayme
according to Law

(See next page for Capt. Barber's Account)

p.31.
Captain Charles Barber's Account.

An account of the Charges tending to the Nansietico Indians
Sep'tr the 4th
1704   This day Coll'o Will'm Tayloe sent
       for me to take charge of the Indian
       prisoners which was ten

5th   I went to Gett Irons made

6th   I carryed the Irons to Coll'o Tayloes
       to put them on the Indians

       To calling a Court to Examine the
       Indians   5: 0: 0

       To calling a Councill of Warr to 5: 0: 0
       dyspose of the women and Children

       to 21 Gall's of Rum spent on
       those that guarded the Indians
       att 5 s per Gall   5: 5: 0

       to 100 Gall'o sider spent on
       do at 9 d   3: 15: 0

       to Calling the Court of Oyer
       and Terminer   10: 0: 0

       to my fees for Executing 5
       Indians att 5: 1: 1 1/2   5: 5: 7 1/2

7'br 6th   to Committm't of 8 Indians
       att 20 por   160

       to Imprisonment of Indians 3
       days att 5 por   120

11th   to Committm't 12 Indians att 20 per 240

       to Imprisonment 20 Indians
       23 dayes att 5 per   2300

8'bor the 4th to Committm't of 28 Indians
       att 20   0560

       to Imprisonm't 40 Indians
       3 dayes att 5   0720

Misc. Records.

p.31.
Captain Charles Barber's Account (continued)

8'ber the 5th	to Releasem't 40 Indians att 20	0960
	to Comittm't 43 Indians att 20 per	0860
8'ber the 9	to Imprisonm't 43 Indian 24 da: att 5 per	5160
	to Releasem't 43 Indians att 20 per	0860
	to the use of my houses and trouble thereof while the Indians was Imprisoned which was 55 da	3000
	To the smith for making 16 pr of Irons and tending	2000
	To the Carpenter for Building the Gallows	0200
	An acco't of the Charge att the Court to Edward Jeffereys Ordinary keeper for drink etc	9479
	to Richard Hill Ordinary keeper	454
	to 3 men hired to tend 6 dayes att 50 per	900
	to 1 man 2 dayes att 50	100
	to 2 women 3 dayes att 20 per	120
	for a man for Leadeing a horse that was prest to Carry provision and Lett	200
		-- -- -- --
		11248

8'ber the 5th	to a Casque of Wine that 30 gall att 5 per	7:	10:	0
	to 5 Bushells wheat Flower att 5 per	1:	5:	0
	to Maj'r Grymes acco't	15:	15:	6
		--	-- -- --	--
		24:	10:	6

Errors Excepted this 7th day)
of Novemb'r 1704 per me   )
                    Charles Barber Sherr R.C.

(see next page)

Misc. Records.

p.31-A

An account of men Imprest to Guard the Indians when I delivered them
to the Sherriff of Essex
To Christopher Petty John Simmons Robert Palmer)
   Luke Hanks John Dalton 2 dayes and one night)
to Mr Wm Woodbridge one day and one night   )
to Do for one Day more   ) According to Law
An acco't of men Imprest to Guard the Indians to)
   the session   )
   to 6 men the first day   )
   to 12 men the second day   )

                        per Charles Barber Sherr R.C.

p.32.

1704 An acco't of the Charge.and trouble which I was att the time
      the Nanzatico Indians were in hold
      to my trouble and Charge att that time which was great   4000

                        per Gerrard Lynch Sub Sherr

p.32
                        8'br An'o 1704
Richmond Ss
      The Clayme of William Underwood Comander of a Comp'a of foot

To two files of men for the takeing three men   )
   and Guarding them one day   ) According to Law

to one bed cord to bind the said Indians   14

to my serjant and 4 men to Convoy 3 Indian prison-)
   ers from Francis Stone to Court 1 day   )
)
to three men to carry the Indians Goods to Court)
   and theire attendance there 2 dayes   ) According to Law
)
to my serjant and 9 men to Convoy the Indian   )
   Women and Children from Mrs Cammooks to Coll'o)
   Tayloes being 2 dayes upon that service   )

                        Wm Underwood

Richmond Ss.   8'br An'o 1704
The Clayme of Capt Alexand'r Doniphan Comander of a troop of horse
in the upper part of Richmond County

to twenty men to Guard the Indians 3 dayes
        and 3 nights   According to Law
to one bed cord 2 Drumm Lines and one piece
        of Manchester cording to bind them
        withall   47

                        Allex'r Doniphan

p.32-A.
                        Octob'r 16th 1704
Richmond Ss
The Clayme of Nicholas Smith on the behalfe of the Troops under his
Command for service done the Country in takeing the Indians
Vizt
Nich'o 6 dayes himselfe and horse
Do Smith 180 lb tobbo Expended on the Soldiers
George Erwin Eight Dayes himselfe and horse
Christopher Ederington 8 dayes himselfe and horse
Fra Sterne for trouble and charge of 7 men and horse three dayes att
        his house to Guard three Indians
Do Starne a horse three dayes to Fetch amunition
Do Starne a Servant man 2 dayes on the service
Fra Williams Six Dayes himselfe and horse
Jn'o Bowen three dayes himselfe and horse
George Erwin 5 dayes himselfe and horse
Benj'a Erwin 4 dayes himselfe and horse
Dan'll White 4 dayes himselfe and horse
George White 6 dayes himselfe and horse
Edmond Maglintia 3 dayes himselfe and horse
James Scott 4 dayes and horse
John Fenner three dayes and horse
                                        Nich'o Smith
for which we pray allowance according to Law

p.32-A
                        8'ber 1704
Richmond Ss
The Clayme of Mrs Jane Cammell Interpreter
to my attendance on Service 5 dayes and nights   1000
                                Jane Cammell

8'ber 1704.
Richmond Ss
        The Clayme of James Sherlock one of the Clks of the arraignm't
to the Commissioners of Oyer and Terminer for the tryale of the
Indians
to my attendance att a Called Court held att Coll'o Tayloes   200
To Eight dayes attendance att the Commission of Oyer and
        Terminer att 200 per day   1600
                                                            - - - -
                                                                1800

                        James Sherlock

p.33.

Richmond Ss   8'ber 1704
To my man and horse for carrying tho proceedings of the Court)
of Oyer and Torminer concerning the Indians to Wmsburgh   )
Charge of Forryage and Gooing and Comoing Exponoos thero being)
in ab't 9 dayes absont   ) 1200
(Noto: No namo shown in above ontry. B.F.)

p.33. Bond. 10th - 1704. 10000 lb tobo. "Tho Condition of tho above
Obligation is such that whoreas tho above bound Garrard Lynch hath
taken upon him the tuition of Sam'll Inglisliby son of Darby Inglith-
by Late of this County deo'ed upon Condition that he shall Learne
the said Sam'll to Read write and Cypher perfectly according to the
tenour of an order of Richmond County Court dated the sixth day of
decemb'r last past x x"
Wit: signed   Garrard Lynch
Geo: Eskridge   Tho x Pannele
Wm Dair   James Ingo
Thomas Dickenson
                        Reo. 3 May 1705

p.33-A. Bond. Dated - - 1705. 5000 lb tobo. "The Condition of this
Obligation is such that whereas Anne Inglisliby Daughter of Darby
Inglishby deo'ed was by an order of Richmond County Court of the 6th
day of December 1704, Ordered to serve the above bound Dan'll McCarty
or his assignos the terme of three yeares he or they doeing theire
Endeavours to Learno the said Anno to Read sew spin and knitt"
Wit:
Thomas Dickinson   signod   Dan'll McCarty
                                         Charles Barber

                        Reo. 2 May 1705.

p.34. Power of Atty. 19 Dec. 1704. John Smallwood of Liverpool in
Co. of Lanc. and Kingdom of England, merchant and Ralph Peters of
Liverpool, Gent., to "our trusty and well beloved Friend Capt John
Green of Liverpool Mariner", to collect debts from Maj'r Francis
Wright of Mochodock and Cap't Richard Drummond and others in Md. and
Va. Said Ralph Peters "being sole Executor of x William Peters late
of Liverpoole afors'd merchant dec'ed who was Copartner with the
said John Smallwood in his lifetime"
Wit: signed   John Smalwood
Robert Mason   Ra: Peters
John Sandeford
                          Rec. 6 June 1705

p.34-A. Power of Atty. 3 Feby 1704/5. Jane paice of Sittenbourne
par. Richmond Co., to "my Trusty and well Beloved Sonn Daniell White
of the aforesaid parish and County planter", to collect debts.
Wit:
Geo Paine   signed   marked by
Timothy x Ick   Jane x Paice
James Storcy
                          Rec. 6 June 1705

p.35. Power of Atty. 20 Feb. 1704/5. "John Loyd of the Citty of
Chester in the Kingdom of England Esq'r x x whereas I am Lawfully
possessed of Interested in and Entitled unto severall Considerable
plantations Reale and personall Estates in the Dominion and Country
of Virg'a which heretofore I Intrusted and Committed to the care and
management of my deare brother Thomas Lloyd who lately dyed there
and upon whose death I am Lawfully Entitled to all his Estate x x
and whereas It is necessary for me att this distance to putt and
Constitute some person or persons In trust to look after and manage
my said Estates and affaires in that Country x x have x x appointed
x x my trusty and well beloved Friend and kinsman Griffin Fauntleroy
Gentl'm my true sufficient and Lawfull attorney x x."
Wit:
Lawrence Clifton   signed   John Lloyd
Will: Halse
William Clifton
George Brereton
Arthur Joynson
Will Heywood

Proved in Richmond County Court by the oaths of Lawrence Clifton and
George Brereton the 6th day of June 1705 and Recorded
                          Test
                          J Sherlock Cl Cur

p.37.

Decemb'r the 19th 1704

Mr Deare
Sir
    I have sent you the writings concerning the ketch and desire you
to goe up to Mr Robison with the Inclosed and do your indeavours to
agree with him for my part of the ketch and what difference is
betweene he and me and what you do I will stand to my quart'r of
ketch Cost 35: 15: 00 and I paid for my part of charges and Repaire-
ing to the ketch 14: 17: 00 so is out of my pockett 50: 12: 0 beside
the loss of the Philadelphia Voyage and other loss I rely believe
above 40 pounds out of my way and out of pockett notwithstanding if
you can agree as he will give you 50 pounds for my part and I to be
att no more charge I will stand to it and I will discharge Mr
Wooseley of the damage I come to by his not minding orders to
Filladelfia so I leave it wholy to your management and you may take
45 pounds before you come away and not agree otherwise you know what
to do about security for my part pray Direct and seale the Inclosed
to Mr Robison and you will oblidge your
Lo: Friend
Nehe: Jones
If it should be small matter betweene you more then what I mention
do not stand
Rec 8 June 1705

p.37. Power of Atty. 11 June 1705. John Ingo of Farnham par. Rd. Co.
to "my trusty and well beloved Friend and Brother James Ingo of the
abovesaid County", to transact business.
On lines 10 and 11 the following appears "or any other Business that
is belonging to me the said John Ingo Green and by these presents x"
The name 'Green' introduced here may possibly be an error in the
original.
Wit: signed   John Ingo
Wm Smoot
Dorrathy x Durran

p.38. Power of Atty. 10 July 1705. "Know all men by these presents
that I Henry Astin of the County of Richmond in the Colony of Virginia
being shortly (with Gods permission) Intended for England" to "my
dear and loveing wife Anne Austin and my trusty Friend Sam'll Godwin
of the County of Richmond" to collect debts and transact business.
Wit:
Thomas Warde   signed   Hery Astin
Richard Thedec
Rec. 5 Sept. 1705

p.38-A Indenture. 19 Oct. 1705. "betweene Thomas Smith of Biddeford
in the County of Devon in the Kingdom of England merchant of the one
part and Patrick Jorn of the Roar (or Rear ?) in the County of
Kilkenny and Kingdom of Ireland of the other part Witnesseth that the
said Patrick Jorn of his owne free and Voluntary will hath bound
placed and putt himselfe apprentice unto the said Thomas Smith",
according to the custom in Maryland, etc.
Wit: his
Charles Hughs   signed   Patrick x Jorn
Will: Wolleman   mark
                          Rec. 26 April 1706

The within Indenture was presented before me this day as witness my
hand and seale of the towne of new Rosse this 9th day of november
an'o Dom 1705

                              Sam'll Pitt Sec'r
                              of New Rosse

p.39.   Power of Atty. 23 July 1706. Augustine Woodward marriner of
Liverpool in behalf of himself and company to "my Friend Rawleigh
Downman of Virginia" to collect debts.
Wit:
George Glascock   signed   Augustine Woodward
Ron'd Lawson

Proved in Richmond Co. by oath of Geo: Glascock 7 August 1706.

p. 39.

Sr
   These are to Will and Require you to appeare for me Phillip Stone
of the County of Richmond att the Court held for the said County next
Ensueing and then and there to do all such business as shall be for
or against me now or hereafter and this shall be your sufficient
Warrent givor from under my hand this 1st day of October 1706
To Mr Thomas Thorne   Phillip Stone
      these

p.39.
Garrard Lynch putts in his place Thomas Thorne his attorney in
Richmond County Court in all actions whatsoever both for him and
against him in the said Court and for soe Doing this shall be his
Warr't as wittness my hand this 5th novemb'r 1706
To Mr Tho Thorne   Gar Lynch
      these

Misc. Records.

p.39-A
9'br 6th 1706

"Execution Issued upon an order of the Court dated the 7th day of
August an'o 1706, granted, to John White against Tho Burke for Two
thousand three pounds of tobbo
Returned Executed on the body of the said Thomas Burke by delivering
him into the common Goale of Richmond County per me
                              James Coward Sub sherr "

p.39-A
"Execution Issued upon an order of this Court dated the 2'd day of
Octob'r 1706 granted to Griffin Fantleroy against John White for
thirteene thousand and four hundred and ninety one pounds of tobbo
novemb'r the 6th 1706
Returned the above precept Executed by Delivering John White into the
common Goale of Richmond County per me
                              James Coward Sub sherr

p.39-A

Richmond Ss
James Westcomb Clk of Westm'nld County Court having Certifyed that
no Execution had issued upon an order of the said County Court
obtained by Wm Curruther against Alex'r Spence Cherrurgeon Execution
hath thereupon Issued against the body of the said Alex'r Spence for
the sume of five hundred and thirty eight pounds of tobbo and Costs
this 7th day of March 1706 (1706/7)
                              Test
                                  Tho: Dickenson
                                         dp't Cl Cur

p. 40. Power of Atty. 5 March 1706/7. Joseph Blake of Lancaster Co.
in Virginia, anchor smith, to "my well beloved Friend Mr Wm Dare" to
collect debts.
                              signed   Joseph Blake
No witnesses shown
on record.
                         Rec. 5 March 1706/7

p.40. Power of Atty. 20 Feb. 1705/6. John Batchellor "of the Citty
of Bristoll Esqr Owner of the good ship or Vessell called the Europe

of Bristoll Burdenned two hundred and fifty tonns or thereabouts
whereof Edward Smith was late Ma'r" to Moore Fantleroy "of Rhappa-
hannock River in Virginia Planter my true and Lawfull attorney for
me and in my name but to the onely use of James Commeline to ask
demand Recover and Receive of and from Henry Austin of Rappahannock
River in Virginia planter" and collect debts from all other persons
on schedule herewith submitted.
Wit: John Bacheler
Benj Deverele
Joseph Williams

Proved in Richmond Co. Court 5 March 1706/7 by oath of Benj'a
Deverell and recorded.

p.41.
"The Deposition of M'r John Doane Aged 58 yeares or thereabouts saith
    That he Intermarryed with one of the Daughters of Coll John
Walker and that by Virtue of a Copy of a Will which was the Will of
the said Coll John Walker attested by Robert Davis als Payne then
Clk of Rapp'ac County Court he recovered a some a Legacy left by the
said Walker to his the said depo'ts wife
    Sworne to in Richmond County Court the 6th day of Feb'ry 1706
(1706/7)

                                        Recorded
                                          Test
                                 J Sherlock   Cl our

p.41. Power of Atty. 18 March 1706/7. John Charteris of Liverpool
Mercht to "my trusty and loving Friend James Ingoe" of Richmond Co.
planter, to receive debts, etc.
Wit: signed   John Charteris
Sam'll Godwin
Aus: Brockenbrough   Rec. 2 April 1707.

p.41-A. Indenture. 2 April 1707. Betw. Sam'll Marsh of Co of Richmond
planter and Griffin Fantleroy of same Co. Marsh to be taught "the
trade or art of a house Carpenter and Joyner". Fantleroy to furnish
"good and sufficient meat drink Cloaths Washing and Lodging during
the said time of his Service"
No witnesses shown   Signature illegible. Appears
on record.   to be a duplicate of original
                                   which was evidently a mere
                                   scratch.
Duplicate entry signed Griffin Fantleroy.
                                 Ack and Rec 2 April 1707.

p. 42-A. Power of Atty. 5 April 1707. Emanuell Cleeve of Richmond Co.,
to James Ingo of same Co., to collect money, tobo, etc. "belonging
unto me as Intermarrying with Patience Nayler Extx of the Last Will
and Testament of Avery Nayler of the same County (her former husband
dec'ed) as likewise all such debts as are due and oweing unto me"
Wit:
Sam'll Godwin   signed   Eman'll Cleve
Wm Mack dannill
                         Rec 3 July 1707.

p.43. Power of Atty. Dated "Rich'd County Rappa'h River Jan'ry 8th
1706", (1706/7) Nath'll Wallplate of Dublin mercht to James Ingo,
to collect debts in Virginia.
Wit: signed   Nath'll Wallplate
David Maguire his marke
Will: Browne his marke

Proved by oaths of David Maguire and Wm Browne 3 July 1707 and recorded the same date.

p.43-A.   22 July 1707
Execution Issued 5 Feb 1706/7 to Capt Charles Barber against Garrard
Lynch for 2354 lb tobo, retd 22 July 1707 satisfied.
                            signed per me James Coward Sub Sher.

p.43-A.   22 July 1707
"Execution issued upon an order of this Court dated the 7th day of
May 1707 granted to Judith Fleming agt Edward Cornwell for her
Freedom Corne and Cloathes Returned Executed and Redeemed with one
steere five years old and one steere three yeares old valued to eight
hundred and fifty pounds of tobbo May the 21th 1707"
Andrew Dew   signed per James Coward Sub Sh:
Robt x Ayres
John x - (Flynn ?)
per me Judith Fleman the above satisfyed.

p.43-A.   "September the 3'd day 1707
We the subscribers do Testifie that a man named Stephen Manerwing
who profest himselfe to be a Resident in north Carolina and did
desese this life in Richmond County and died the first week in november and was Buryed in the Church yeard of Sittenburne parish in the

above said County, Nabuchedenesor Jones and John Tysett do Testifie
that the abovesaid Stephen Manerwing did declare that he had a son
named John and a Daughter named Hanah living in the said North
Carolina; Manerings son and Daughter, Wittness our Hands the day and
yeare above

Nabu Jones
marked by
John x Tysett
marked by
Nathaniell x Hall

The above deposition was Sworne to in Richmond County Court by the
above named Nab'u Jones John Tysett and Nathan'll Hall and upon
the motion of -(illegible)- Bluhead on the same was admitted to
Record "

pages 44. 44-A. 45. Account of Capt. Thomas Beale to Nat: Davis and
Comp'ny. This is a long list of merchandise with prices. It is very
interesting from that standpoint but too much to be included here.
Dated Virginia 19 June 1705. Recorded 2 October 1707. See next entry.

p.45-A. "Virginia March the 13th 1702/3 Exch: L 62: 9 s.
Att Thirty Dayes sight of this my third of Exch' my first and second
not paid pay unto Capt Tho's Beale Ex'r of Mr Wm Colston the summe
of Sixty two pounds and Nine shillings Sterl Make good payment and
place it to your owne account

Sr
Your humble Serv't
David Gwyn

To John Loyd Esq'r Mercht
in the Sitty of Chester

Recorded amongst the Records of Richmond County Court this 2'd day
of October an'o Dom 1707

Test

Rec'ed of Capt Thomas Beale first and second bills of Exchange Drawne
upon John Lloyd Esq'r Merchant in Chester (by Major David Gwyn) for
Sixty two pounds nine shillings the which bills I promise to be
accountable for according to order as Wittness my hand this 23'd
June 1705

Nath'll Davis

Recorded amongst the Records of Richmond County Court this 2'd day of
October an'o Dom 1707

Test   "

p.45-A. Power of Atty. 9 Sept 1707, Thos Houlston of the Kingdom of England merchant to"my Friend Charles Barber of the parish of Farnham and County of Richmond" to collect accounts.
Wit:
James Fushee   signed   Tho's Houlston
Alex x Fleming

Proved by oathes of James Foushee and Alex'r Fleming in Rd Co Court 1 Oct. 1707.

p.46. Power of Atty. 20 Sept. 1707. Wm Atkinson of Whitehaven in the Kingdom of England mariner to "my loveing Friend Edward Barrow of the County of Richmond in the Colony of Virginia Gentleman" to collect a/cs from William Dickson of Richmond Co. mariner for divers goods.
Wit:
Will Browne   signed   Wm Atkinson
William x Carter

Proved 1 Oct. 1707 by oath of Wm Browne in Rd. Co. Court.

p.46-A. Power of Atty. 10 Oct. 1707. "Joseph Smith late of Richmond County mercht" to Nicholas Smith of Rd. Co. to collect a/c of Charles Ashton of Potomack gent.
Wit: signed   Joseph Smith
Wm Thomas
Wm x Grant

Proved in Rd. Co. Court by oaths of Thomas and Grant 4 Feb, 1707/8.

p.47. Power of Atty. 20 Sept 1707. Jno. Naylor merchant to Capt Wm. Barber of Rd. Co. to collect a/cs.
Wit: signed   Jn'o Naylor
John Tarpley
Jno Spurstow   Rec. 4 Feb. 1707/8

p.47-A. Power of Atty. 12 Feby 1707/8. Josia Poole of Liverpool Gent to John Naylor of Liverpool to take possession of a plantation of 500 acres lying in the County of Baltimore in the province of Maryland known by the name of Upton Court.
That David Poole and Josia Poole had given a power of atty to Jeffery Roby (this name may be Proby) late of Liverpool Gent impowering him

to dispose of the plantation but he being since deceased, poer of atty
now issued to Natlor.
Wit: signed   Josia Poole
Dan'll Collet
William x Woodcock
Robert x Leigh

Proved in Richmond Co Court 5 May 1708 by oaths of Daniell Collet and
Robert Leigh.

p. 48-A. Power of Atty. 13 Feb. 1707/8. "John Smallwood of Liverpoole
in the County of Lancaster merchant and Ralph Peters of the same gent,
Exec't of the last will and Testament of William Peters late of
Liverpoole aforesaid merchant deceased" to John Naylor of Liverpool,
merchant, to receive from Maj'r Francis Wright of Mochodock and
others, debts, etc, due the said Wm Peters deceased.
Wit:
Ja Looker   signed   John Smalwood
Dan'll Collet   Ra Peters
Robert x Leigh

Proved in Rd. Co. Court 5 May 1708 by oaths of Collet and Leigh.

p. 48-B. (this page not numbered in the original). Power of Atty.
1 Nov. 1707. Sam'll Hartnell of the City of Bristol merchant and
John Thomas of the same city mariner, to Nicholas Smith of Rappa.
River in Virginia planter, to collect a/cs from William Ayres of
Rappa River in Va. planter, Henry Brewton and David Berrick both
of Richmond Co in Va. planters.
Wit: signed   Sam'll Hartnell
John Walker   John Thomas
George Blake

Proved by the oath of George Blake in Rd. Co. Court 7 July 1708.

p. 48-B. Power of Atty. 20 Sept. 1707. James Puckle notary and
Tabellion dwelling in London issued Power of Atty of George Purvis
of London mariner to Capt Charles Smith of Rappa River in Va mercht
to collect a/c from Coll John Battles (John Battaile) of Rappa River,
also "from the widdow of Maj'r David Gwyn of Rappahannock River"
and others.
Wit: signed   Geo Purvis
Walter Cooke
Justin Magrath
John Black   (see next page)

Misc. Records.

George Purvis' Power of Atty (continued)
Proved 7 July 1708 in Rd Co Court by oath of John Black.
"Proved in Richmond County Court by the oath of Walter Cooke the
first day of Sept'r an'o 1708".

p.50.

April the 16th 1707
Mr Edward Bromlow is Dr.

To 5 galls of Sydar att 8 per	040
To accomadating yourselfe and 2 men 4 months	
at 240 per month	1960
To y'r part of Tho Jenkins board att	040
To boarding Jn'o Brabin 10 days att	033
To 6 pr mens stockings att 50 per	300
To y'r part of Mr Dares fees	300
To y'r part of Mr Thornes Do	150
To making a fine shirt and 1 Corse do	030
To 1 pr of mens stockings att	050
To 20 days work att 40 per	800
	2703

To Contra

by one bushel of Flower att	050
By 2 galls and 1 qt Rum att 80 per	180
By paid James Coward for 2 levys att 46	092
By paid do for Clarks fees	084
By paid for a pr of Cart Wheels	300
By 1 Childs Coat att	075
By paid Tho Jenkins	150
By serch and Coppy 3 pattens att 40 per	120
By paid Rich'd Fristoe for goeing to the office	045
by your trouble in Goeing to the office	060
by 22 days work att 40	880
by Ball'a due to Gabriell alloway	667
	2703

Richmond Ss
    Pursuant to an order of Court the 6th day of May last we whose
names are here unto subsoribed being mett att the house of Gabriell
alloway have perused all the acct both of plaintiff and defend't and
do find that the said Edward Bromlow stands Indebted to the said

Edward Bromlow stands Indebted to the said Gabriell alloway 667 pds
of tobbo given under our hands this 19th of June 1708

                              Jos Deeke
                              Will Barber
                              Charles Barber

Recorded amongst the Records of Richmond County Court
                         Test   J Sherlook Cl Cur

p.50. Power of Atty. 1 April 1708. "John Dudlestone of Bristoll
Baronett" to "my Loving Friend Mr Robert Valx of Popes Creek on
Potomack River Virginia" to collect debts.
Wit:
Robt Edwards   signed   John Dudelestone
Stephen Harvey

Proved in Rd. Co. Court 7 July 1708 by oath of Robt Edwards.

p.50-A. Power of Atty. 10 Oct. 1707. Edward Foye of the City of
Bristol merchant to "my trusty and well beloved friend Paul Micou
mercht" to collect debts.
Wit: signed Edw Foye
     the mark of
William WT Tillier Jun'r
     the mark of
Patrick PD Daly
     The marke
William T Tillier Sen'r

Proved in Richmond Co. Court 1 Sept 1708 by oaths of William Tillier
Son'r and Wm Tillier Junr.

Note. Paul Micou was a French doctor. He was an ancestor of mine, so
I may add (with a slight blush) that he was pretty good at collecting
debts,particularly from the widows and orphans of his patients. B.F.

p.51-A.
                                          London Anno 1707
Tobaccos Imported for acc't of Mr Joseph Dykes being 11 hh'ds rec'ed

Misc. Records.

here per the George Brig'a Thomas Ma'r a Virginia".
Then follows list of hogsheads with marks, custom expenses, etc.
Entry signed "London Sept'r 1707 Errors Excepted per Hamlett
Robinson". See next entry.
                                    Rec. 11 Sept 1708 in Rd. Co. Court.

p.52-A. "Tobacco Received per Mr William Ayres for the use and upon
the proper accep't of Capt John Thomas of Bristoll". 14 hhd listed.
                          signed   Henry Brereton

"Sworne to in Richmond County Court by Henry Brereton the 2d day of
February an'o D'm 1708 and Recorded Test
Examined per order Court by M: Beckwith Cl Cur "

p.53.

A List of Debts due to Mr Tho Woodyates Estate as appears by his books.

				Tobbo	
Mrs Jane Baker	5.	4.	10	0836	overcharged in book 0160
Mad'm Win'd Griffin	15.	05.	00	0	
Nath'll Thrift	04.	14.	3	0754	overcharged 0172
Mary Teton	00.	01.	3	0010	
Mad'm Deek	02.	05.	11	0367	
Mrs Lynch	07.	03.	9	1150	discompted 0020
Mr Jenings	07.	7.	9 1/2		
Mr Job Hamon Jun'r	04.	19.	6	0796	
Mr Joseph Taylor	02.	04.	0	0352	
Mrs Henry Webster	00.	10.	01		
M'r Ed: Jones	00.	15.	03	0122	discompted 0122
Mr Jn'o Jones	00.	14.	8	0117	
Elmer Hightower		04.	00	0032	
Cap't Tarpley	00.	07.	00	0056	
Garrett Lynch	00.	05.	0	0040	Lost 0040
Cap't Barrow	00.	10.	0	0080	
Cha Dodson	02.	11.	9		
Jn'o Pynes	16.	13.	10	2681	Discompted 1596
Mr Martin Hamon senr	04.	04.	0	0032	Disc'ted 0032
Hen Clark	01.	16.	0	0288	
M'r Wm Morgan	00.	01.	03	0010	
Capt Brereton	00.	05.	3	0042	
Mr Gaythings	00.	08.	0	0064	

                              (continued)

Misc. Records.

Debts due Tho. Woodyates Estate (continued)

Mr David Berrick	02. 03. 5 1/2	0348	discompted 0348
Mad'm Travers	00. 06. 00	0048	
Mr Deeke	05. 07. 00	0856	overcharged in books 0221
Mrs Eliz'a Hill	03. 03. 9	0510	
Simon Taylor	00. 05. 7	0044	
Rich'd Appelby	00. 07. 3	0088	
Garrott Lynch	00. 04. 3	0034	Lost 0034
Jn'o Sherlook	00. 10. 0	0080	/ 0080
Eow'd Jones	02. 18. 0	0464	discompted per Judgmnt
Mr Tho Suggitt	00. 16. 4	0130	
M'r Breoking	03. 11. 6	0572	

To Goods as per Inventory	8820
To tobbo debts as per Ledger	10438
	- - - -
	30262

An account of what Debts not rec'd vizt

Madam Griffin	15. 5. 0
Hon Jenings	7. 7. 9 1/2
Cha: Dodson	2. 11. 9
	- - - - - - - -
	25. 4. 6 1/2

Lost 938 discompted 2526	3461
by the Ex'rs owne acco)	
made and appeare to us)	6674
by funerall Charges	1198
by Judg'mts agt the Estate for	16124
	- - - -
	30285

In obediance to an order of Court held for Richmond County the sixth
day of May and Continued to the first day of Sept anno Dom 1708 we
whose names are hereunto written have audited and stated the accounts
due to and from the Estate of the said Thomas Woodyates dec'ed as
above may appeare Wittness our hands this second day of October anno
Dom 1708

                          Will Woodbridge
                          Edward Barrow
                          Geo: Heale
                          Jos. Deeke

              Rec. 15 March 1708/9

Misc. Records.

The Estate of Thomas Bendrey dec'ed

To a winding sheet	00:	10:	0
To a coffin	01:	05:	0
to 10 gall'o Rum Expended att the dec'ed funerall att 6 s per gall is	03:	00:	0
to 4 Bushells of wheat att 4/per	00:	16:	0
to 50 lb of Butter att 6 d per	01:	05:	0
To 40 lb of Sugar Expended att the funera'll of the dec'ed att 9 d per	01:	10:	0
To 600 lb of sweetsented tobo pd Peter Kippax) for preaching the said dec'ed funerall) Sermon att 12 s 6 d per Ct)	03:	00:	0
To Maj'r Gwyn his Coroners Fee	00:	13:	4
To My trouble in looking after the said dec'ed) Corps one night and halfe a day in the) woods untill the Coroners Inquest had sat) upon in and after two days and two nights) untill it was Interred and also for the) trouble of my house and what I paid persons) for assisting me in the doeing thereof in) all)	02:	10:	0

John Crask

Rec. 15 March 1708/9

Note: It looks to me as though Mr. Crask had had an exciting and
interesting time, had given a handsome entertainment and was now
being paid for it. All of which was doubtless approved by the
appreciative guests.   B.F.

p.54. Power of Atty. 11 Dec. 1708. Sam'll Richardson of Liverpool,
merchant, to Wm Everard "of Liverpoole Mariner Mast'r or Comand'r of
the good ship the Content of Liverpoole", "in my name But also of
Thomas Americ and James Halsall of Liverpoole merchts" to receive
from George Glascock of Rappahannock River in Virga, mercht, 13000
lb tobo according to a note of the said Glascock dated 27th Sept.
1707.
Wit: signed   Samuell Richardson
Thomas Boulton
Thomas Boulton
John Sandeford

Proved in Rd. Co. Court 1 June 1709 by oaths of Thomas Boulton and
Thomas Boulton.
                        Test M: Beckwith Cl Cur

p.54-A. Note. 27 Sept. 1707. Signed by George Glascock to Sam'll
Richardson for 13000 lb tobo to be paid March next. Witnessed by
Rawl. Downeman and Tho. Glascock.

p.54-A.

                                    Liverpoole Decemb'r the 11th 1708
Mr George Glascock
Sr
    I desire you to deliver the goods as under or Effects to Mr William
Everitt and his receipt shall be your discharge from your Frend and
Serv't

                                    Sam'll Richardson

1 punch bowle
1 Carte Saddle
5 yds Cartey'r
1 Rasor
1 pr Wosted stockins
1 pr Gloves 1 bridle
1 axx and 1 one howe

                    Truly Recorded Test Marma: Beckwith Cl Cur

p. 55

January the first day 1708
        These are to Certifye to all persons to whom it may Concerne
that I John Oldum of the County of Richmond have received of Richard
Rout Jun'r of the same County the Just sum of four thousand three
hundred and thirty pounds of Tobacco it being my full part and share
of my fathers estate and I the said John Oldum do by these presents
acquit and discharge the aforesaid Richard Rout from all debts dues
and demands due unto me from the beginning of the world unto this
day as Witness my hand and seale the day and year first above written
Wit:
John Williams   his
John x Harris   John x Oldum
                                      marke

                    Rec. 6 July 1709.

p.55.   Virginia August the 6th 1707
                          Exchange for 19 lb
Sr
   At Thirty days sight of this my first of Exchange my second and
third not paid, Pay or cause to be paid unto Osman Crabb or order
the Just sum of nineteen pounds sterling money of England it being
for the like value Received, and place it to account as by advise
from
                                   Yr Servant
                                   Wm Addison

To m'r John Smallwood
Merchant in Liverpoole
Endorsm'ts
   Osman Crabb
   Lyonel Loyde
   Tho: Nelson

Liverpoole in) By this Publick Instrument of Protest, Be it known
Com. Pat. Lane) and made manifest unto all persons That upon the
                  seventeenth day of Decemb'r Anno Dom. - 1708 I John
Sandeford Notary and Tabellion Publick dwelling at Liverpoole aforesaid and by Royall authority duly admitted and sworn at the Instance
and Request of m'r John Pemberton of Liverpoole merchant went to the
house of m'r John Smallwood of the same place merch't and tendered
him the Originall bill of Acceptance Whereof the above written is a
true Copy, Word for Word, Who denyed to accept the same saying he had
no Effects of the Drawers in his hands x x x.

At a Court held for Richmond County September the 7th 1709
At the mo'con of Cap'tn Geo Eskridge the within bill of Exchange
subscribed Wm Addison together with the Protest thereon is admitted
to record
                          Test Ms Beckwith Cl Cur
                          Examined per Ms Beckwith Cl Cur

p. 55-A

Richmond County
            In obedience to an order of Court bearing date the
second day of June 1709 wherein it was ordered that A Jury should goe
upon the land in difference between James Toone by his nearest friend
John Fan plantife and John Miller deft to survey according to the
most known and reputed bounds thereof the land aforesaid x x and find
the Defend't a trespasser and that the said Def't hath Comitted
damage upon the said land to the value of five shillings sterling as

witness our hands and seals this fift day of July 1709.

Fran: Lucas   John Rankin
John Leaman   Jn'o x Battin
Stevens Gupton   Job x Hammond
Bar't: Rich'd Dodson   Christopher Petty
Jn'o x Buckston   Jn'o Simmons
Thomas x Dodson   Richard Branham

p.56.

Richmond So't
        Pursuant to an order of Court bearing date the 8th June 1710
Wee whose names are under written being summoned as Juryers in a
difference between Capt'n Nicholas Smith and m'r Nathaniell Pope
pl:ts and John Combs and Henry James Defend'ts have surveyed the
land of the plts: it being a patent granted to Wm Yarrett and Francis
Wittington for five hundred and eighty acres dated the 29th July
1650 and wee find one of the Def'ts (Viz't) Henry James a Trespasser the sum of five shillings sterling. Witness our hands this
twenty first of June 1710

George Payne foreman   Thomas Richardson
Tho x Brooks marke   Fra: James   x
James Scott   John Mason   x
Joseph Mellinton his marke   Charles Chill
Thomas Paise   John Jenings
Cornelius Edmunds   George Erwin

                Wm Thornton Sur'y'r

p.56. Appointment of Wm Thornton as Surveyor of Richmond Co. 27th
April 1710.

p.56-A. Feb. 10 1709/10. Thomas Fitzhugh petitions to build a water
grist mill on his land adj Claybournes run. It is ordered that Charles
Colo and John Jones value 1/2 acre belonging to Edward Watts opposite
and make report to next Court.

"Richmond Ss   28 Feb'r 1709/10
        In obedience to the with (within) order wee the persons within
appointed have viewed and valued half an acre of the within named
Edward Watts land to Five shillings and have delivered the within

mentioned Thomas Fitzhugh possession thereof
                                    Charles Cole
                                    John x Jones

At a Court held for Richmond County September the sixth 1710
At the motion of George Eldridge in behalf of Thomas Fitzhugh this
order together with the report hereon Endorsed is admitted to record
                           Test M: Beckwith Cl Cur "

p.57. Proclamation. 6 July 1710. Col. Alexander Spotswood regarding
certain legal rights of the subjects of Queen Anne.

p.58. "Know all men by these presents that I Francis Williams Sen'r
do acquitt and Release and discharge Hanna Charlton from all servi-
tudes due to me my heirs Executors and from all men that shall Lay
any Claims of Services of her from the beginning of the world to this
day as Witness my - and Seale this ninth day of October one thousand
seven hundred and ten
Test   his
Jo'n Barnard   Francis M Williams
Rich: Claxton   mark

And Also I give unto Hannah Charlton her Daughter Arn, as Witness my
hand from year above wrighten as Witness my hand and seale this present
day and year Above wrighten
Test   his
John Barnard   Francis M Williams
Richard Claxton   mark
James Peed "
                           Rec. 6 Dec. 1710

p.58-A
                           "March the 5th 1710
The mark of John Knights hoggs and Cattle is an under keel and an
over keel in the right ear, and a Cropp and a slitt in the left
                                        his
                                  John x Knight
                                        mark
                           Rec. 7 March 1710/11

p. 58-A. Indenture. 9 March 1710/11. "Between Mary Clayton formerly
Mary Butler of the parish of Sittenborn in the County of Richmond

within the Dominion of Virginia of the one part and Henry Ravnall and
Martha his Wife of the same parish and County within the Dominion of
Virginia aforesaid of the other part Witnesseth that the said Mary
Clayton hath and by these presents doth bind and put her Daughter
Fogg Butler as an apprentice and Servant to the said Henry Ravnall
and Martha his said Wife to serve them in any lawfull Inployment as
they shall sett her about for the space of fourteen years and six
months from the date hereof". The girl to receive food, clothing, one
year's schooling, etc.

Wit: signed   Mary x Clayton
Marrnaduke Beckwith   Henry x Ravnall
Willian x Simms   Martha x Ravnall

                         Rec. 2 May 1711.

p.59.   "Sr
        Please to record the mark of William Richards which is a
crop and slitt in the right Eare and a swalo fork in the left"
                    Rec. 6 June 1711.

p.59. Proclamation. 28 April 1711. Col. Alexander Spotswood.
Marked "A precept for the due holding of Courts and for Conveying
Criminalls".
                    Rec. 6 June 1711.

pp. 60 - 65-A. Twelve pages of commercial accounts. Various items
mdse charged to the following:

p.60 .	16 April 1709	Mr Nathaniell Pope	8. 11. 6
	20 July 1710	Col'o William Fitzhugh	1. 16. 4
	-	Mr Robert Harrison	4. 03. 11
p.60-A	9 Nov. 1710	Dennis Raudone	3. 05. 09
	30 Sept 1710	Mr Jn'o Mees	1. 16. 2
p.61	20 May 1710	Mr Benj'a Strother	24. 4. 9
p.61-A	- 1710	Mr Augustian Smith	3575 tobo
p.62	7 Oct 1710	Mr Dannil Sild	06. 03. 06
	26 June 1709	Mr Henry Crue- (?)	02. 09. 02
p.62-A	16 Sept 1711	Mr Larking Chew	12. 11. 08
p.63	6 Aug 1710	Mr Robert Ingles	1. 16. 2
	24 June 1711	Mr Nich'o Brint	3. 10. 03
	17 Sept 1709	Capt George Andersson	2. 7. 7
p.63-A	11 Sept 1708	Mr Joseph Allimond	12. 5. -

Commercial Accounts (continued)

p.64	1 Aug	1711	Cap't Jn'o Washington	13.	16.	2
p.64-A	30 Sept	1710	James Henderkin	3.	7.	2
	25 Feb	1709	Mr Benj'a Berryman	1.	9.	8
p.65	4 Sept	1710	Tho: Striblin	6.	15.	1
	6 June	1710	Mr Sam'll Hickman	2.	14.	5
p.65-A	23 Oct.	1710	Mr Jn'o Somerfeild	1.	2.	9
	27 Oct.	1708	Mr Robert Garden	2.	14.	4
	16 Feb.	1711	Jn'o Kemp the Smith	-	7.	-

Above a/cs all proved in Court 4 July 1711 by oath of Benj'a Deverell.

Note: Perhaps the dates shown in the record were when the accounts
were due rather than when they were made. Note the dates on Capt.
Washington's account and that of John Kemp.   B.F.

p.66. Bond. 16 Aug. 1710. Dan'll Fawcett ship carpenter to John
Pemberton merchant in Liverpool L 100., to guarantee bills of Exchange
for L 20. drawn on Thomas Fawcett, L 30. drawn on John Cunningham
merchant in Liverpool, both bills payable to John Pemberton and "being
for the proper use and acco't of William Tayloe of Virginia".
Wit:
John Wilkinson   signed   Daniell Fawcett
John Garnett

                         Rec. 10 July 1711.

p.66-A
                         Virginia August 16th 1710 Excha for 20
D'r Bro'r
    Att Thirty days after sight of this my fourth of Exchange and
my first second nor third of the same Date not paid, pay unto Mr
John Pemberton merch't of Liverpoole or order for the use and on the
proper account of Coll'o William Tayloe of Virginia the summe of
twenty pounds sterling money of England for value Rec'ed att time
make good paym't and place it to account of
                         Dr. Bro'r
                         Daniell Fawcett

                    Rec. 10 July 1711.

Same page. Bill of Exch on Mr John Cunningham merchant in Liverpool.

p.67. "Execution Issued upon an order of this Court Dated the third
day of May one thousand seven hundred and eleven, Granted to James
Hutchinson against John Pound Jun'r for four hundred pounds of
Tobbacco and Costs of Suite

Returned Executed, Richmond Ss In obedience to the above precept
to me Directed, I have arrested the body of the above named John
Pound Jun'r on the tenth day of this Instant as above I am Comanded,
Given under my hand this 30th of July 1711

John Doyle   Sub Sher   "

Rec. 30 July 1711

p.67

Richmond Ss
In obedience to an order of sd Court bearing date May 2d 1711 It was
ordered that we the subscribers sometime between this and next Court
should audit and state all accounts between Mr Thomas Hewlett as
Guardian to one of the Orphans of John Baylis dec'ed and John Jones
and Elizabeth his wife in pursuance to which we have audited and
stated the said account and find that the said John Jones and Elizabeth his wife stands Indebted unto the said Thomas Hewlett as guardian
aforesaid in the summe of five thousand nine hundred and sixteene
pounds of tobbo, given under our hands this 23d day of May 1711

John Tarpley
Will: Woodbridge

Rec. 13 Aug. 1711

p.67. Power of Atty. 20 June 1711. Marmaduke Beckwith of Richmond
Co., to "my well beloved friend John Tayloe Gent" to collect debts.
Wit:
Tho's Dickinson   signed   Marmaduke Beckwith
Aus Brockenbrough
Rec. 3 Janry 1711/12

p.67-A.

Richmond Ss
Articles of agreement Indented concluded and agreed upon by and
Betweene Elizabeth Harman late of Westmorland County of the one part
and Edmond Moolenshy of Richmond County of the other part.
Eliz Harman agrees to serve sd Edmond two years, she to receive

clothing etc and he to "acquitt and discharge her from the fines
penalties and forfeitures that by Law may be Imposed upon her for
having of a Bastard child, maintain the said Child dureing said time"
etc,
Wit: her
Wm Reid   signed   Eliza x Harman
Dan'll Dillon   mark

Rec. 6 March 1711/12

p.18. Patent for Naturalization. 6 Feb. 1711/12. Mr James Foushee.
Includes "and James Foushee a naturall borne subject of the French
King having settled and Inhabited for severall yeares in the County
of Richmond in this Colony and now made application to me for the
benefitt of Naturalization and before me taken the oathes prescribed
by Law", etc.

signed   A. Spotswood

Rec. 5 March 1711/12

p.68-A. "These are to Certifie to all persons x x that I james Oldham
of the County of Richmond have Received of Richard Rout of the same
County", 4330 lb. tobo., "which is the full part of my fathers Estate
due unto me x x". 31 March 1712.
Wit: signed   James Oldham
John Sabre
Tho Rout   Rec 2 April 1712

p.69.

"May 7th 1712
      Henry Bruce of Sittenburne parish in Richmond County aged fourty
eight yeares or thereabouts Deposeth and sayeth that William Bruce
the son of this Deponent and Mary his wife was borne the one and
thirtieth day of October in the yeare of our Lord one thousand Six
hundred and eighty nine and that his said son William Bruce, and
Motrem Wright the son of Motrem Wright late of Sittenburne parish in
Richmond County were Christened in one Day, and that to the best of
this Deponents knowledge or beliefe the said Motrem Wright was younger
then your Deponents said son Wm Bruce And further he sayeth not
                                        Hen Bruce
Sworne to in Richmond County Court the 7th day of May 1712 and
admitted to Record   Test
                                        Jno Tayloe D Cl

p.69.

May 7th 1712
Elinor Thomas aged Fifty eight yeares or thereabouts deposeth and
saith that att the time when Motrem Wright Jun'r the son of Motrem
Wright the elder dec'ed was borne she lived with the said Motrem
Wright the elder on Rapp'ac Creek, and that it is, since the said
Motrem Wright the Younger was borne twenty two yeares in Jan'ry last
past and no more having a son of her owne borne the July following
and further she saith not

                                   her mark
                           Elinor x Thomas

Sworne to in Richmond County Court the 7th day of May 1712 and
admitted to Record
                           Test
                               Jno Tayloe D Cl

p.69-A

May 7th 1712
Mary Leasure wife of Bartho: Leasure aged fourty yeares or there
abouts deposeth and sayeth that Motrem Wright the younger the son
of Motrem Wright the elder, is (if he had lived) twenty two yeares
of age in Jan'ry last, and that the reason she has to show for the
same is, that she had a Daughter borne about a week or thereabouts
after the said Motrem Wright the younger, and that she was twenty
two yeares old in Jan'ry last and no more, and further she saith not

                                   her
                           Mary M Leasure
                                   mark

Sworne to in Richmond County Court the 7th day of May 1712 and
admitted to Record
                           Test
                               Jno Tayloe D Cl

p.69-A

May 7th 1712
Mary Bruce the wife of Henry Bruce aged fourty seven yeares or there
abouts Deposeth and sayth, that shee this depon't had a son borne
before Motrem the younger the son of Motrem Wright the elder late of
Rappa'ac Dec'ed, and that her said son to the best of her knowledge

or Rememberance was twenty and two yeares old in last October and no
more, and that Motrom Wright the younger was borne in the month of
Jan'ry Following And further she sayeth not

                                        her
                                Mary M Bruce
                                        mark

Sworne to in Richmond County Court the 7th day of May 1712 and
admitted to Record

                                Test   Jno Tayloe D Cl

Att a Court held for Richmond County the 7th day of May 1712
The said Depositions of Henry Bruce Elinor Thomas Mary Lesure and
Mary Bruce, att the motion of Joseph Belfield were ordered to be
Recorded and are Recorded

                                Test   Jno Tayloe D Cl

p.69-A. "Know all men by these presents that I Warren Cary of the
Continent of Virginia x x do make x x and appoint my Loving Brother
Richard Cary of Bristoll my true and Lawfull attorney" to collect
accounts in Virginia. 27 Feb. 1711/12.
Wit:
Robert Boyd   signed   Warren Cary
Thomas Haynes

Proved in Court by oaths of Boyd and Haynes and recorded 14 May 1712.

p.70-A. "Whereas a suit at Law brought by Edward Barrow of Richmond
County Gent'n against Gilbert Metcalf of the same County Gent x x x
for certaine slaves Detained by the said Metcalfe from the said plt.
Whereupon a Jury brought in a special verdict upon the whole facts
of the case" before Judgmt was issued the "parties to the Estate Mr
Richard Metcalfe dyed possest of", to my (Robert Carter's) examination and settlement. "x x the papers produced on both sides The Will
of Gilbert the Grand Father the long Entercourse by letters between
Mr's Metcalf and this Richard her son and after his death to his
Relict Mrs Barrow, also the letters of the said Richards Brothers to
him and likewise Richards long Possession, his Claime to his Uncle
the Alderman of York his Estate".
"Upon the whole it is my opinion that Barrow recover the negroes
claimed in his Declaration x x That in the mean time Gilbert have x

the said slaves". Metcalf to pay for use of slaves until delivered.
Dated 2 June 1712.

signed   Robert Carter

"And Foras much as Mrs Jane Metcalfe Daughter of the said Richard
and sister to the said Gilbert and now maintained by the said Gilbert
claiming of theire said Fathers Estate as her portion from the said
Barrow, to prevent further Trouble hath agreed to stand to my Determi-
nation relateing to her Claime out of her said Fathers Estate and the
said Barrow agreeing x x". Barrow to settle all matters with Gilbert
Metcalf by Nov. 15th next. etc. Dated 2 June 1712.

signed   Robert Carter

Rec. 7 Aug. 1712.

p.71-A

To the Worship'll the Court etc
Richmond Ss
The account of Edward Turbervile and Anne his Wife Executrix with
the Will anext of John Sise deceased of all and singular the goods
and chattels which came to theire hands that were of the said
Decedent, and of theire payments and Disbursements out of the same
as followeth
    x x

To the sume of	10047
To tobacco paid by John Easter due to the sd Estate	876
To tobacco paid by Robert English due to do	118
To tobacco paid by John Birkett due to the same	50
	11091

x x allowance for such Debts and payments as they have paid out x x	3893
To a Judgm't obteyned by John Dalton and Mary his wife Exor'x of William Brockenbrough dec'd paid with cost of suit	1004
To a Judgment recovered by Sam Cox with cost thereon	665
To a Judgment obteined by Alexander Spense with Cost	676

p.72.

To a Judgm't with Costs paid to Thomas Griffin	676
To a Judgment of John Grimsley obteynd per Warrent	75
To John Sise his obligation paid to Cap't Thomas Ward	1300

(continued)

Settlement of the Estate of John Sise (continued)

To 240 paid William Woodford for phsick administered
    to the said dec'd in the time of his last sick-
    ness   240
To Secretarys Fees   40
To Clerks Fees   85
To our Comicon for paying and receiveing at 10 lb
    tobo per Ct   1100
                                             - - - -
                                         9848

                    Errors Excepted by
                    E Turbervile

                Rec. 6 Aug. 1712

p.72. "The Deposition of Patrick Doran aged 40 yeares or thereabouts
being Examined and sworne saith
    That last night he lay att the house of James Story in this
County where he saw William Reid, Well and also this morning Drinking
Sider at the same house well, to his Judgment, who also Desired your
Depon't not to tell the Court where he was eot and further saith not
this 4th day of September 1712
    Sworne in Richmond County Court the fourth day of September 1712
and Ordered to be Recorded
                    Test M Beckwith Cl Cur

p.72.
        The Estate of Giles Mathews July 30th 1712   Dr
Smiths acco't)
      vs   )
Mathews Est   )
To 4 1/2 Ells Browne Linon att 20   090
To 1/4 throd   009
To 5 yds fine stuff to Mary Mathews   100
To 3 ells browne Linon   060
To paid the Tresher for threshing the wheat   228
To a q'rt of Rum to Mr Mathews   018
To 1/2 bushel of wheat   020
To a peck sault   015
To 2 gallons and a p't of Rum   127
To 4 lb Sugar   040
To 2 1/2 ells Dowlas to Mary Mathews   090

                (continued)

Estate of Giles Mathews (continued)

To 3 yds Scotch Cloths to Do   090
To a muzlen hankerchief   030
To 2 Aprons to Do   050
To John Steele 200 for bringing howie Robin (Howie Robin)
    a serr't man belonging to the Estate   200
To Mary Jeffereys 2 gall'o mollasses   060
To 2 qts Rum   036
To Goods belonging to Mary Mathews delivered to
    John Higdon apraised to   710
To Court Charges about Mathews Estate   340
                - - -
To Mary Mathews part of the Estate which   2313
was not appraised Delivered to John Higdon
by me
                Nich'e Smith

Per Contra
by 34 bushels wheat att 40 per bushell   1360
by 155 lb of pork att 2: per   0810
by Mary Mathews Estate according to appraism't   3810
                - - -
                5480
                2313
                - - -
        Balla' Due   3167

Att a Court held for Richmond County the 4th day of March 1712
This account was sworne to in Court by Capt Nich'o Smith and upon
the motion of John Higdon it was admitted to Record
                Test
                  M: Beckwith   Cl Cur

p.73.

Debtor Mr George Alsup his Account Curr'o

1705/6	Feb: 25	To Cash paid his Exch to Tho: Bagwell	-:	7:	-
	March 13	To do paid do to Robt Bristoll	17:	4:	-
1707	Apll 12	To Do paid Do to Hen: Scott	0:	9:	-
	16	To Do paid Do to Wm Syer	17:	19:	0
	Octr 20	To Do paid protest Tho Smith Junr) bill on Tho Smith Sen'r for 50 -) sent by the Northampton)	0:	3:	9

			L	36:	2:	9
1708	Septr 10	Balla due to Mr Geo: Alsup	L	8:	18:	9
				45:	01:	6

Errors Excepted

Robert Dunkley

Recorded amongst the Records of Richmond County Court the 7th day of May 1713

Test Tho's Dickinson dept Cl Cur

p.73.

Richmond Ss

Pursuant to an ord'r of Court dated the fourth day of June 1712 we whose names are hereunto Subscribed being Sumoned by the Sherriff of this County have mett on the Land of Mr Rawleigh Travers (together with the surveyer of this County) the 28th of June 1712 and did then and there survey and Lay out the said Land according to the best of our Judgments and the Courts order Given under our hands and seals the day and year above written

David Berrick form'n   And Dew
James Suggitt   Mark Tune
Giles Webb   Barth: Rich'd Dodsen
John White   Charles Dodson
Martin Hamon   John Fann
Jobe x Hamon   Symon Taylor

Richmond Ss

Pursuant to the said Order I did together with the said Jury Survey and Lay out the Land of Mr. Raw: Travers, Beginning att a point on Moratico Creek called the Island point and Running up the said Creek according to its severall Courses unto a Gutt that parts this Land and the land of William Acres thence up the said Gutt x x

near the path which leads from Mr George Glascocks to the said Wm
Aeres x x^h, etc.

Surveyed this 4th of June 1712
per Cha: Barber Su'r R: C:

Recorded 2 July 1712

p.73-A

Richmond Ss

Pursuant to an order of Court Dated the second day of aprill 1712
we the subscribers being sumoned by the Sherriff of this County having
mett att the house of Cap't Edward Barrow and being first Swoare
before Mr Austin Brockenbrough did in Company of the surveyor of this
County survey and lay out the Land where Capt Edward Barrow now lives
according to the best of our Judgments Courts order and said Patent
but in one of our Courses having an elder patent presented unto us by
John Mezingo who said we was within the bounds of the said patent,
but by Consent of the said Mozingo and Capt Edward Barrow we proceed-
ed on our Courses without marking untill we were out of the said
patent as we were Informed. Given under our hands and seals this 20th
of May 1712

William x Carter	John Kelly F'm
John x Bowen	John Champe
Thomas x Williams	Hen Bruce
Thomas x Patty	Jacob Simmons
John x Muse	Thomas x James
John x Muse Jun'r	Francis x Williams

Report of Survey. 20 May 1712. Signed by Cha: Barber, Surveyor of
Richmond Co. 719 acres and 126 perches of Land. Adjs land of William
Marks, a Path near Ed: Mozingoes fence, Rappa Run, etc.

Rec. 2 July 1712

p.74

Richmond Ss

In obedience to an order of Court dated the 2d day of May 1711
which is the continuance of sundry orders formerly made in a Difference betwixt William Woodbridge plt and Thomas Glascock defend: we x
x being sumoned by the sherriff x x did in Company of the Surveyor
of this County x x lay out the land of the plt which he Claymes by
a patt: granted to Paul Woodbridge for six hundred acres of Land
dated the 18th November 1664 but were stopt by the defend't he pro-
ducing an elder pattent and alleadging we were within the bounds of

the same which said patent is granted to Cap't Moor Fantleroy for
5350 acres of Land and Dated the 22d of May 1650 part of the land
Contained in the said patent lying above a part below Farnham Creek
which last part Containes 2750 acres by surveying of which both
parties did there alleadge would end the Controversie, which (with
the assistance of the said Surveyor) we did do according to the
Courses and Distances therein Expressed and found that we were not
within the bounds of the same when Thomas Glascook stopt us, after
which we surveyed the lands of the plt aforesd and do find that the
defend't aforesaid hath done damage thereon to the value of five
shillings sterl, Witness our hands and seals this 2d day of june
1711

And: Dew Foreman	Fran: Lucas
James Suggitt	Stanley x Gower
John Gower	Wm x Smith
Richard Bramham	David Berrick
Will Smoot	Mark Tune
Job x Hamon Sen'r	Fra: Yeats

William Thornton Surveyor

Rec. 4 July 1711

p. 74-A

Mr Edward Jones Dr

To tobbo paid James Bidlecom	741
To do rec'ed of John Battin	500
To do rec'ed of Thos Tayler	110
To do rec'ed of Mr Jn'o Alloway	230
To ditto of Rotherick Jones	74
To ditto of Martin Fisher	76
To ditto of Simon Taylor	47
To ditto of James Phillips	4000
To ditto of William Meekes	56
To ditto of Steven Gubton	90
To ditto of Joseph Gold	246
To ditto of Gilbert Cresswell	53
To tobbo rec'ed of Sem Cox	800
To ditto of Mrs Jane Baker	872
To ditto of Rob'n Blewford	15
	- - - -
	8210

(continued)

Edward Jones' Account (continued)

P'r Contra   Cr
By tobbo paid Coll Geo Tayler   721
By ditto of Ed Smith   580
By ditto Richd Jesper   248
By ditto Mrs Glascook   508
By ditto for Clks fees   285
By Leveys an'o 1700   275
By tob'o paid Abra: Goard   204
By tob'o paid Job Hamon   250
By ditto paid Mr Hayes   225
By ditto paid John Muse   62
By ditto paid Mr Hamlett Robinson   650
By ditto James Parsons   115
By paid Edward Jeffereys   2266
By Trouble   1000
By the Ball's of Mr Brockenbroughs acct   953
                                                   - - - -
                                                     8342

Decemb'r the 1st 1712
On persuall of the accounts that was produced to me by John Dalton
and Edward Jones do find the accounts between them as above, without
the Judgment that the said Dalton obtained of the said Jones mentioned in the bill of Complaint, my opinion on the whole matter is that
if Edward Jones make oath that he hath not directly nor Indirectly
received Either of the Estate of William Brockenbrough or of the said
Dalton any tobbo other then what he is made Debtor for in the above
acsount that then he have a Decree according to his prayer in his Bill
                                              G Eskridge

                   Rec. 5 Feb. 1712/13.

p.75.
These Following Interrogations was put to Mr Richard King by William
Barber Charles Barber and Stanley Goar.

First   Mr Richard King you being an antient Man and an old stander
          in these parts, did you Ever hear George Haslook dec'ed
          Grand Father to Tho: Freshwater say that the line which part-
          ed his land and the land of Tho: Robinson dec'ed, went by
          his Clear ground which was under the hill near the said
          Haslooks house

Answer   I being a boarder in Geo: Haslooks house heard him the said
          Haslook say that his line Run by his Clear Ground side where

Interrogations (continued)

stood a small hoghouse

2'dly   Did you Ever hear Tho: Robinson dec'ed say that the land
which Joyned Geo: Haslooks line was his the said Robinsons
land

Answer   Yes I heard him say so severall times for that I was going
to buy the said Land of him

These following Interrogations was put to Mr Richard Branham by
William Barber, Charles Barber and Stanley Goar

First   Mr Richard Branham you being an Antient Man and Son in Law
to Geo: Haslook dec'od did you Ever hear him the said Haslook
say that under the hill where Tho: Freshwater dec'd father
to Tho Freshwater built his house, the line which bounded
his Land and parted it from Tho Robinson land Run

Answer   No, George Haslook was dead before I came into the Countrey

2'dly   did you ever heare Tho Freshwater dec'ed say that he had
built his house near his Line

Answer   Noe

3'rdly   Did you ever hear the said Tho Freshwater dec'ed say he must
ask leave of Mr Sam'll Bayly to Clear into his Land to give
air to his house

Answer   Noe

4'thly   did you never hear Tho Freshwater dec'ed say that the land
wher Charles Barber house now stands was Mr Samll Baylys
Land

Answer   I dont remember anything of it

5'thly   Was it not generally reported among the neighbours that the
land where Charles Barbers house and plantation now is was
Mr Sam'll Baylys Land and before he marryed Mr Robinsons
Daughter it was accot'd the said Robinsons Land

Answer   Yes I have heard the land where the said Barber house stands
called Robinsons neck

Interrogations (continued)

6thly   did you ever hear Geo: Haslock dec'ed say that the spring
         where Tho: Freshwater now Fetches water was Robinsons spring

Answer   Noe

7thly   Did you Ever heare Tho: Freshwater dec'ed call the spring
         where Tho Freshwater now Fetches water Robinsons Spring

Answer   I do think I have heard the said Freshwater call it
         Robinsons Spring

8thly   was not the Spring where Tho: Freshwater now Fetches water
         notoriously knowne by the name of Robinsons Spring

Answer   it was comonly so Called

9thly   did you ever hear Tho Dyes say that in the upper end of the
         Island stood the Corner tree of the Island where he lived

Answer   Yes that I have

These Interrogatories Following was putt to William Lee by Wm Barber
Charles Barber and Stanley Gower

First   Did you ever hear Tho: Freshwater dec'ed say that the house
         where he lived stood Just by his line meaning the land
         where he lived

Answer   Noe

2'dly   Did you ever hear Tho Freshwater dec'ed say that the Land
         where Charles Barbers plantation now is was Mr Tho Robinsons
         or Mr Sam'll Baylys

Answer   Noe

p.76
3'rdly   Did you ever hear Thomas Freshwater dec'ed call the Spring
         where Tho Freshwater now Fetches water Robinsons spring

Answer   No

4th   did you ever hear Francis Goar dec'ed say that on the hill
         side neare the old field where Charles Barbers Plantation

Interrogations (continued)

            now is stood a line tree of his

Answer   Yes I have

5   Did you ever know that mr Fra Goare took away some timber
            which the German Docter gott near Cha: Barbers Q'ter and
            that he said it was on his land

Answer   Yes

p.76.
These Following Interrogateryes was put to Mr David Berrick by
William Barber, Cha: Barber and Stanley Goare.

First   Mr David Berrick you being about Buying a parcell of Land of
          Mr Henry Austin did you hear him the said Austin say that
          the land on the left hand on the path which Leads from Cha:
          Barbers Q'ter to Capt Heales was Francis Goares Land

Answer   Yes

2'dly   have you not heard it Generally Reported that the plantation
          where Charles Barber lives was Mr Sam'll Baylys Land

Answer   Yes

3'rdly   Did you not always hear the spring where Tho Freshwater
          Fetches water Called Robinsons Spring

Answer   No

Mr Richard Branham
Can you tell where stood a hog house belonging to George Haslock
which Mr Richard King mentions
Answer   Just att the mouth of a branch making out of the marsh Just
below the old orchard

Pursuant to an order of Richmond County Court bearing date the fourth
day of Septemb'r 1712 which is the Continuance of a former order of
the said Court dated august the 6th 1712 wee the Subscribers mett on
the 8th day of September 1712 att the house of Capt Charles Barber and
having Sworne such Evidences as were produced before us have taken
and Returned their Depositions as above. Given under our hands the

Misc. Records.

Interrogations (continued)

said Eighth day of September 1712

> Jos Deeke
> John Tayloe
> Edward Jones
> Sam'll Samford

Rec. 5 Feb. 1712/13

p.76-A

The Estate of Mr Sam Cox   Dr

To the ballance of an account takeing Date the 20th) Aprill 1713 stated and settled before the) auditors due to me)	58.	00.	9
To a farther acco't of Expense &c stated also) and allowed by said auditors)	20.	12.	8
To a farther account of Expence and Charges in Great) Brittain as by account of particular am't to)	11.	16.	9
	90.	10.	2

Per Contra

By what of the said Coxe's Estate hath come to my) hands and I Retaine in part satisfaction of) my said Debt)	(left blank)		
By what I have Received out of the Inventory and) Appraisem't said Estate 9276 lb tob att 8) per 100)	37.	02.	1
By one Negro wo:	26.	-	-
By a bill of Exch'a not in the Inventory	10.	05.	-
By one Barrell Tarr		12.	6
By 35 lb tobo of Job Stapleton		02.	10
By 58 lb bread; John Taliaferro 15/ per Ct		08.	9
By 65 lb tob: Will Prootor		05.	3
By 960 lb tob James Strother att 8/	3.	16.	9
By Yett (or thett) due to Benja Deverell	11.	17.	-
L	90:	10.	2

Errors Excepted
per Benj'a Deverell
7'tember 1712

Rec. 6 August 1713.

p.77.

1707   The Estate of Mr Sem Cox   Dr

To Coll Fitzhugh Jugment   16. 10.
To Nich'o Phillips Judgment   17. 11. 3
To John Taliaferro Judgment   6. 02.
To George Downing Judgmt   16. 00. 11
To Capt Nich'o Smith Judgmt   05. 09. 6
To Henry Long   02. 00. 00
To Jervis Taylors Judgment   09. 16. 00
To Benj'a Doverell   90. 10. 2
                                                  - - - - - - -

                                                  lb tob
To Cost on Coll Fitzhughs Judgment   102
To Do Nicho Phillips   061
To Do John Taliaferro   113
To George Downing   57
To Do Nich'o Smith   61
To Do Jervis Tayler   101
To Alex Spence Judgment and Costs   1751
To Doctor Jackson Judgment and Costs   1121
To Edward Turberville Judgm't and Cost   2016
To Thomas Evins Judgmt and Cost   4084
To Robert Taliaferro Do   856
To Henry Berrey Judgmt and Cost   1964
To George Pleyberry Judgment and Cost   814
To Tho Evins Charges per Judgment   63
To George Alsup Do   63
To John Hall digging the grave   50
To Mrs Eliz'a Taliaferro   330
To John Somervell   500
To John Clay   1000
To William Soale   830
To Mark Rymer   270
To Wm Ankram att   -
To Richard Hill Judgment   660
To Will Anderson for Coffin and horse   300
To Clarks Fees   1041
To Daniell McCarty attor: Fees   900
To Grace Fillpin attending Mr Cox in his sickness 100
To James Strother   200
To Expence about the Estate   -
To Commission   -

                    Per Contra   Cr
By the appraisement of 3 negroes L 43 in tob
By Edward Goldmans Noat   L 5
By a bill of Exchange   L 10. 5

                    (continued)

Estate of Mr. Sem Cox (continued)

By a barrell of Tarr   12/6
by 58 lb bread Jn'o Taliafero   8/9   tob att

By the Inventory and appraisement of the said Estate
    in tobacco   29064
By tobaco Rec'ed of Thomas White   16589
By   Do   Sam'll Hoyles   1613
By   Do   Wm Hainett   650
By   Do   Robt Inglish   880
By   Do   George Brenaugh   339
By   Do   Rich'd Perell   460
By   Do   James Higgins   590
By   Do   John Corbin   500
By   Do   Thomas Norman   229
By   Do   Mr Hawkins   250
By   Do   Jos Simmans   640
By   Do   Steven Sebastian   150
By   Do   John Spencer   050
By   Do   James Strother   210
By   Do   Job Stapleton   035
By   Do   William Proctor   065
By   Do   James Strother   960
By   Do   George Phillips   100

Errors Excepted per George Downing
Benj'a Deverell

Recorded 6 August 1713

1710   The Estate of Mr Sem Cox Dec'ed Dr to Benj'a Deverell Vizt

To an account in Court the ball is   L   58: 0: 0
To Thomas Pannell going to Northumberland
    to serch the Records   1: 2: 6
To 12 gallons Sider   00: 12: 0
To Edward Turbervile making bonds   00: 15: 0
To Mr Owen Jones for his funerall 500 lb tob
    att 8/ per 100 lb   02: 00: 0
To 1 lb Candles   00: 00: 9
To John Davis Sherriff a per accot 1682 tob   7: 10: 0
To Rum att the last appraisemt   0: 01: 10
To Marg't Taliafero a Gold Ring when she
    acknowledged the land   1: 00: 00
To a boat lent Mr Coxe and not Returned   4: 00: 00
To Mr McCarty 1000 lb Tob   4. 00. 00
- - - - - - -
79: 3: 5

(continued)

Miso. Records.

Estate of Mr. Sem Cox (continued)

      Per Contra
By what has come to my hands before what is paid Viz't
by a Bill of Exch'a   10: 5: 0
by a barrell of Tarr   -   12: 6
by 35 lb tob Job Stapleton   -   2. 10
by 58 lb bread Mr Jn'o Taliafero att 15 per Cent   -   8: 9
by 62 lb tob Will Proctor   -   5: 3
by what I have had out of the Estate that was
    appraised vizt: in tob: and 9276 att 8/
    per 100   37: 2: 1
                          -- -- -- -- -- --
                                                                 48: 16: 5
By abated for acco't of the boate   - 10: 0
                          -- -- -- -- -- --
                                                                 49: 6: 5
                Ball L 29: 17: 0
      Errors Excepted this 30th March 1711
                   per Benj'a Deverell

            Rec. 6 August 1713.

p.78

Richmond Ss
Pursuant to an order of Court we the Subscribers have Examined the
within account of Benj'a Deverell agt the Estate of Sem Cox dec'ed
and find the said account Rightly stated x x Wittness our hands this
17th day of May an'o Dom 1711
                  Fra Slaughter
                  Jonath Gibson

            Rec. 6 August 1713

p.78-A.
Octob'r 1711   The Estate of Mr Sem Cox dec'd is Debt'r to Benj'a
Deverell for sundry charges in Great Brittaine vizt

To advice in Bristoll Relating to Mr Sem Cox's will   0: 5: 0
To horse hire and Expence in Journeying to London   7: 19: 3
To Cash paid att Doctors Comons for proving the said
    Cox's Will   3: 12: 6
                           -- -- -- -- -- --
                                                                11. 16: 9
          Errors Excepted per Benj'a Deverell

           Recorded 6 Aug. 1713.

Misc. Records

July the 2: 1698
                    Mr Richard Metcalfs Estate   Dr
                                                                  Tobo
To paid Mr Bertrand for Funerall Sermon   1000
fine Coffin   0400
paid M'r Henry Seagar for Rumm &c   2787
Paid Doct'r Paul Micou for his attendance on the
    said dec'ed   1500
Balla of his owne account amt 29: 18: 6 in tobo
    att 10 per Cent   5985
Receiving of 4193 a 10 per Cent   0419
Levys Quittrents, Clks fees Sher &c   -
                                                             - - - -
                                                               12091

Articles Disallowed by us in Capt Barrows account

Two 60 gall'o Casks of boyled Sider   1500
To mourning cloaths for the Children and bought of
    Young Smith and Blanch flower   2000
Wheat meat Butter Sugar and other Expences suitable
    to Occasion att the funerall of said dec'ed
    and appraism't   5000
Paid Doctor Paul Micou for Cureing Gilbert Metcalfs
    leg   0500
Cloaths and other necessaries for children bought
    of Nath Davis   51: 07: 9
Charges of Law Suite and my trouble   12. 10. 0
10 per Cent of 542: 10: 6 paying and Receiving   54: 05. 0

                        Per Contra   Credit
By a list of Debts due to the Estate Listed in the
    Inventory   4193
Cropps made the yeare of Mr Metcalfs decease   -
10 hhds of tobo a Nominy plantation amounting to
    neat 5182   5182
By 2 do att Rapp'a plantation N't   1100
By paid Mr Bertrand att do plantation   1000
                                                             - - - -
                                                               11485

Richmond Ss
Pursuant to an order of Court Dated the 3d day of June 1713 we the
subscribers have mett at the house of Mr Edward Barrow the 15th day
of the same month and having audited all the accounts produced by
Comp'lt and Resp'o and stated and adjusted the same as it is herewith

Exhibited to your Worships we have disallowed severall articles
because they were Debts Contracted by Anne Barrow one of the Resp't
in her widdowhood therefore we think the orphans are not Chargable
with them and some other charges which were a part of the Estate
not Inventoryed and appraised and others that we think no legall
Charge &c. Vizt: for mourning Cloaths and Cloaths &c Bought of Nath:
Davis and syder and wheat meat x x"

                              signed   John Tayloe
                                        Austin Brockenbrough
                                        Jos: Belfield
                                        James Ingo

                      Rec. 5 Aug. 1713.

p.79. Power of Atty. 11 Aug.1713. "Benjamin Deverell agent to Mr
John Beacher and Comp'a Merch'ts in Bristoll late of Richmond County
in the Colony of Virginia" to George Eskridge Gent to collect debts.
Wit:
James Strother   signed   Benj'a Deverell
Joseph Strother
                      Rec. 2 Dec. 1713

p.79-A. Power of Atty. 24 Nov. 1713. "James Jackson of Belfast in
the Kingdom of Ireland" te "my Son in Law John Sloss of Belfast"
to manage er dispose of real estate "in the County of Richmond in
the Northern Neck of Virginia, all which I hold x x which said
patents were granted to Andrew Jackson my Brother late of Lancaster
County in Virginia aforesd Clerk dec'd to whom I am heir"
Wit:
Rich'd Kelsick Jun'r   signed   James Jackson
John Parrett
Henry Collin
Thomas Smith

Statement in Latin by Ja: Perry (Jacobus Perry) Notary Pub.

Proved in Richmond Co. Court 3 March 1713/14 by oaths of John Parrett
and Thomas Smith

Further proved in Richmond Co. Court 7 April 1714 by oath of Richard
Kelsick Junior.

p.80-A

Richmond Ss
Pursuant to an order of Court dated the 8th of Ap'll: 1714 we the
subscribers have mett and Considered the accounts of Mr Robert
Singleton and John Pound Jun'r and do find the Ball'a due to the
said Robt Singleton 1418 pds of tobo given under our hands this 10th
day of Ap'll 1714
Detail of a/c follows.   signed   Will Barber
                                                  Cha: Barber
                                                  Robert Tomlin

p.80-A

Richmond Ss
An Execution Issued upon an order of this County Court dated the 4th
day of July 1706 ag't the body of John Browne att the suite of Martin
Sherman for four hundred and ninety pounds of tobacco and Costs, and
was Returned the 21st day of July 1714 in these words: Richmond Sct
the above named John Browne is not to be found within my Baylywick
per John Doyle Sub Sherr

p.80-A
                    " August the 4th 1714
The Deposition of John Alton aged 20 or thereabouts being sworne saith
that the first day of Aprill in the yeare 1709 came on board the ship
Elizabeth Cap't John Hodge Comander, then Riding att anchor in the
Kingdom of North brittain, a Lad named John Browne who the day after
his coming on board, Indented with the said Cemander to serve him or
his assigns seven yearse, as the Depon't hath often heard the said
Com'dr and the saylers and the said John Browne himselfe say, and that
he was always reckoned a servant for seven yeares to the best of the
Depon'ts knowledge and further saith not
                                          Signum
                                    John x Alton "

p.81.
July 1714   The Estate of Mrs Patience Cleve dec'ed   Dr
To a Coffin   00: 12: 0
To 2: Gallon Rum att the funrall of the dec'ed   00: 12: 0
To a young hogg   00: 07: 0
To my trouble in Burying and att the appraisement
   of the dec'ed   00: 05: 0
                                                      - - - - - - -
                                                        01: 16: 0
                    Errors Excepted
                        per Henry Bruce

                Rec. 7 July 1714

pages 81*A. 82. 82-A. 83. Tobacco accounts of Mr. John Jones. 1708 to 1712. Recorded 6 October 1714.

p.83-A

Worshippfull Gentlemen

Mr William Thornton haveing signified to me that he Desires to Lay down his Survey'rs place and has Recommended Cap't Edw'd Barrow to be a fitt and proper person to Execute the same and being Informed by others of his abillity in that Siense

I doe hereby Depute Constitute and appoint the said Cap't Edw'd Barrow Surveyor of the Upper Presinques of Richmond County In the stead and place of Mr William Thornton untill further orders x Given under my hand and seal this 18 day of March 1714

Wm Buckner Su'r Gen'll

To the Gentlemen of the
Court of Richmond
      Ex'a   Rec. 6 April 1715

p.83-A.
"Shipped by the Grace of God in good order and well Conditioned by Peter Kippax in and upon the good Ship called the Sarah and Hannah whereof is Master under God for this present Voyage Wm Finch and now riding at Anchor in Rappa: River and by God's Grace bound for London to say One hhd of Stem'd Tobacco being marked and numbered as in the Margent (P.K. 11-4) and are to be delivered in the like good Order and well Conditioned at the aforesaid Port of London (the Danger of the Seas only excepted) unto Mr Richard Lee or to his Assigns, he or they paying Freight for the said Goods at Six pds per Tunn with Primage and Avarage accustomed. In Witness whereof the Master or Purser of the said ship hath affirmed to three Bills of Lading, all of this Tenor and Date, the one of which three Bills being accomplished the other two to stand void, And so God send the good ship to her desired Port in safety, Amen"
Dated in Virginia 9'br: 4th 1713.
" Quaintity Rec'd Quality unknown per W Finch "

Rec. 6 April 1715.

p.84. Power of Atty. 3 July 1714. Thos. Monteith of Glasgow to Thomas White "in the Parish of Hannover Richmond Countie Virg'a" to collect debts. Signed by Thomas Monteith. Witnessed by Mathew Thornton and John Eliot. Proved in Richmond Co. Court 2 June 1715 by oaths of both witnesses.

p.84. Indenture. 11 Aug. 1715. Nicholas Muse planter of one part and William Woodward of the other part. Woodward agrees "to bind my Son Thomas Woodward unto Nicholas Muse and Mary Muse his Wife or the longeth liver of them untill he come to the Age of Twenty One Yeares x x the said Thomas Woodward being eaight Yeares onto the 14 day of Febuary before the date hereof". Muse agrees among othings "to learn him to read the Bible and also to learn him the Trade of a Carpenter and Cooper in the last Two Yeares that he hath to serve".
Wit:

Richard Claxton   signed   William Woodward
James Sandie   Nicholas x Muse

Rec. 7 Sept. 1715.

Note: Difficult for Muse, who could not write while Woodward could.
                                                                    B.F.

p. 84-A. Indenture. 1 Aug. 1715. Thomas Thornton of Cittenborn Par. Rd. Co., Carpenter, on the one part and Mary Williamson, widow of the same Par. and Co., on the other part. Mary Williamson binds over her Daughter Mary Williamson an apprentice and servant to Thornton until she "bee full Eighteen Years old she being now five years of Age". Thornton agrees among other things that "Susanna Wife of the afore-said Tho shall indeavour to instruct and teach the said Servant to read in her Mother tongue and at the Expiration of the said terme which shall bee in the Year of O'r Lord God One thousand Seven hundred Twenty Eight to bestow on her a compleat Suite of Cloths fit and decent for one of her Condition"
Wit: Signed thus:
Henry Bruce   Mary x William (seal)
Mathew Thornton
                                Rec. 5 Oct. 1715.

p.85. Duplicate of above signed by Thomas Thornton.

p.85-A

Richmond Ss/
              To the Wo'pfull the Court
The humble Peticon of William Carter sheweth/
That your Pet'r last February Court was security for Eliz'a Williams's Admon of her husband John Williams Estate, which upon the appraism't thereof amounted to Four Pounds Four shillings
That your Pet'r hath already paid upon Acc'tt of the said Estate as by

Account here in Court ready to be produced may appear 1305 lb of
Tobacco

> Your Pet'r therefore humbly prayes
> that the Wo'pps would be pleased to
> discharge him from his aforesaid
> Security Ship
>   And he shall pray &c

P'd to Cap't Nich'o Smith on Acc'tt of Cap't Daniell McCarty	561
P'd to Jos: Carpenter (possibly Jas: Carpenter)	600
P'd to Mr Beckwith	50
P'd Sec'ys Fees	40
	1251
Do to more Clerks Fees	54
	1305

Rec. 1 Feb 1715/16

p.86. Power of Atty. 11 Jan. 1715/16. Thomas Wills of the City of
Bristol, mercht., to John Bagge "of Essex County in Virginia Clk" to
collect debts in Virginia "and farther whereas the said Constituent
hath received powers and orders by letters bearing Date at Bristoll
the 20th of July One thousand Seven hundred and fifteen from Mess'rs
Benjamin Coole, George Whitehead and Richate Coole (sic) March'ts in
Bristoll to buy a certain quantity of Tobacco and to pay for the
same by Bills of Exchange". Rev. Bagge authorized to buy the tobo
and draw the Bills of Exchange.
Wit: signed   Thom's Wills
Jn'o Elliott
Thomas Commery

Proved in Richmond Co. Court 5 April 1716 by oaths of the two
witnesses.

p.87. Power of Atty. 29 May 1716. John Spicer of Richmond Co. Gent. to
Daniell Gaines of Essex Co to transact business, particularly to "make
over unto Fransis Smith of the County of Essex (according to the tenor
of my bond to the said Smith) two hundred acres of Land being part of
my tract of land lying in the County of Essex"
Wit:
John Berryman   signed   Jn'o Spicer
Wil Robinson
Tho: Clark   Rec. 6 June 1716.

p.88. Drawing. A surveyor's plat marked "December the 12th 1701
Surveyed for the Davenports (Mr George Mr Wm and Mr Fortunatus) A
tract of Land Containing 1000 Acres Sittuate Lying and being in
Richmond County on the Northward Side of the main Swamp of Morattico
Creek". Adjs land of Richard Merryman, etc. "Surveyed and Divided into
three Equal Parts by me"

                                signed   Edwin Conway

"Att a Court held for Richmond County the second Day of May 1716
Aut the Motion of George Davenport this survey made by M'r Edwin
Conway is Ordered to be Recorded
                                Test M: Beckwith Cl Cur "

p.88-A.

Richmond Co Ss/
To all Christian People to whom these presents shall come I Francis
Williams of the parrish of Sittenbyrne in the County aforesaid Planter
x x for divers good causes x x but more Especially for good Service
done and performed by Hannah Charlton unto me Have Manumitted,
Released and sett free x x Catherine Charleton Mary Charlton and
John Charlton of and from all and all manner of Service and Vassallage
whatsoever x x". Dated 1 August 1716.
Wit: signed   Francis x Williams
Jno Davis Jun'r
Mathew x Beane   Rec. 1 Aug. 1716

p.89. Indenture. 5 Dec. 1716. Sarah Phillips, widow and Relict of
James Phillips late of the parish of Sittenbourne, Richmond County
of the one part and Marmaduke Beckwith of the same Co. of the other
part. Mrs. Phillips binds her son, James Phillips, as an apprentice
and servant to Beckwith until he arrives at age of 21, "he being
Nine Years of Age the twenty fourth Day of November last".
Wit: signed   Sarah Phillips
Jno Pound Jr   Marmaduke Beckwith
                              Rec. 5 Dec. 1716.

p.89. Power of Atty. 24 March 1715/16. Joseph Hincks of the County
of Chester, mariner, for self and Company of the ship Dalphin (sic)
to Master William Fantleroy of Richmond Co to collect debts in Va and
Maryland.
Wit: signed   Joseph Hincks
Jn'o Tarpley
John Hipkings   Rec. 5 Dec. 1716

Misc. Records

p.90. Power of Atty. 1 Nov. 1716. Edmund Jenings Esq'r., agent and
attorney for the Right Honourable Catherine, Lady Fairfax, Proprietor
of the Northern Neck in Virginia, to George Eskridge of Westmorland
Co., Gent., to receive Quit Rents, etc.
Wit: signed   E Jenings
Robert Jones
Tho: Thorne   Rec. 6 Dec. 1716.

p. 90-A.

Andrew Laughinghouse	Dr.
To 8 yds Druggett at 60	480
To 6 yds Searge at 40	240
To 2 yds of Linning at 20	50
To 1 pr Stockings at	30
To 5 hanks moheir at 10	50
To 2 Night Caps at	40
To 1 hatt at	70
To 10 skeins of thrid	10
To 9 yds Coll'd Fustion at 24	216
To 11 yds 1/4 Dowlas at 40	450
To 4 yds 1/2 Druggett at 60	270
To 1 yd and 3/4 Linning at 40	70
To 1 yd 1/4 fustian	25
To 1 hank of Silk at	30
To 5 doz: vest buttons at 20	100
To 3 doz: Coat Do: 20	60
To 2 hanks of Moheir	20
To 1 p: Gloves at 40	40
To 1 yd 1/4 Linning at 30	30
To 1 pr Wosted hose	100
To 1 point of Rum (sic)	10
To 1 qt: Do at	20
To paid the Taylor	200
To 1 fine Shurt	300
To 1 Mare	1200
To 1 gold Ring	900
To your bill paid James Butler	600
To your Com'dations	1000
	- - - -
	6611
	452
	- - - -
To the Ballance due	6159

(continued)

Misc. Records

Andrew Laughinghouse's Account (continued)

Per Contra   Cr.
By 3 bushells of salt   144
By 1 pr Wom's shoes   48
By 2 hanks of Moheir   20
                                                                    - - -
                                                                      212
By 6 yds of Searge Returned at 40 per yd   240
                                                                    - - -
                                                                      452

Errors Excepted
per me Eliz: Seale

Att a Court Continued and held for Richmond County the sixth Day of
June 1717
Eliz'a Seale in open Court made oath that this Account is Just and
true and that she never received any satisfaction for the same, but
what Creditt is given for and at her Motion it is admitted to Record
Test M: Beckwith Cl Cur

p.91

Thomas Paton Feb: 10th 1713/14   Dr.

To 1 Gun   500
To 1 Peticoat Silk   200
To 4 yds of Stript Lin'g 30   120
To 1 pr fine wost'd hose Wom's   60
To your Diet   100
                                                                    - - -
                                                                      980

Errors Excepted per
me Eliz: Seale

Rec. 6 June 1717.

p.91. John Camock about 40 years old upon his Oath saith that he had
an old bagg in his possession at his Mothers house a Considerable
time in which he kept his Writings and also a Gold Ring in a paper
which Bagg was so kept by him in a Chest wherein there was a parcell
of Linnen Containing - yards and other things: that the said Chest
was broken open and severall things taken out particularly the said
Linnen, Bagg and Ring: that M'r George Uriell having lost an hatt
att the same time when the before mentioned things were lost told him

that if ever he discovered his lost Goods it would be by means of his
said Hatt which was very remarkable having a Notch cutt in the brim
of it and some other particular Mark under the hatband; That after
the robbing of his Mothers house he heard her Complain of loosing
some Camlett out of her Chest that he hath soon the said Camlett
before and to the best of his Judgement it was much like the Camlett
now produced by Elizabeth Furlong which she had of Fargus Maden the
Prisoner: that the aforesaid Ring new lost was stollen twice from him
before, one time from him before, one time he found it in the Prisoners possession and another time in the possession of a Woman which
he was suspected to keep Company with and was then taken out of the
same bagg (now produced) wherein it was when last lost; That upon
your Depon'ts asking the Prisoner where the hatt was which he were
on Sunday he went and fetcht the hatt now produced and delivered it
to the Deponent.

Note: Could there possibly be a more perfect example of our Colonial
simplicity of mind than this item ? In this hard day and time attempt
to steal a conspicious article of wearing apparel and then wear it in
the most conspicious place that could be selected. Not to mention
having to listen to the Episcopal Morning Service while adorned with
the stolen 'hatt'.
    Now I've never tried to steal anything from a suspicious old
lady. God Forbid ! - there are cheaper ways of earning a dishonest
living. But I have been an innocent bystander when old ladies were,
or thought they were robbed. Stupid honesty never appeared in so
glamrous a light as on these occasions.   B.F.

p. 91-A. Mary Green about 17 upon her oath saith that she lived at
M'rs Cammocks when the Hatt now produced, which she particularly
knows by a Notch cutt in the edges of it, was bought by George
Uriell, that it was in a chest at her said Mistresses, that to the
best of her rememberance about a Day or two before the house was
robbed she saw the said Hatt in the aforesaid Chest, where it usually
lay.

p.91-A. Eliz'a Furlong about 29 upon her oath said that she lett
the Prisoner have two Yards of red serge, for which he promised her
three Yards of Cloth Serge and afterwards brought her three Yards
of Camlett now produced, and told her he had it of Cap't Smith for
Cloth Serge

p.91-A. Doot'r Paul Micou aged about 50 upon his Oath saith that
sometime since he sold a parcell of Camlett to M'rs Cammock, that
likewise he sold some of the same unto one Tho's Petros in Essex;

that he gott a peice of the said Camlett from said Petros upon
Comparing whereof with the said Camlett Exchanged by the Prisoner
with said Eliz'a Furlong and now produced he verily believes it to be
some of the sd Camlett sold to said M'rs Camook: that John Cammook
sometime since haveing lost a Gold Ring, and suspecting the Prisoner
and a Woman in Essex County who he was suspected to keep Company
with, applyed himself to the Depon't for a Warrant to search, which
being granted and the said Womans Chest search't therein was found
the said Ring, which she Confest was given to her by the Prisoner.

Note: This is a suggestion for genealogists. No more than a mere
suggestion. There was a man named Cammook who settled in Maine and
who was said to have been a nephew of the Earl of Warwick. This Mrs.
Cammook appears to have been the mother in law of Dr. Paul Micou
and to have been the wife of Warwick Cammook. This combination of
names, to which my attention was called by Miss Elizabeth Hawes
Ryland, seems worthy of a search by at least one of the many descendants of the old Huguenot doctor. According to this he was born about
1664 and therefore must have been eye witness to some horrible and
bloody things before he came here to peacefully squabble over camlett
and notched hats, and to collect accounts from the widows and orphans
of his deceased patients. He does not seem to have been paid for the
only cure we actually have record of, that being of Gilbert Metcalf's
leg. See page 54 this volume.   B. F.

p. 91-A. (Note: Now we have Francis' identification of the "Hatt".
Conclusive to say the least. B.F.)
Francis Stern aged about 15 upon his oath saith that the Hatt now
produced he verily believes was belonging to M'r Uriell, which he is
induced to believe by reason that he waited upon him when he kept
Store at M'rs Camooks and often brushed the same, and particularly
took Notice of its being motheaten under the hat band.

Records of Richmond County, Virginia. Court Order Book No. 6. p.249,
6th October 1714.

Maden   Upon the petition of Fergus Maden against Marg't
  vs   Camook for his Freedome Corne and cloathes accord-
Camook   ing to Law, the said Fergus Maden having made oath
Extr Estate   in Court, that he had rec'ed no more then three
15th 9'ber 1714   barrells of Indian Corne and five yards of ozen-
                     brize in part thereof, Judgment is thereupon
granted him against the said Margarett Camook for the sume of thirteene shillings and four pence or the value thereof in goods and a
well fixt muskettor fusee of the value of twenty shillings and Costs
als Ex'o.

                       (See next page)

Richmond County, Virginia, Records. Court Order Book No. 6, page 274.
6 April 1715.

Maiden   Whereas Fargus Maiden was by warrant of Nicholas Smith Gent
Whipt   one of the Justices of this Court com'itted to the County
              Goal on suspition of stealing severall things from John
Camook and being now brought before his Majestys Justices here present,
Upon hearing the evidence of John Camook, Mary Green, Elizabeth Furlong, Paul Micou and Francis Sterne against the said Fergus Maiden
and what he had to say in his defence, are of opinion that he is
guilty of petty Larceny, and it being sufficiently proved he is a
person of evill fame, It is thereupon ordered that the Sherriff forthwith carry him to the Com'on whipping post and give him thirty nine
lashes on his bair back well laid on, and after haveing soe done to
remain'd him to prison where he shall continue without bail or main
prise untill the next Court, and that he shall have other thirty nine
lashes, and then remain in Goal untill he give such security for his
good behaviour as the Court shall approve of.

Ibid. page 276. 7 April 1715.

Maiden discharged   Whereas an Order past Yesterday for the whipping
giveing security   of one Fargus Maiden for Petty Larceny as also
                      that he should remain in Prison without bail or
mainprise untill the next Court, and then to be whipt again, and after
that to remain in Goal, untill he should give security for his good
behaviour, but the Court upon mature deliberation had, are of opinion
that he has been sufficiently punished for the Crime aforesaid, It is
therefore ordered that upon the said Fargus Maidens giveing security
according to the aforesaid order, the Sherrif release him out of
Custody.

Note: Justices this day
John Tarpley, Edward Barrow, Nicholas Smith, Wm Thornton and Richd.
Taliaferro.

Misc. Records. p.92
Att a Court held for Richmond County this Sixth Day of Aprill 1715
                              Present
        John Tarpley   )   Wm Thornton   )
        Edward Barrow   )   John Tayloe   ) Gent Justices
        Nicholas Smith)   Rich'd Taliaferro)

James Blackabee this Day filed his Bill in Chancery and therein sett
forth that he is seized of 250 acres of Land x x and that sundry
persons pretending an Interest in the same threaten to bring his

Title into Question as soon as some aged persons now liveing are dead
and therefore for preservation of the Evidence of his Title prayes a
Com'ission to be directed to some Gentlemen to take the Examinations
and Depositions of his Witnesses and the same to be returned to this
Court that they may remain among the Records thereof for a perpetual
Evidence x x.

                              Copy Test
                                        M: Beokwith   Cl Cur
p.92

Richmond Co: Ss/
The Exeou'oon of the within Comi'con appeares in the schedule hereunto annexed

                              Jn'o Tarpley
                              Tho: Griffin
                              Tho: Glascook

p.92.

Richmond Co: Ss/
The Examination and Deposition of Robert Christopher aged 63 years
of age or thereabouts taken before us whose names are hereunto
Subscribed and Seales affixed by Virtue of a Com'ission out of his
Majesties Court of Chancery for the County aforesaid unto us directed
Interrog:
Did you know one Robert Leatherland late of this County and where-
abouts he lived
Answer
Yes I did know Robert Leatherland but did not know where his habita-
tion was
Interrog:
Did you know of any Children he had, and what were their Names
Answer
I knew one James Leatherland who was reputed the son of the aforesaid
Robert Leatherland
Interr: 3.
Was he the Eldest Son of the aforesaid Robert Leatherland
Answer
Yes, the Eldest Son, and all that I know of
Interr.4.
Was that James Leatherland the same person of whom James Blackabee
purchased the Land he now lives on
Answ'r
Yes I believe he was. I know no other that laid any Claim
Interr 5
How long since is it you saw the aforesaid James Leatherland
Answ'r
It is near a twelve month since I saw him

Interr: 7.
Of what age do you think the aforesaid James Leatherland may be
Answ'r:
As well as I remember he told me he was about Thirty

Aprill the 30th 1715
By vertue of the Com'iscon hereunto annexed the above Examination
and Deposition was taken before us
                       Wittness Our hands and Seales
                              Jn'o Tarpley
                              Tho: Griffin
                              Tho: Glascock

p.92-A

Richmond Co: Ss/
The Examination and Deposition of Anne Christopher Aged 54 yeares of
Age (sic) taken before us whose names are hereunto Subscribed x x.

Interr: 1
Did you know one Robert Leatherland late of this County and where-
abouts he lived
Answ'r
Yes I knew him, for it was said he marryed my Sister by the Mother
side and they lived together as man and wife, and his habitation was
sometimes att John Motts and sometimes att Batt: Woods
Interr: 2:
Did you know of any children he had, and what were their names
Answ'r
Yes I knew a Girle he had named Ann that he had by his Wife before
he marryed my Sister, and another Boy I heard he had, but do not
know his Name, which Boy as the aforesaid Robert Leatherland writ my
Father dyed as they were goeing upp to Stafford, and one James
Leatherland which he had by my Sister, as she said
p.93.
Interr: 3
Was the said James Leatherland the Eldest Son of the aforesaid Robert
Leatherland
Answ'r.
Yes, he was the Eldest Son to my knowledge, after he writt my Father
word that his Son dyed goeing to Stafford, and I never knew or heard
of any other son he had
Interr: 4.
Do you know James Leatherland of whom James Blackabee purchased the
Land whereon he now lives, to be the Son of the aforesaid Robert
Leatherland who married your Sister
Answ'r
Yes I know him to be the same, for he alwayes came to see me, and
allwayes called me Aunt.

Misc. Records.

Interr: 5.
How long since is it you saw the aforesaid James Leatherland
Answ'r:
About this time twelve months
Interr: 6
Of what age do you think the aforesaid James Leatherland may be
Answ'r
I think nigh Forty
                                    Aprill 30th 1715
By vertue of the Com'icon hereunto annexed the above Examina'con and
deposition was taken before us. Wittness Our hands and seales
                                    Jno. Tarpley
                                    Tho: Griffin
                                    Tho: Glascock

Att a Court Continued and held for Richmond County the 7th Day of
July 1715
The within Depositions of Robert Christopher and Ann Christopher as
also the Order of Court hereto annexed are ordered to be Recorded
                            Test   M Beckwith   Cl Cur

p.93

Att a Court held for Richmond County the seventh Day of September 1715

William,Simms this Day filed his Bill in Chancery and therein sett
forth that he is seized of a Tract of Land in Sittenburn parish in
this County the bounds whereof are in a great measure decayed and
worn out, and there being severall aged persons now liveing who well
know the antient bounds thereof and not being likely long to live, if
they should dye before their Testimony given he and his Posterity
might hereafter be in danger of loosing all or a great part of his
said Land for want thereof: Therefore he prayed an Order to be directed to some persons of Creditt and Repute to take the Examination and
Depositions of his Witnesses and the same together with this order
to be returned to the next Court to the end the same may be entered
upon the Records thereof, there to remain in perpetual rememberance
Whereupon it is Ordered that Edward Barrow, Nicholas Smith, John
Tayloe and James Ingo or any three of them doe meet sometime between
this and the next Court upon the said Simms aforesaid Land and take
the Examination of all such persons upon Oath as shall by him be
produced before them to give their Evidence relateing to the said
bounds x x and that they return such Examinations x to the next
Court x x.
                        Copy Test   M: Beckwith   Cl Cur

p.93-A

Richm'd Ss/ October 5th 1715
Pursuant to an Order of this Court dated the seventh day of September
last wee Edward Barrow, Nich'o Smith John Tayloe and James Ingo have
this day mett at the house of William Sims and taken the Deposition
of John Mews and William Carter as followeth

John Mews aged Eighty two Yeares Deponing saith That old Roger
Cloathworker about three years after he sold the Land now in possession of William Sims to James Browne Sen'r the said Cloathworker went
with him the Deponent to the head of a Branch now known by the Name
of William Sims Spring Branch and showed him a line of Marked Trees
from the head of the aforesaid Branch to the Back Line of said Cloath-
workers Land and told the said Deponent that Line was the Bounds of
the Land he sold to the said James Browne Sen'r and further saith not

                                                    mark
                                        John   M   Mews

Note: 1715
        82
       - - -
       1633 That's right far back. B.F.

p.94.
William Carter aged Sixty two Yeares deponeing saith that James
Browne Jun'r told him the Depon't that at the head of a branch now
knowne by the name of William Sims Spring Branch and show'd him a
Sorewey Oak tree and from thence to the Road, to a White Oak, and
that the said James Browne said that was the Line of the Land that
his Father bought of Roger Cloathworker, and further saith not

                                                    mark
Edw'd Barrow   William   W   Carter
Nich'o Smith
Jn'o Tayloe
James Ingo

p.94
Richm'd Ss/
In Obedience to an Order of Court dated the second day of May 1716
Wee x x did in Company with Capt. Charles Barber Surveyor, Did Survey
x x the Land of Henry Burdett due to him the said Burdett by a Deed
from Mr William Fantleroy Dated June 1673 the 3 Day. Given under our
hands and Seals 9 day of May 1716

Richard Bramham	Thomas x Freshwater	James Ingo
John faver	Evan x Thomas	Will Sisson
David Berrick	Austin Brookenbrough foreman	George Gaydon
New'n Brookenbrough	Martin x Sherman	John Seaman

p.94. Surveyor's Statement. 8 May 1716. By Charles Barber, Surveyor, re. land of Henry Burdett, 534 acres 60 perches, adj. land Mr. Wm Smith, etc. See foregoing entry.

p.94-A. Power of Atty. 24 April 1717. John Watkinson of Liverpoole, mariner, to "my trusty Friend Mr Moore Fantleroy of the County of Richmond" to collect debts.
Wit: signed   John Watkinson
Jno Tarpley
                         Rec. 4 Sept 1717.

p.95
                         Sepber the 4 1717
Robert Rymer cheife meate of the Charfild Snow aged thirty three yeares Doth heare make oath before this Cort of Justis that on Saturday Night the 24d of Aug't 1717 a Flatt belonging to George Warton Drove from the said Snow by Distress of Weather with sundry Goods to the vallue of 7 lb or thereabouts she halling out heer fore thaught by thatt Reason was Lost
                                       Robert Rymer

sworn to in Richmond County Court the 4th Day of September 1717 by Robert Rymer and ordered to be Recorded
                         Test   M: Beckwith   Cl Cur.

p.95.
                         Sep'ber the 4'd 1717
Peter Mishine Gunor of the said Snow Aged forty foure Yeares Doth heare make Oath before this Court of Justis that on Saturday Night the 24'd Aug't 1717 a Flatt belonging to George Warton Drove from the said Snow by Distress of Weather with sundry Goods to the Vallue of 7 lb or thereabouts she halling out hur fore thought and by that Reason was Lost
                              Peter   x   Mishim

                  Rec. 4 Sept 1717.

p.95. Deed of Gift. 4 Sept 1717. "Gilbert Metcalf of the Parish of North Farnham in the County of Richmond Gent for x Naturall Love and affection which I have and bear unto my loveing Wife Susan Metcalf and Anne Fauster her Daughter x x Have Given x x unto the said Anne

Fauster from and after the Decease of the said Gilbert Metcalfe and
Susan his Wife without Issue of their Bodyes x x two negroes named
Peter and Judith x"
Wit: signed   Gilbert Metcalf
Jn'o Metcalfe
John Bramham   Rec. 2 Oct. 1717

p.95-a. Power of Atty. 25 July 1717. "John Becher Thomas Longman
William Attwood and Innys all of the Citty of Bristoll Merchants
and Rachaell Deverill of the same Citty Widdew Relict and Exer'x of
the last Will and Testament of Benjamin Deverill late of Virginia
Merchant dec'ed" to "Mr Richard Johnson of York River in Virginia
aforesaid and Mr Samuell Skinker of Rappahannock River in Virginia"
to "receive of and from Samuell Mathews of Rappahannock River" and
other persons in Va., accounts contracted for or transacted by the
said Benjamin Deverill decd.
Wit: signed   John Becher
John Darracott   Thos Longman
John Twitt   Wm Attwood
Richard x Shinglar   Jers Innys
Mosley Battaley   Rachall Deverill

Proved in Richmond Co. Court 2 Oct 1717 by oaths of John Darracott
and Mosley Battaley.

p.96. Deed of Gift. 5 Dec. 1717. Margaret Story of Richmond Co. to
"my son James Story" various personal possessions including two gold
rings.
Wit: signed   Margrett Storey
John Merton Jun'r
Alvin Mountjoy   Rec. 2 April 1718.

p.96*A. Power of Atty. 12 Nov. 1717. "Sarah Walter of the Citty of
Bristoll Widow Executrix of the last Will and Testament of my Husband
Jn'o Walter late of the same Citty Mariner Dec'd" to "my sone Rob't
Walter of the Citty of Bristoll Marriner" to receive a/cs from Joseph
Bayley Planter of Va. and others.
Wit: signed   Sarah Walter
John Thomas
Israell Howell
John Williams

Proved in Richmond County Court 2 April 1718 by oaths of Jno Thomas
and John Williams.

p.97. "To all Christian People to whom these presents shall come I
Paul Micou of Essex County in Virginia send Greeting in Our Lord God
Everlasting, Know Ye that I Paul Micou for and in Consideration of
the Love good Will and Affection which I have and do beare towards
my Loveing Dauther Margaret Fantleroy have Given and Granted and by
these presents Do freely clearly and absolutely Give and Grant to my
said Dauther and the heirs of her Body Lawfully begotten five Negroes:
viz: Peter Darbe Marjory Sarry and Tulip To have and to hold all the
said Negros unto my said Dauther and the heirs of her Body for Ever,
Provided that in Case my said Dauther should dye without heirs of
her Body that the said Negros shall revert to me and my heirs
        In Testimony whereof I have hereunto set my hand and Seale this
third Day of June 1718 "
Test   signed   Paul Micou
Jn'o Gilbert
Tho's Turner   Rec. 4 June 1718

p.97-A. Accounts of "The Sloope Millford In Berbados". 1716.
Recorded upon oath of Mathew Pope, 2 July 1718.
p.99-A. "Mathew Pope late Master of the sloop call'd the Milford
owned by John Hawkins of Essex County" makes oath that he has not
held any property pertaining to the sloop. Refers to suit depending
betw Hawkins and Himself in Essex Co. Court.

                        Rec. 2 July 1718

p.99-A. Power of Atty. - May 1718. John Watkinson of Liverpool,
mariner, to "my trusty Friend Mr Newman Brockenbrough of the County
of Richmond in Virginia" to collect debts.
Wit:
Wm Downman   signed   John Watkinson
Travers Downman
Proved by oaths of both witnesses in Richmond Co. Court 6 Aug. 1718.

p.100.   Providence February the 10th 1715/16
        Then Rec'd of M'rs Sarah Tallipher one Chest Wearing Cloaths
three hundred heavey peices of Eight one Silver Tankard and three
porringer and Six Spons the which I premis to Deliver to Maj'r Parent
Trott in Bermudas the freight being already paid having sign'd to Two
Receipts of the same Tenor and Date the one being Accomplished the
other to stand Void the Danger of the Seas only Excepted
                                per Jona: Tucker
Recorded 6 August 1718 on motion of Nicholas Smith Gent
                                M: Beckwith Cl Cur
            (See next page for note)

Note: The following may give an indication of the value of Mrs.
Taliaferro's pieces of eight. It is taken from a letter written by
Sir William Gooch, dated Virginia, 9th February 1739/40, to the
Lords Commissioners of Trade and Plantations.

Great Britain.
Public Record Office. London.
Colonial Office 5. Volume 1324. page 373.

"From 1661 to 1700". x x "In the first mentioned Year an Act passed,
that Pieces of Eight which were Good and of Silver should pass for
five Shillings Current Money: And as there is no mention made of any
other Species, I conclude, the People, at that time, had little Gold,
or any other than Spanish Coin amongst them.
     But however that might be, it is certain Pieces of Eight passed
currently for five Shillings without weighing, and less Prices, it
must be presumed, in Proportion until the year 1710, when at a Session
of Assembly, Begun and Held the 15th of October, It was Enacted, that
Pieces of Eight of Mexico, Seville and Pillar, Ducoatoons of Flanders,
Eou's of France or silver Lowis, and Crusadoes of Portugal, with all
Halves, Quarters, and lessor Pieces of the same, should Pass at three
pence half Penny the Penny-Weight".

Richmond Co. Misc. Records.
p.100.
Deed of Gift. 7 Aug. 1718. John Bowen Son'r of Richmond Co.
To Daughter Sarah Bowen #attle"to be given at her day of marriage or
     att the Day of my Death".
To Daughter Mary Bowen, cattle and furniture at day of marriage or
     his death, as above.
To Daughter Elizabeth Bowen, cattle as above.
To Son John Bowen all the rest of Estate at day of his death.
Wit:
Richard Claxton   signed   John x Bowen Senr.
Franois x Williams Junr.
                              Rec. 7 Aug. 1718.

p.100-A.
Att a Court held for Richmond County the Fifth Day of March 1717

Mrs Catherine Gwin this Day filed her Bill in Chancery and therein
sett forth that her late husband dec'd David Gwin some time before
his Death and after the Publication of his last will informed her

that there was in his Escrewtore thirty Pounds in ready money and
that by reason he had not left his Daughter Catherine any Lands that
he did order her to buy his said Daughter with the said Money One
Young Negroe, and that she should have the same over and above her
proportionable part of his personall Estate which Orders and Directions were spoke to her in the presence of severall Witnesses, Therefore Prays an Order to be Directed to some Persons to take her Deposition and others for the Manifestation of the premises aforesaid etc
Whereupon it is Ordered that Charles Barber and John Tayloe Gent doe
meet some time between this and the next Court and take Depositions
as aforesaid and that they return the same with this order annext
thereto the next Court to be held for this County

Copy Test   Ms Beckwith Cl Cur

The Execution of the within order appears in certain schedules hereunto annexed   Chas Barber
                                          John Tayloe

Interrogatones Exhibited to be Administered to the Witnesses to be
produced and Examined on the behalf of Katherine Gwyn Jun'r by vertue
of the annext ord'r of the Wo'p'full Court of Richmond.

1st Interr   Did you know David Gwyn Gent Dec'd ?

2'd Interr   Doe you know or can you remember any directions or order
              which the said David Gwyn gave on his Death bed for the
              disposing or laying out of any and what sume of Money
              which was in his Scrutore and to whom was such directions
              given, and for what purpose and for whose use was the
              said money to be laid out

3'd Interr: Was the said David Gwyn at the time of such directions
              or Order given as aforesaid in perfect Sence and how
              long was the same before the time of his Decease and
              whether it was before or after the Publication of his
              last Will in Writing ?

4th Interr   Was any and what Sume of Money pursuant to the aforesaid
              Order of the said David Gwyn laid out and disposed of
              and by whom and what was bought or purchased therewith
              and for whose use or Service ? Declare the Truth and
              all that you know relating to the premises to the best
              of your knowledge, Relief and Rememberance.

(see next page)

Depositions taken 28 March 1718

Katherine Gwyn Widow being Sworn and Examined Deposeth and saith to the First Interrogatory that she well knew David Gwyn dec'd in the said Interrogatory named, he being her Husband.

p.101-A. To the second Interrogatory the said Depon't saith that the said David Gwyn some few Days before his Death bid this Depon't fetch his Will which was in his Scrutore, which she accordingly did, and he haveing lookt on the same sometime told this Depon't that since he had not left his Youngest Daughter Katherine any Land, he said he would have this Depon't as soon as conveniently could be after his Decease buy her a Young Negroe and that there was money enough in his Scutore for that purpose, or Words to the like effect

To the third Interrogatory the said Depon't saith that the said David Gwyn at the time of such order as aforesaid given to her was in perfect Sence to the best of her knowledge and apprehension but how long it was before his Decease she cannot particularly remember, but is certain it was a Considerable time after the Publication of his last Will in Writing

To the Fourth Interratory the said Depon't saith that pursuant to her said dec'd husband David Gwyns Order as aforesaid she did sometime after his Death lay out seven and Twenty Pounds of the Cash aforesd and therewith bought a Young Negroe Girl, now a Woman called Moll, which she bought for the particular use and service of her aforesaid Daughter Katherine according to the said David Gwyns aforesaid directions given to this Depon't And further this Depon't saith not

Katherin Gwynn

Sworne before us
Cha: Barber
John Tayloe

p.101-A
William Fantleroy Gent being sworn and Examined Deposeth and saith to the First Interrogatory that he did know David Gwyn in the said Interrogatory named, he having marryed this Depon'ts Mother

To the Second and Third Interrogatoryes the said Depon't saith that the said David Gwyn a few Days before his Death being in his perfect sence to the best of this Depon'ts knowledge and apprehension, did in this Depon'ts hearing Order his Wife as soon as conveniently could be after his Decease to buy a Young Negro for his Daughter Katherine, saying he haveing given his two other Daughters Land and his said Daughter Katherine haveing none, for that reason he would have a

Negro bought for her which she should have over and above her part
of his other Estate, and told her that there was Money enough in his
Scrutore for that purpose, or words to the like effect

p.102. To the Fourth Interrogatory the said Depon't saith that sometime after the said David Gwyns Death his widow did goe down the
River in order to goe on board a Negroe Ship called the Eagle Galley
to buy Negroes as this Depon't understood and was informed, and when
she returned brought up some Negroes, and amongst the rest a Negroe
Girl, now a Woman call'd Moll, who this Depon't understood his
Mother bought pursuant to the Order of her said dec'ed husband David
Gwyn for the use and service of his said Daughter Katharine, but how
much the said Negroe Girl cost this Depon't doth not know, and
further this Depon't saith not.
                                        Wm Fantleroy
Sworn before us
Cha's Barber
John Tayloe   Rec. 7 Aug 1718
                         Test   M: Beckwith Cl Cur

p.102.

July the 2'd 1718
The Estate of George Gaydon   Dr
                                                     Tobo
To funerall Expences   500
To the Charge of Administra'con   150
To Judgm't paid John Harris   3541
To paid John Champe   500
To his Leavy   38 1/2
To 8 Months Board at my house   800
                                                     - - - -
                                                     5529 1/2

To my charge and Expence
To Clerk and Sherr fees

Per Contra   Cr.
By Goods by Appraysm't   L 18. 5. 0
By Tob'o recd of John Fleming   64
By Tobo recd of Rich'd Apleby   94
By more rec'd of Charles Lewis   602

                    (continued)

Estate of George Gaydon (continued)

By more recd of John Branham   541
By more recd of Michall Meldrum   785
By more recd of Mr Taffe   200
                                                         -- -- --
                                                         1825
                              recd of Mr Barrow   100
                                                         -- -- --
                                                         4211

                There is due from Charles Lewis   648
                Peter Duncans Bill   450

Sworn to in Richmond County Court the Seventh Day of August 1718 by
Martin Sherman and ordered to be Recorded
                              Test   M Beckwith   Cl Cur

p. 102-A
                    Wm Underwoods Estate Dr
To paid Capt Smith for Levies   101
To paid Thos Harp'r for a Coffin   100
To pd to Mr Beckwith   312
To pd Rich'd Tutt by Ord'r of Cap't Smith   200
To pd Margarett Birk by ord'r Court   274
To pd M'r Jn'o Dunwidde   49
To the Funerall Charges   454
                                                         -- -- --
                                                         1490
                    Per Contra   Cred't
By Goods according to Appraism't by the Inventory
       return'd   88. 12. 4
            Errours Excepted per John Underwood
                         Wm Underwood

                    Rec. 3 Sept. 1718

p.103. Account of Estate of James Spendergrass Dec'd amounting to
640 lb tobo submitted by John Smith. Includes item paid to Henry
Harford 60 lb tobo.
                    Rec. 3 Sept. 1718.

p.103. By agreement made this 19th day of September 1718 between us Subscribers the Negros belonging to the Estate of James Scott are to be divided Viz:
Elizabeth Scott is to have Harry Dick Bobb and Tony
James Scott is to have Little Will, Nany and Nerro
Paul Scott is to have Great Will Pheby and Little Nany
Margaritt Scott is to have Hannah and Jeany

Paul Micou
Wm Monroe
Elizabeth x Scott

Rec. 1 Oct 1718

p.103. Deed of Gift. 1 Oct. 1718. Elizabeth Rogers widow of Nicho Rodgers late of this County Deceased. "I give to my sone John Ford sone of John Ford deceastt" furniture and cattle to be delivered to him at age of 24 years.
To "my sone Wm Ford" 20 pounds Sterl. and cattle to be delivered at age of 24 yrs.
To "my Daughter Patience Ford" 20 pounds and cattle at day of marriage or age of 18.
Wit: signed   Elizabeth Rodgers
James Nelson

Rec. 1 Oct. 1718.

p. 103-A. Deed. 29 January 1718/19. George Newman of Sittenbourn Par. Rd. Co., Planter and Elizabeth his wife to John Newman of same Par. and Co. Planter, for L 60. Sterl., a negro man named Robin and a negro woman named Rose.
Wit: signed   George Newman
Sam'll Godwin   Elizabe. New   (sic)
Wm x Clary   Rec. 4 Feb 1718/19

p.104. Deed. 30 January 1718/19. Duplicate of above in reverse.

p.104-A. William Woodbridge Admin'r of the Estate of James Samon late of this County deceased. Debtor. Amounts to L 15. 0. 2 and includes payment to Elizabeth Taffe 880 lb tobo.
Rec. 5 Feb. 1718/19

p.105. The mark of William Skrines for Hogs and Cattle. Recorded 5 February 1718/19.

Misc. Records.

p.105. Power of Atty. 31 Dec. 1718. "Mary Plumer Widdo the sole
Executrix of my deceased Husband Thomas Plumer of the Parish of
Kingston and County of Glocester" to "my well beloved Friend Mr
James Ingo of the County of Richmond" to collect accts in Essex
and Richmond Counties.
Wit: signed   Mary Plumer
Robert Singleton
Joshua Singleton   Rec. 4 March 1718/19

p. 105#A.

Richm'd Ss: Novb'r the 4th 1718
George Hopkins aged Fifty years or thereabouts deposeth and saith
That at the time when Mr Thomas Loyd (since deceased) received into
his possession the Plantation belonging to Mr Mottrom Wright of
Lancaster County (since deceased) sittuate upon Rappa Creeks in
Richmond County now in the possession of Joseph Belfield that then
there was on the aforesaid Plantation one dwelling house fourty five
foot long and twenty foot broad with Girders and Sawed halfe Joice
and Rafters two rooms on a floor Stairs and a Closet, planked above
and below, a double brick chimney and brick Closet plaister'd with
lime and hair above and below
     One kitchen about thirty foot long plaister'd with lime and
hair below another small house a Celler with a good roof over it
all in a good Condition, a good Stilhouse and another good small
house by it.
     A good large Tobacco house under the hile another large new
Tobacco house Called the press house and further the Deponent saith
not
                              signum
                         George x Hopkins

Sworn to in Richmond County Court the Fifth Day of March 1718 by the
above named George Hopkins and at the motion of the above named
Joseph Belfield was ordered to be Recorded
                              Test M: Beckwith Cl Cur.

p. 106.

Richmond Ss: Novb'r the 4th 1718
Thomas Cooper of Westmorland County "Aged Fifty Years or thereabouts
deposeth and saith" - as foregoing deposition - "and the reason he
have to know the above is that about two years before the said Loyd
had the possession of the Plantation aforesaid your Deponent lived

on the Plantation and was often at it and afterwards at it to the
taking of it by Mr Thomas Loyd and further your Deponent saith not
                        signed   Thomas Cooper

Sworn to in Richmond County Court 5 March 1718/19 by Thos. Cooper
and recorded.

p.106. Richmond So. Novb'r the 4th 1718. "Mary Burress Wife of
Mathew Burress aged about Thirty Eight Years deposeth and Saith" - as
foregoing depositions. Signed Mary Burress. Sworn to in Rd. Co. Ct.,
5 March 1718/19 by Mary Burroes and recorded.

p.106. Surveyors plat. Marked "A Plott of Land belonging to Robt
Hopkins and Arthur Dye". Plat shows lands making up 84 1/2 acres.
Further marked "February 11th 1707/8 Then Surveyed and Devided the
above Platt of Land att the Request of the said Hopkins and Dye".
Signed "per Edwd Barrow".

p.107. Further: February 11th 1707/8. "Then Survey'd for Mr Robt
Hopkins and Mr Arthur Dye a parcell of Land being part of a Dividend
of Land Sould by Mr James Williamson deceased unto Mr Robert Hopkins".
Adj "to a Stake in an ould field in the Line of Coll'n Fleet" etc. By
Edw'd Barrow. Recorded 5 March 1718/19.

p.107-A. By order of Rd. Co. Court, 5 Feb. 1718/19, the subscribers
have settled a/c betw Thomas Faulkner (ffalkn'r) and the Exors of
"Mr Aug'tine Brookenbrough decd Admr of the Estate of Thomas Dickenson
son dec'ed". Settlement of a/c includes: Dr. To Shadrick W'ms bill
if paid 3450.
                        signed   Wm Fantleroy
                                  James Ingo

p. 107-A.

March the 31th 1719
An Account of what Tobo I have paid for the Estate (of) Ann Dodson
Deceased
To funirall Charges att   800
To buring of my Sister Mary Dodson   800
To Thos Reed   020
To Mr Newmon Broookenbrough   040

(continued)

The Estate of Ann Dodson (continued)

To Capt Woodbridge   040
To John Simpson   200
To Jeames fowshe   090
                                                     - - - -
                                                     1890

per me Charles Dodson

Recorded 1 April 1719.

p.107-A.   24 Nov. 1718. Affidavit of Robt. Whitlow regarding a suit
in Chancery depending between Wm Hancock and Wm Robinson concerning
a Bill of Exchange drawn by James Robinson upon Wm Robinson. English
business detail in the suit. An appraisal of long list of mdse, ect.

p.109. Power of Atty. 10 Aug. 1719. Saml. Skinker to Charles Burges
of Richd Co. Mercht. A long complicated entry concerning Deverell
Estate.
Wit: signed   Sam'l Skinker
Tho's Turner
Benja Strother
Wm Strother Jun'r   Rec. 2 Sept 1719.

p.110-A. Deed. 15 August 1719. George Hopkins "in Consideration of
the naturall Love and Affection which he hath and beareth unto his
Loveing Wife Frances Hopkins and her Daughters Katherine Dye the wife
of Avery Dye and Charity Bayly the Wife of William Bayly" settles
certain negroes upon them at his death. "and the first child that the
said Phillis (one of the negro women) shall have unto the said
Charity Bayly dureing her life and after her Decease to Mackmillion
Bayly son of the said Charity Bayly", he failing in heirs to "Frances
Bayly daughter of the said Charity Bayly".
Wit:
John Newman   signed   George x Hopkins
Kathrin x Kendall
                             Rec. 2 Sept 1719.

p.111. Settlement of Estate of Will'm Sims deceased, 30 June 1719.
Total 8792 lb. tobo. Includes: tobo
To pd Mary Jefferys   400
To pd John Morton for plank for a Coffin   50

(See next page)

Estate of Wm. Sims (continued)

To pd Mr Ingoe   90
To pd Mr Jn'o Bagg   312
To pd Charles Bruce by Ord'r of Court   339
To pd Capt Walter King   509
To pd Martin Kemp per Ord'r of Court   186
To pd Dan'll Jefferys   45
                          Errors Excepted
                            per Nicho Smith

                   Rec. 4 Nov. 1719

p.112. "I Wm Baptie Junr doe hereby acknowledge to have had and rec'd
of and from George Hopkins full satisfaction of all Claims and
Demands due from the said Geo Hopkins on the Acco't of John Baptie
Dec'd x x 20 Day of Feb'y 1719"
Wit: signed   Wm Baptie
Avery Dye
Michael x Wildey
Sam'll Godwin   Rec. 2 March 1719/20

p.112. 1719 The Estate of Wm Rogers decd Dr. Total 2021 lb tobo.
Includes:
To pd And'w Scrimshar   30
To pd Tho's Turner Judgm't   680
To pd Char: Spee for Oath   60
To pd Doot'r Turners Do   135
                    Errors Excepted per me
                        Edw'd Moseley

                   Rec. 2 March 1719/20

p.112-A. Power of Atty. 20 Feb. 1719/20. Rachell Deverell of the
City of Bristoll Widow and Jeremiah Deverell of the same City Surgeon
(Two of the Executors named in the last Will and Testament of Benja-
min Deverell sometime of the said City of Bristoll and afterwards of
Virginia dec'd and who have duly proved the same)" to "our well
beloved Friend Charles Burges of Virginia aforesaid Merchant" to
collect accounts.
Wit: signed   Rachell Deverell
Will'm Strotton   Jerem'h Deverell
Alexand'r Parker

Proved in Rd. Co. Court by oaths of witnesses 4th May 1720.

                              December 1719
Received of Mr John Spicer Gent Seven Negros Darkiss, Bobb, Hannah,
Humphry, Phillis, Bess and Sue and nine head of Cattle, four Cows
and Calves and a young Steer, Nine Barriells of Corne and five
Bushells of Beanes Rec'd per me
                                        Wm Griffin Carp'r
Received this Estal of Wm Deane
                         Rec. 1 June 1720

p.113. Deed of Gift. 1 Nov. 1720. Jane Thorne of Richmond Co. "in
Consideration of the tender Love and Naturall affections that I bear
for and towards my Dear Children Susanah Thorne and Merryman Thorne"
gives personal property (handsome for this period) to be delivered
to the girl at 18 and the boy at 21.
Wit: signed   Jane Thorne
Jno Ham'ond
Thomas Lewis   Rec. 7 Dec. 1720.

p.114.
The Estate of Mr Thos Fitzhugh Dec'd in Tob'co is   Dr

To a Judgment of Stafford Court granted to Mr Jn'o
        Dynwiddy March 10. 1719   898
To Do to Mrs Anchoram March 10 1719   1322
To Do to Mr Charles Burgess March 10 1719   5039
To Do to Mr John Bagg March 9th 1719   1832
To Do to Mr James Cordiner March 10 1719   962
To Do to Mr Robert Hamilton June 8 1720   1152
To Do to Mr Gustavus Browne June 8th 1720   1917
To Do to Mr John Allan June 9th 1720   2103
To Do to Coll Lee for Fitzhughs orphans June 9th 1720   4982
To Do to Mr Henry Butler June 8th 1720   532
To Do to Mr Jos: Eaton June 8th 1720   552
To Do to Mr Thos James June 9th 1720   627
To Do to Mr Mungo Roy June 9 1720   327
To Do to Capt Parkes   1231
To Will'm Hall for Hirelings wages June 1720   1600
To pd John Willson 1720   300
To Do to George Monke 1720   200
To Do Fran: Warrington as per an acc't prov'd Octob: 1719   700
To Leavys due when he Dyed Octob: 1719   1248
To Charges on the Money Judgm'ts Granted to Mess: Thornton,
        Lee, Strother, Fitzhugh, Megill and Wain   475
To payd James Ireland a sh: fee 1720   015
To 10 per Ct for receiving the Tob'o and Contra   417
                                                              -- -- -- --
                                                              30431

Misc. Records.

The Estate of Mr. Thomas Fitzhugh (continued)

Per Contra
Per hhs of old Tob'o N't with Caske   1442
Per Rec'd of Mr Benj'a Bullet   1622
Per Do of James Ireland   107
Per Do of John Simson   385
Per Do of Richard Johnson   322
Per Do of Jos King   202
Per Do of Mary Anchoram   094
                                                              - - - -
                                                                4574

Henry Fitzhugh

At a Court held for Richmond County
the first day of March 1720
Henry Fitzhugh Went One of the Executors of the Last will and Testam't
of Thomas Fitzhugh deced x x made oath that the above acco't was Just
and true, and that he never received any Sattisfaction for the same
xx that the ballance due to him which amounts to Twenty Six thousand
and two hundred Fifty Seaven pounds of Tobacco, might be settled in
money, on Consideration of which the Court doth value the said
Tobacco at two pence per pound which amounts to two hundred and
eighteen pounds sixteen shillings and two pence and at the motion of
the said Henry Fitzhugh the said Account is ordered to be Recorded
Test   Mr Beckwith Cl Cur.

p.114-A.

The Estate of Mr Thos Fitzhugh Dec'd   Dr
To a Judgment of Rich'd Court to Henry Fitzhugh   148. 9. 6
To Do to George Fitzhugh   41. 9. 8
To Do to John Fitzhugh   5. 0. 0
To Do to Mr Wm Thornton   55. 6. 9
To a Judgm't of Staff'd Court to m'r Frans Strother   12. 0. 0
To Do to Coll Lee for Fitzhughs Orphans   27. 15. 8
To Do to Do for Arrearages of quitrents   13. 9. 0
To Do to mr Robert Hamiton   14. 6. 8
To Do to mr David McGill   6. 8. 0
To Do to Capt Winn   6. 2. 7
To Do to M'r John Bagg   0. 12. 0
To payd Simon Smith for a Justices Order   0. 7. 6
To payd mr Alexander Parker   11. 0. 0
To payd mr Alexand'r Scott a Funerall Sermon   5. 0. 0
To payd Major Berriman a Lawyers fee   1. 19. 0
To Do to Dan'll McCarty Esq'r   1. 4. 0
To a Servant Man Named Sam'll Ridgway which does not)
     belong to this Estate but by mistake was In-   ) 8. 0. 0
     ventoried and apraised to   )
                                                       - - - - -
                                                      358. 5. 4

Miso. Records

Estate of Mr. Thos. Fitzhugh (continued)

per Contra.
Per the Inventory of the Estate apraisd to   569. 11. 0
Per 5 Heifers and 2 Bulls not apraised   7. 0. 0
Per 4 Stears of 3 years old each   5. 0. 0
Per 2 Barren Cows which the widow says she kild
        before the apraism't   --   --   --
Per an old watch and pr of Leather baggs   1. 0. 0
Per a Cane without a handle   0. 5. 0

                        Henry Fitzhugh

Recorded 1 March 1720 on oath of Henry Fitzhugh Gent.
                        Test M Beckwith   Cl Cur

Note: This date 1720/21.

p. 115↓
Stanley Gower Deceased is Debtor in November the 12th day 1718

To funerall Charges at   02. 0. 0
paid to mr Lenard Hill Curent money   21. 0. 4
To a Debt due to my Selfe   04. 5. 8
paid to Roger Rooker   00. 10. 9
paid to Nicloas Christopher   01. 05. 0
paid to John Bramham   00. 04. 0
paid to hensfill Broos   00. 05. 0
                                                      -- -- -- -- -- --
                                                      29. 13. 1

A List of Tobacoe paid in 1718
To Capp'tt Charles Barber   0095
To William Phillips   0150
To David Williams   0015
To John faver   0015
To John Peycraft   0600
To Gilbert Metcalfe   0245
To Gilbert Metcalfe   0065
To William Phillips   0030
To francis Yeats   0037
To John Bramham   0146
To Jeames Deboard   0100
To Danll hornby   0370
To John Pound Juner   0800

                    (continued next page)

Estate of Stanley Gower (continued)

To John Bryant   0030 1/2
To Thomas Phillips   0018
                                                        - - - -
                                                        2717

Creditt to the above Acc'tt 1500 pounds of Tob'c
                              At a Court held for Richmond County
                              the fifth day of Aprill 1721
John Gower in Open Court made Oath to the Truth of this account and
att his Motion is admitted to Record
                              Test M: Beckwith Cl Cur

p.115-A. The Estate of John Daly dec'd Dr. Amounts to 659 1/2 lb.
tobo. Includes "To Anne Reynolds 100". Recorded 2 August 1721.

p.115-A. The Estate of Alexand Clayton. Totals 800 lb tobo. Includes
"To Ruth Canterbury ord'r of Court 500" and "By John Russell 300".
Submitted by Dan'll Hornby administrator and Recorded 4 Oct. 1721.

p.115-A.   November the 1st 1721
When M'r Deeke Lay on his Death bead I asked him what must be done
about that Negro that was Catys. Then I asked againe if I must buy
her one, and his Answer was that he left a great Charge of Children
and if I Could to buy one but I must do as I Could and if I Could
not She must have One of them that there was to the best of my
Remsmberance
                              Catherine x Suggitt

Sworne in Richmond County Court the First Day of November 1721 by
Catherine Suggitt, and Ordered to be Recorded
                              Test M: Beckwith Cl Cur

p.116.
Sir:
    In all the Suites petitions and Complaints depending in Richmond
Court brought against us by Tho's Mountjoy, John Moulton and Mary his
Wife, Alvin Mountjoy Orphants or Children of Alvin Mountjoy deceased
We desire and require you will withdraw all such pleas as you have to

the said Suites or petitions already Entered or pleaded and suffer
Judgements to pass for the Complainants Non Sum informatus or other-
ways for the Complainants for their filial portions or ratiable parts
of their said fathers estate, and for your so doing this shall be
your Sufficient Warrent from

                                    Your Loving Friends
                                       Jos: Belfield
                                       Mary x Belfield

Sep'r the 14th 1721
To Cap'n George Eskridge

                           Rec. 2 Nov. 1721
                           Test M: Beckwith Cl Cur.

p.116.

Richmond Ss.
Pursuant to an Ord'r of Court dated the 5th of Octob'r 1721 We the
subscribers have sett apart and devided the Estate of Mr Jos: Deeke
Late of this County dec'd between Katherine Suggitt and Eliz'a Deeke
Ex'rs of the Last Will and Testament of the said Jos: Deeke, dec'd
as followeth
To James Suggitt and Katherine his Wife we have allotted x x (a long
     list of personal property).
To Eliz'a Deek we have allotted x x (a further long list of personal
     property)
Given under Our hands this 20th of November 1721
                                    Cha: Barber
                                    Robert Tomlin

                     Recorded 3 January 1721/2.

p.116-A. Further division of Estate of Joseph Deeke.

p.117. Power of Atty. 7 Nov. 1721. Thomas Seale of Liverpool, Sarah
Prescott, widow, of the same place admx of Ralph Prescott late of
Liverpool, merchant, deceased, Henry Mason of Wigan in Lancaster Co.
(England) Gent., Brother and admr of Robert Mason late of Liverpool,
merchant, deceased, to Travers Downman of Moraticoe near Rappahannock River, Virginia, Gentleman and William Downman of the same
place, Gent., his Brother, to collect debts in Virginia. " and know
yee Further that I Thomas Willis of Leverpoole aforesaid Esq'r and
I the said Thomas Seel, who are the acting assignees of the Commissioners in a Commission of Bankruptcy awarded and executed against Daniel
Willis of Leverpool aforesaid merchant (who was a partner x x with

me the said Thomas Seel and with the said Ralph prescot and Robert
Mason in severall of the Debts goods and Effects before mentioned)"
joins with Sarah Prescot and Henry Mason in above power of atty.
Wit:
Rich'd Blevin   signed   Thos Seel
William Kenwrig   Sarah priscott
William x Martin   Henry Mason
                                           Tho Willis

At a Court for Richmond County, 4 April 1722, proved by oaths of
William Kenwrig and William Martin and recorded.
                            Test   M: Beckwith   Cl Cur.

p.118.   October the 12th 1714
I the subscriber doe own to have received from m'rs Ann Green all
Dues belonging to me by Right of Hester my Wife Likewise I doe acquit
and Discharge the abovesaid mrs Ann Green Relick of m'r Richard Green
des'd from all Debts Dues and Demands bills bonds and acc'ts from the
beginning of the wourld to this present Date Witness my hand the
Day and yeare above written
Testis   John Gower
David Berrick
Sam'll Pound

5th April 1722. At the motion of John Bramham this receipt was
admitted to Record
                            Test   M: Beckwith   Cl Cur

Note: For those who desire a background of the British nobility, not
to mention royalty, just check back on that item. You will be reward-
ed full share and more.   B.F.

118-A. Power of Atty. 10 April 1722. Edward Little, Merchant, of
Bristol, to Robt Tomlin of Richmond Co., to collect debts.
Wit:
Elizabeth Tomlin   signed   Edward Little
John x Swilivan

Proved in Richmond Co. Court by oaths of witnesses 2 May 1722.

p.118-A. Indenture. 5 Feb. 1722/3. Nathaniel Mason of No. Farnham
Par. Richmond Co., of one part and Thomas Dale, Carpenter, of the
same Par. and Co., of the other part. "Nathaniel Mason hath and with

the Consent of his Aunt Million Downman put himselfe an Apprentice
to the said Thomas Dale from this Instant untill Five years be Expired to Learne the Art and Trade of a Carpenter". Dale binds himself "to give the said Nathaniel Mason one new suit of Kersey vz:
Coat, Vest, and Britchis, Two Shirts, one new pair of Shoes, one new
pair of Stokins, one new hat, Itm Carpenters Tools, Broad ax, ads,
handsaw, fre Drawing knife, Augar and hammer".
Wit:

Travers Downman   signed   Tho Dale
Thomas Barber

                     Rec. 6 Feb. 1722/3

p.120. Power of Atty. 9 March 1720/21. John Beecher Esqr and William
Wraxall merchant both of the City of Bristol, Exors of last W and T
of John Walker of the same city, mariner, dec'd., to Nicholas Smith
of Virginia, merchant, to dispose of properties in Virginia.
Wit:

Stephen Papps   signed   John Becher
Arthr Muresy   Wm Wraxall

Proved in Rd. Co. Court, 3 July 1723, by oath of Stephen Papps and
recorded.

p. 120-A. "John Davis Jun'r Dec'd Dr to Mrs Susanna Taylor widow".
Account 1719 to 1722. Totals L 59. 16. 8
Debits include:
1721 To Tob'o paid of hers to Elias Fennell 100 lb   0: 12: 6
Credits Include:
By paid John Knight   0: 10: 0
According to Court order of 3 July 1723 the above a/c was settled
19 July 1723.

                                signed   Wm Fantleroy
                                          James Ingo

                     Rec. 7 Aug. 1723.

p.121-A. Surveyor's Plat. The table includes:
F is Tho's Pettys Corner a white oak
G is a small Red oak near Jno Mortons one of Jenkins Corners
K is John Mortons Corner
L is an ash in a branch of C- branch one of Henry Haws Corners
M is Wm Jenkins house
N is Henry Haws house

                     (see next page)

Continued from page 89.

O is Law: Bakers house   (sic)
P is John Mortons house

"Surveyed for Wm Jenkins Henry Haws and Lawrence Barker (sic) 771
acres of Land It being a pattent formerly granted to Harman Skelderman for 800 acres 153 acres of which Land the said Skelderman Sole
which John Morton now Claimes the other part of the pattent he the
said Skelderman in his last Will and Testament bequeathed among his
children which are the Wives of the said Jenkins Haws and Barker and
they the said Jenkins and his wife Haws and his Wife Barker and his
Wife being willing to know Each part hath with one Consent and
assent freely agreed to Survey and Devide the same which I have Done
as the above figure Describes x x and the Lines of John Morton which
said Land is Sittuate in the parish of Cittenburn and County of
Richmond and on the branches of Rapp'a Creek"
"Surveyed the 12th of October 1714 per Cha's Barber Sur' R.C."

At a Court held for Richmond County the second Day of October 1723
At the Motion of Elizabeth Jenkens Mary Grimstead and Ann Commins
this Survey and plat of Land is Ordered to be Recorded
                              Test   M: Beckwith Cl Cur

p.122.
"Memorandum
Pursuant to an Order of Richmond County Court Granted to Henry Street
Orphan for L 22: 4: 3 1/2 Dated the 6th Day of Nov'r 1723 I as guard-
ian to the said Orphan have Rec'ed for his part the Following articles
of the adm'r Out of which I am to account for and pay One Third part
of what Debts shall be brought against the Dec'ed Estate"
Account in detail follows. Household goods and stock.
                              signed "per me Richard Barnes"

p. 122-A. Power of Atty. 21 Nov. 1723. Evan Thomas of Rd. Co. planter
to   Wm. Moulton of same Co. to collect debts "from all and Every
person or persons whatsoever from the South Side of Rapp'a River to
the Southermost part of South Carolina".
Wit:
John Morton   signed Eavan x Thomas
Richard x Alderson

                    Rec. 4 Dec. 1723.

(see next page)

p.123.
"To all To whom these presents shall come know ye that whereas Rich'd
Alderson of the County of Lancaster by his last Will and Testament
amongst other things Gives and Devises the Remainder part of his
Estate unto his Son Richard in which part was a Woman Slave named
Penelope also whereas Christopher Edmons Intermarried with Marg't
the widow of the aforesaid Alderson who in a Clandestine manner
absented Out of the aforesaid County of Lancaster and Carried away
with him the aforesaid woman Slave Penelope and Christopher and John
Children of her the said Penelope". Therefore Rich'd Alderson appoints
Wm. Moulton of Sittenbourne Par., Rd. Co. attorney to apprehend the
woman slave and her children. Dated 5 December 1723.
Wit:
Jno Tayloe   signed   Rich'd x Alderson
Dan: McCarty
Marmaduke Beckwith
G. Eskridge   Rec. 4 March 1723/4
Cha: Barber   Test   M: Beckwith Cl Cur

p.123-A. Power of Atty. 18 Jan. 1723/4. Wm Cleiveland Esq., of
Liverpool, merchant, son and heir of Ald'rn John Cleiveland late of
Liverpool, merchant, deceased, to William Beverley of Essex Co., to
dispose of two tracts of land. Whereas one Timothy Hay of Rappahannock River in Essex County within Virginia planter in or about the
year One Thousand seven hundred and Ten being Indebted to the said
John Cleiveland in a considerable sume, Coll'o Robert Beverley late
of Rappahannock aforesaid Gentleman dec'ed then attorney or sollicitor
for Garrett Minor late of Rappahannock aforesaid merchant dec'd who
was attorney and agent for the said John Clieveland did for and
Towards dischargeing the said debt so Due to the said John Cleiveland
Recover and get from the said Thomas Hay (sic) for the use of the
said John Cleiveland Two Tracts plantations or parcels of Land the
one whereof consisting of 118 acres lying or bounding upon the Mill
formerly call'd Tandie's alias Rowzes and now or late Brooks and the
other consisting of 210 acres lying and being in the Forrest some
Distance from the first and had the same conveyed over to him and his
heirs for the use of the said John Cleiveland and his heirs by a
certaine Deed now in the hands of William Beverley of Rappahannock
aforesaid Gent Son and heir of the said Coll'o Robert Beverley and
inrolled or Registered in the Register Book of Essex County.
Wit:
Edward Manwaring   signed   Wm Cleiveland
Rob't Maddock

Proved by oath of Robt Maddock 19 May 1724 in Court of Essex County
                          Test   W Beverley Cl Cur

Proved by oath of Edward Manwaring 1 July 1724 in Court of Richmond
County.   Test   M: Beckwith Cl Cur

p.124-A. Power of Atty. 13 June 1723. "Mary Luke of the City of
Williamsburg Wife and Lawfull Attorney of George Luke late of Hampton
in the County of Elizabeth City Esq'r" to Marmaduke Beckwith of
Richmond County, Gentleman, to collect debts.
Wit:
Tho Griffin   signed   Mary Luke

Proved 2 Sept 1724 by oath of Thomas Griffin in Richmond Co. Court.
                            Test   M: Beckwith Cl Cur

p.125-A. Petition of John Tayloe Gent, 5 Aug. 1724, setting forth
that he intends to erect a Grist Water Mill on the swamp called
Shorts, and prays that one acre of land may be assigned him out of
Cary's land on the point that makes the fork between Shorts and the
Bridge Quarter Swamp.
        Charles Barber and Robert Tomlin Gents are ordered to view and
value the land.

Richmond Ss/
Pursuant to the within Order wee have mett at the place where John
Tayloe Gent Intends to Erect a Water Mill and viewed an acre of Land
belonging to Mr Carey which acre of Land wee vallue to the price of
Five shillings Sterling Given under our hands the 2'd Day of
September 1724
                            Cha Barber
                            Robert Tomlin

Recorded amongst the Records of Richmond County the Second Day of
September 1724.
                    Test   M: Beckwith Cl Cur.

                            The End.

Richmond County
Virginia

Clerk's Office,
Warsaw, Va.

Record Book marked "Fines, Examination of Criminals Tryalls of
Slaves &c from March 1710 to -"

p.1.
At a Court held for Richmond County the Seventh Day of March One
thousand Seven hundred and Tenn
                          Present
     Samuell Peachey   William Woodbridge)
     John Tarpley   John Tayloe   and) Gent Justices
     Charles Barber   John Taverner   )

George Erwin being sum'oned to show cause why he did not appear as a
Juryman on the Land in difference between William Fantleroy Plt and
Mathew Thornton Defend't, he this Day appearing, but showing noe
sufficient Cause why he did not appear, It is therefore Ordered that
he be fined Two hundred and Fifty Pounds of Tobacco to her Majesty,
which the sheriff of this County is hereby Ordered to Collect of him,
upon refusall of payment by Distress, and that the said sheriff
Account for it with William Byrd Esq'r her Majestys Receiver General
in this Country.

p.1. John Bowen fined 250 lb tobo as above.

p.1. John Fennell fined 250 lb tobo as above.

p.2. William Smith fined 250 lb tobo as above.

p.2. James Lockhart fined 250 lb tobo as above.

p.2. At a Court held 2 May 1711.
                          Present
     Samuell Peachey   William Woodbridge)
     Alexander Doniphan   William Thornton   ) Gent
     John Tarpley   and   ) Justices
     Charles Barber   Thomas Griffin   )

p.2. Griffin Fantleroy fined 200 lb tobo for not appearing "being
returned upon the Pannell of the Grand Jury to attend this Court"

p.3. James Ingo fined 200 lb tobo as foregoing.

Fines, etc.

p.3. At a Court held 3 May 1711.
                                Present
     Samuell Peachey   Charles Barber   )
     Alexander Donaphan   William Woodbridge) Gent Justices
     John Tarpley   William Thornton   )

Downing etc   George Downing, William Seale and William Sims being
fined   by order brought before this Court to answer to what
               should be objected against them Relateing to the
breaking open the Prison of this County and Rich'd Clatherbucks
makeing his Escape from thence; On hearing the Evidence of James
Ingo, James Wilson Samuell Short Elizabeth Smith and Martha Hayton
in this behalfe, and the said George Downing, William Seale and
William Sims being separately Examined and offering nothing materiall
in barr of what was laid to their charge in this matter are of
opinion that they are guilty of the Fact aforesaid; It is therefore
Ordered that they be each of them fined One Thousand pounds of
Tobacco to Our Sovereign Lady the Queen, and that each of them give
good and sufficient Security for their good Behaviour One Year

p.3. Geo. Downing with Henry Berry bound in L 10 Sterling to keep
the peace.

p.4. William Seale with William Berry bound as above.

p.4. William Sims with Thomas Dickenson bound as above.

p.4. At a Court held 7 August 1712.
                                Present
     Alexander Doniphan   Joseph Deeke   )
     John Tarpley   George Heale   ) Gent
     Charles Barber   and   ) Justices
     Edward Barrow   Thomas Griffin   )

p.4. Richard Hill fined 2000 lb tobo "for keeping an Ordinary without
Lycence".

p.5. At a Court held 6 August 1713.
                                Present
     Alexander Doniphan   Joseph Deeke   )
     John Tarpley   William Woodbridge) Gent Justices
     Charles Barber   Thomas Griffin   )

"John Champ being Sum'oned as a Juryman to Survey and lay out the

Land in dispute between John Lomax Plt and Henry Butler Defend't and appearing accordingly upon the said Land, but Refusing to be Sworne It is Ordered that he be fined the sume of Two hundred pounds of Tobacco x x ".

p.5. "Joseph Minton the same"
"Cornelius Edmonds the same"
"William Carter the same"
"Daniell White the same"
"Maxfield Brown the same"
"Matthew Burrows the same"
"Daniell Jeffereys the same"

p.5. At a Court held 2 September 1713
                              Present
Alexander Doniphan   Edward Barrow   )
John Tarpley   Nicholas Smith and) Gent Justices
Charles Barber   Rich'd Taliaferro   )

p.6. Thomas Thornton fined 200 lb tobo for not appearing to serve as a Juryman.
     Leonard Dozier the same.

p.6. At a Court held 6 January 1713/14.
                              Present
John Tarpley   Jonathan Gibson   )
Charles Barber   Richard Taliaferro) Gent
Nicholas Smith   and   ) Justices
William Thornton   Thomas Griffin   )

p.6. "James Welsh of the Parish of North Farnham in the County of Richmond being presented by the Grand Jury for publick selling of Brandy by Retail in the Race Ground of Thomas Dews in the said Parish and County on the 23'd and 24th Days of October last Contrary to Law, was returned by the Sheriff not to be found in his Bayliwick and now failing to appear" is fined 2000 lb tobo.

p.7. "Andrew Dew of the Parish of North Farnham in the County of Richmond being Sum'oned to Answer the Presentment of the Grand Jury against him for Publick selling of Cyder by Retaile, in the said County and Parish the 23'd Day of October last past, Appeared in Court and Refusing to undergo the punishment the Law directs" is fined 2000 lb tobo.

p.7. "John Caine of the Parish of North Farnham in the County of
Richmond being sum'oned to Answer the Presentment of the Grand Jury
against him for the Publick Selling of Cyder by Retaile in his house
x x the 5th Day of September last past, Appeared in Court, and
Refusing to undergo the Punishment the Law directs x x" is fined 2000
lb. tobo.

p.7. "Thomas Bayles of the Parish of St Maryes in the County of
Richmond being sum'oned to Answer the Presentment of the Grand Jury
against him for publick selling of Cyder by Retaile in a Race Ground
and att his own house in the said Parish and County the last of
August last past Appeared in Court and Refuseing to undergo the
Punishment the Law directs" is fined 2000 lb. tobo.

p.8. "William Dalton of the Parish of Sittenburne in the County of
Richmond appeared in Court to Answer the Presentment of the Grand
Jury against him for the Publick Selling of Cydor by Retaile on a
Race Ground in the said Parish and County the last day of August last
past, and Refuseing to undergo the Punishment the Law directs" is
fined 2000 lb. tobo.

p.8. "James Strother of the Parish of Maryes in the County of
Richmond x sum'oned x for the publick Selling by Retaile of Cyder in
his house in the said Parish and County the 28th Day of October last
past, Appeared in Court and refuseing to undergo the Punishment as
the Law directs" is fined 2000 lb tobo. Major William Robinson goes
bond for Strother for the fine.

Note: There must have been right much fun and frolic around Richmond
County the fall of 1713.   B.F.

p.8. At a Court held 8 April 1714.
                              Present
        John Tarpley   William Woodbridge)
        Charles Barber   Jonathan Gibson   ) Gent Justices
        Edward Barrow   Thomas Griffin   )

Tayloe sherr   "In an Action of Trespass between John Lomax Plt and
   fined   Henry Butler Defend't the Order for a Survey with a
                Jury in this Cause not being Complyed with att the
Motion of Dan'll McCarty Attorney for the Plt, It is Ordered that the
Shoriff of this County for his default therein be fined the sums of
One Thousand pounds of Tobo"

Fines, etc.

p.9. At a Court held 5 May 1714.
                          Present
    Alexander Doniphan   William Thornton   )
    Charles Barber   Moore Fantleroy   ) Gent
    Edward Barrow   Jonathan Gibson   ) Justices
    Nicholas Smith   Richard Taliaferro   )

p.9. Arthur Dye fined 200 lb tobo for not appearing as a juror.

p.9. "William Littman being brought before this Court the seventh
Day of Aprill last for raising malitious and scandalous Reports of
Elizabeth and Frances the Wife and Daughter of Charles Hill, did then
Contemptuously goe away from the said Court after his appearance
Whereupon it was then Ordered that the Sheriff of this County should
apprehend the said Littman, and him safely keep till he should give
Security for his appearance at the next Court to Answer for his said
Comtempt; And the said Littman now appearing x x but offering nothing
materiall to Excuse himself" is fined 500 lb tobo. John Doyle goes
his bond.

p.10. At a Court held 2 Dec 1714.
                          Present
    William Woodbridge   Jonathan Gibson   )
    John Tayloe   Rishard Taliaferro) Gent Justices

p.10. Thomas Hooper fined 200 lb tobo for not appearing to serve as
a juror.

p.10. "John Heaford being bound over to this Court by John Tayloe
Gent one of his Ma'ties Justices of the Peace for this County on
Suspition of Hogg Stealing, and he now appearing" is ordered to give
security for good behavior for one year. George Gaydon goes his bond.

p.10. The same for Benjamin Hinds. Thomas Thorne goes his bond for
L 10. Sterling.

p.11. The same for William Phillips Junior. George Gaydon goes his
bond for L 10. Sterling.

p.11. At a Court held 7 January 1714/15.
                          Present
    Alexander Doniphan   John Tayloe   )
    Edward Barrow   and   ) Gent Justices
    Nicholas Smith   Moor Fantloroy   )

(For proceedings see next page)

Fines, etc.

p.11. 7 Jan. 1714/15.

Jones   John Jones having been Com'itted Prisoner to the Goal
Acquitted   of this County by Vertue of a Warrent of John Tarpley
             Gent one of his Majesties Justices of the Peace for this
County on suspition of killing one Richard Garrett; this Day the
Court haveing taken the said matter into Examination, and having
heard the Evidence of Griffin Humphreys on behalf of the King against
the Prisoner, no sufficient Cause appearing to them upon the said
Evidence to remove him to the Publick Goal; He is therefore Ordered
to be acquitted

p.12. At a Court held 4 May 1715.
                         Present
    Alexander Doniphan   Edward Barrow   )
    John Tarpley   and   ) Gent Justices
                           Nicholas Smith   )

p.12. Ordered that William Bayley Constable for not duely Executing
a Warrant Granted by John Tayloe Gent x x against William Smith
Cordwainer to Answer the Complaint of Austin Brookenbrough is fined
100 lb tobo.

p.12. William Smith Cordwainer fined 500 lb tobo "for Contemning a
Warrant"

p.12. At a Court held 1 June 1715.
                         Present
    John Tarpley   John Tayloe   )
    Edward Barrow   and   ) Gent Justices
    William Thornton   Richard Taliaferro)

"Whereas Margarett Richardson was by Warrant of John Tarpley Gent
one of the Justices of this Court Com'itted to the County Goal on
Suspition of Murdering her Bastard Chile which by her own Confession
she privately buryed and being now brought before his Majesties
Justices here present was Examined by the Court as followeth
Evidence includes:
p.13 "Court, Who was the Father of the Chile "
     "Answ. One John Stanley
     "Court. Was you ever married to the said Stanley"
     "Answ. No"

(See next page)

p.13. "Mary Bluford Aged 38 yeares or thereabouts being Sworn and Examined" makes a statement.

p.14. "Mary Bradey Aged 25 yeares or thereabouts" the same.

p.15. "George Bluford aged 47 yeares or thereabouts" the same.

p.16. The Prisoner remanded to Prison to be conveyed to Williamsburg for trial by the Gen'll. Court.

p.16. George Bluford and Mary his wife give bond L 20. Sterl. to appear at Gen'll Court in the case.

p.16. Mary Brady gives bond as above.

p.17. Notice of a Session of Oyer and Terminer held at Richmond Court House 13 June 1715 to try Negro Will, a slave belonging to William Robinson Gent, he having made an assault upon the body of Richard Copley and stolen silver money valued at L 5, Sterling from him.
p.18. Also another indictment was preferred agt the said Will for breaking Goal. Upon evidence against the negro, he was acquitted. The evidence offered by John Doyle.

p.19. At a Court held 7 July 1715.
                              Present
        Alexander Doniphan   William Thornton)
        Edward Barrow   and   ) Gent Justices
        Nicholas Smith   John Tayloe   )

p.19. "John Davis Junr of Sittenbourn Parish haveing been presented by the Grand Jury for being a Common Disturber of the Peace, this Day appeared in Court to Answer the said Presentment, but offering nothing materiall to discharge himself from the same, It is therefore Ordered that the said John Davis be fined the Sume of Five Pounds Sterling to our Sovereign Lord the King". Matthew Davis and Edmond Molinchy go his bond for L 100. Sterl. that he keep the peace for one year and one day.

p.19. "William Griffin of Sittenbourn Parish haveing been presented by the Grand Jury for not keeping lawfull Measures in his Mill, this Day appeared in Court to Answer the said Presentment but offering nothing materiall in Barr thereof, It is therefore Ordered that he be Fined Fifteen shillings to Our Sovereign Lord the King"

p.19. "Wobley Pavey being Presented by the Grand Jury for being gen- erally Suspected to live in Adultery with Sarah Yeats, It is therefore

7 July 1715.
p.19 continued. - Ordered that the said Webley Pavey enter into Bond
with good and sufficient Security in the Sume of L 50. Sterl for his
dismissing the said Sarah Yeats from her dwelling and Cohabitation
with him in his house as alsoe for his restraining himself from re-
sorting to or frequenting her Company, and that the Sheriff take him
into Custody and him safely keep untill he shall give such Bond with
Security as abovesaid; Whereupon the said Webley Pavey appeared in
Court and together with David Berrick his Security Acknowledged
themselves Indebted to Our Sovereign Lord the King his heirs and
Successors in the Sume of Fifty pounds Sterling to be Leveyed of their
Lands and Tenements, Goods and Chattels if the said Webley Pavey did
not Comply with and fulfill the purport and Contents of the above
Order"

p.20. "Francis Williams being presented by the Grand Jury for being
generally Suspected to live in Adultery with a Mulatto Woman" - word-
ing as in foregoing item. Francis Williams, John Bowen and Francis
Williams Junr enter into bond L 100 Sterl. that he fulfill Court
Order in the case.

20. "John Champ being presented by the Grand Jury for being generally
Suspected to live in Adultery with Mary Carter" ordered to give bond
for good behavior. Bondsmen not shown on record.

p.21. "Richard Copley haveing been Com'anded by James Phillips one of
the Under Sheriffs of this County to assist him in the apprehending
of one James Elkins who for Contempt of Authority was by this Court
Ordered to be taken into Custody, the said James Phillips this Day
made Complaint to this Court that the said Richard Copley not only
denyed giveing his Assistance, but alsoe used severall threatening
Speeches to him, and likewise Assaulted and beat him, the said Rich'd
Copley appearing but offering materiall to Excuse himself" order that
he be fined L 10. Sterl., be imprisoned one month and give security
for his good behavior.

p.21. The following fined 15 shillings each for not clearing roads.
John Champ Surveyor of Highways betw Court House and Charles Beaver
    Dam.
William Carter Surveyor of Highways betw Charles Beaver. Dam and
    Gravelie Run.
James Wilson Surveyor of Highways betw Court House and Rappahannock
    Run.

p.22. Richard Copley this day discharged from order for fine and im-
prisonment upon his humble submission.

This Book marked "Fines etc" continuos to page 353.
The last date 20 May 1754.

INDEX

Charleton, Cath: 60
           Hannah 33, 60
           John 60
           Mary 60
Charteris, Jno. 20
Chew, Larkin 34
Chill, Cha: 32
Christopher, Anne 67, 68
             Nicho: 85
             Robt. 66, 68
Clark, Hen: 27
       Tho: 59
Clary, Wm. 78
Clatherbuck, Richd. 94
Claxton, Richd. 33, 58, 73
Clay, Jno. 51
Claybourn's Run 32
Clayton, Alex: 86
          Mary 33, 34
Cleeve, Emanuell 21
Cleve, Mrs. Patience 56
Cleiveland, Jno. Wm. 91
Clifton, Lawrence 16
         Wm.   16
Cloathworker, Roger 69
Cooke, Walter 24, 25
Cole, Cha: 32, 33
Collet, Danl. 24
Collin, Henry 55
Colston, Wm. 22
Combs, Jno. 32
Commeline, Jas. 20
Commins, Ann 90
Connary, Tho. 59
Conway, Edwin 60
Coole, Benj: 59
        Richd. 59
Cooper, Tho: 79, 80
Copley, Richd. 99, 100
Corbin, Jno. 52
Cordiner, Jas. 83
Cornwell, Edw. 21
Coward, Jas. 19, 21, 25
Cox, Sem 40, 45, 50, 51, 52
          53
Crabb, Osman 31
Craske, Jno. 6, 10, 29
Cressey, Tho. 1
Cresswell, Gilbert 45
Crosse, David 1

Crue, Hen: 34
Cunningham, Jno. 35
Currency Valuations 73

Dair, Wm. (or Dare) 15, 19
Dale, Thos. 88, 89
Dalton, Jno. 13, 40, 46
        Mary 40
        Wm. 96
Daly, Jno. 86
      Patrick 26
Dare, Mr. 25
Darracott, Jno. 71
Davenport, Fortunas 60
            Geo: 5, 60
            Wm. 60
Davis, Jno. 52
       Jno. Jr. 60, 89, 99
       Matthew 99
       Nath'll 22, 54, 55
       Robt. 20
Davis als Payne 20
Deane, Jno. 20
       Wm. 83
Deare, Mr. 17
Deboard, Jeames 85
Deek, Mad'm 27
Deeke, Eliza: 87
        Joseph 26, 28, 50, 86, 87
        94
Deeke see Dykes
Devorell, Benj: 20, 35, 50, 51,
          52, 53, 55, 71, 82,
          Jeremiah 82
          Rachael 71, 82
Dew, Andrew 10, 21, 43, 45, 95
Dickinson, Thos. 15, 19, 36, 43
           94
Dickson, Wm. 23
Dierham, Thos. 2
Dillon, Danl. 37
Dinwiddy, Jno. 83
Dinwiddie see Dunwiddie
Doctor's Commons 53
Dodson, Ann 80
        Cha: 27, 28, 43, 81
        Bart: Richd: 32, 43
        Mary 80
        Thos. 32
Doniphan, Alex. 8, 14, 93, 94, 95, 97
          98, 99

www.ingramcontent.com/pod-product-compliance
Lightning Source LLC
Chambersburg PA
CBHW021902020426

42334CB00013B/438